D0934261

FALLING APART

FALLING APART

The Rise and Decline
of Urban Civilisation

by

ELAINE MORGAN

SOUVENIR PRESS

Contents

1 Declaration of Interest

Over the last century the tide of wealth and influence, as well as the tide of power, flowing into the world's largest cities and conurbations has been so powerful that the sense of being peripheral – of belonging to places that are haemorrhaging power and population and youth and hope – has not been confined to rural populations. It has spread to towns, to once-prosperous and declining cities, to whole economically blighted regions both urban and rural, and it has been growing more acute. It is not always easy for individuals to live out their lives in such declining communities without some part of the sense of failure and inferior relative status being internalised – just as it is not easy for an urban immigrant to become integrated into a powerful and thriving metropolis without feeling himself to be, in some real and personal sense, more important and significant than the country cousins he left behind. It is part of a universal pecking-order as old as civilisation.

However, we are going through a period of growing equality when pecking orders quite as venerable as that have been unexpectedly capsized. Our masters have recently learned to be wary of declaring themselves superior to coloured people, or to women. They have yielded up to these groups (often with the gravest misgivings) appreciable quantities of political and economic power.

But even though the dominance of whiteness and maleness has slightly abated and the heavens have not yet fallen, they still cannot contemplate without a shudder the prospect that the dominance of centralism might be similarly eroded. The frequently quoted line 'Things fall apart. The centre will not hold' is uttered always on a note of apocalyptic doom, as though the metropolitan conviction of an intrinsic superiority to rustics and stagnating provincials and the mountainy men and the small town hicks, now going on five thousand years old, had scarcely yet suffered a scratch.

One of the reasons is that, at least over the last half-century, the vast majority of the quantities of books falling from the presses about the generally admitted malaise of the cities has been written by city-dwellers, totally committed to urban life and urgently seeking solutions for contemporary urban hang-ups. It might even be thought axiomatic that nowadays nobody without that urban experience and commitment should have the temerity to write about cities at all. It is far from axiomatic. It is like saying that only criminals should write about crime; that no one under seventy should be listened to on the subject of geriatrics; that unless you hold stocks and shares your views on capitalism are worthless.

This is a book about cities from the outside.

You might conclude from that, that the views expressed in it are partial and biassed. Of course they are. I will grant you that point freely if you will grant me the corollary – that all the books written about cities from the inside are biassed in precisely the same degree. And there are a lot more of them. If this one serves no other purpose, it may help to redress the balance.

It would be absurd to claim that this is a field where the on-looker sees most of the game. There are innumerable things about great cities which can only be thoroughly understood by people who spend their lives in them, just as there are many things about the sea which can only be appreciated by navi-gating it. On the other hand there are always some aspects which can be most clearly perceived from the sidelines. For example it is not easy for a navigator in mid-ocean to take depth-measurements of tidal movements and establish whether the water beneath him is growing deeper or shallower. If you want to see with the naked eye whether or not the tide has turned, the simplest method is to stay near the edge of the water, and keep still in one place and watch.

PART I

General

2   Urban biology: Primate into hive?

The city is, among other things, the place where the ethologist gets deeply discouraged and the economist comes into his own.

In urban society, less and less of the actual daily behaviour of men and women can be illuminated by pointing out: 'That response is specific to the mammals, or the primates, or the anthropoids.' Most of it is far more pertinently described by saying: 'That is the typical behaviour pattern of a factory hand, a consumer, a private employer, a bureaucrat or a commuter.'

Those bloodless isotypes are undoubtedly waiting around the corner for us, but it might help us to keep a sense of perspective if we spent one chapter in considering whether the biologist has, or has not, anything useful to contribute to the study of urbanism.

The attempt, of course, is constantly being made. No scientist who has studied the evolution and development of animal behaviour takes kindly to being turned back at the outskirts of the city and told that beyond that point his discipline ceases to be relevant. He may still be listened to when he talks about sex and when he talks about babies, but many people feel that for ninety-nine percent of the problems which occupy the urban consciousness, any insight we get from apes is only going to be marginally helpful. To talk about the Stock Exchange as a jungle and the office worker on the 8.15 as the hunter going forth to win sustenance for his mate and her young is a high falutin' and old-fashioned metaphor that doesn't get anybody very far.

One spirited counterploy has been to protest that the jungle metaphor doesn't work because urban *Homo sapiens* behaves not like a jungle animal but like a zoo animal; 'other animals do behave in these ways under certain circumstances, namely when they are confined in the unnatural conditions of captivity. Clearly the city is not a concrete jungle, it is a human zoo.'

Some classic observations and experiments have indeed been made along these lines. For instance, it was discovered that when a herd of deer confined on an island increased their numbers and could not disperse at will, even though the food supply was ample for all, some of them began to drop dead of a mysterious disorder which left no visible mark. When post-mortems were carried out it was discovered that their adrenalin glands were pathologically enlarged, suggesting they had died of stress.

Then there are the experiments with rats conducted by F. A. Barnett and others. It appears that if you keep a pack of rats in a confined space large enough for all their physical needs, feeding them well and protecting them against infection, their numbers will go on increasing until eventually, though they still have plenty to eat and drink and room enough to move around and build their nests, their society becomes demoralised. The males fight violently, sometimes to the death; the rules governing the rank order no longer hold. Sexual behaviour becomes deviant; and the young may be aborted or neglected, or attacked and devoured. As with the deer there are sudden deaths from no visible cause. The parallels with contemporary urban problems are striking – increase in violence, contempt for the law, breakdown of family life and social cohesion, sexual permissiveness, baby battering, nervous breakdowns and the stress diseases that threaten to become as much a hazard of city life as the plague once was.

Are we to accept then that the zoo theory of city life is a tenable one? Unfortunately there are two major weaknesses in it. One is that what resemblances there are between behaviour in cities and in zoos apply only to the *pathological* aspects of human life, and even there there is an awful lot of loose thinking going on.

Take the following statement 'Under normal conditions in their natural habitats wild animals do not mutilate themselves, masturbate, attack their offspring, develop stomach ulcers, become fetichists, suffer from obesity, form homosexual pair bonds or commit murder. Among human city dwellers, needless to say, all of these things occur' . . . and, of course, the same things happen among caged animals. But it is not true that non-captive animals *never* masturbate or form homosexual pair bonds (read about Konrad Lorenz's gay geese), or commit murder. Nor is it right to imply that human beings only grow fat or kill one another when they live in cities, or that the incidence of fetichism and self-mutilation correlates in a positive way with the size of human settlements.

However, the really glaring difference between the city and the zoo is that the modern city has no walls and that even when cities did have walls they were not designed to keep the insiders in but to keep outsiders out. If you built a broad bridge from the deers' island to the mainland, or tunnelled an exit for Barnett's overcrowded rats, it would be very surprising if those thoroughfares were not used by ex-captives eager to escape and disperse. Yet every time you build a broad new highway from a rural hinterland to an overcrowded city the net result is to speed up the rate of migration *into* the city and overcrowd it still further. Nobody ever coined a platitude by saying 'all roads lead from Rome'. To depict the whole conurbation as a vast cage full of unwilling captives is to turn the actual situation precisely inside out.

Other anthropologists approach the problem in a different fashion. They admit that the typical social structure of an anthropoid is not always easy to perceive in a modern metropolis, but they argue that it may still be seen if we can only learn to ignore the irrelevancies. So they prefer to examine a person's interactions with the small circle of his kin, colleagues and acquaintances scattered around the city (or around the state, or the nation, or the world), treating these as his 'tribe' and the thousands in between as non-existent. Given all these provisos, it is possible to assume that species-specific human behaviour remains unchanged. The modifications in it are felt to be fortuitous departures from the norm, occurring only because in so many places it just happens that there is an uncharacteristically large number of individuals living very close together.

This is fair enough, except that these allegedly atypical aggregations are due at any moment now to comprise over fifty percent of the species, and the atypical interactions for many people occupy over fifty percent of their waking hours. This is the point where the economist plausibly makes his take-over bid, as the man who really knows what makes human beings tick, on the grounds that what is happening to them now has no parallel anywhere in the history of life on earth.

However, that too is not entirely true. The parallel is such a naïve and obvious one that few reputable scientists have bothered to make any reference to it for decades. Yet, if you took a child from a primitive tribe and transported him to the centre of Tokyo, New York, London or Berlin and asked him to say something about the inhabitants, his very first impression would undoubtedly be 'there are millions of them'. And if you had stationed him on top of a skyscraper, fifty to one he would spontaneously reinvent the old cliché: 'Look at them, they are just like ants'.

Now a century or so ago this insect parallel used to be a great favourite with Victorian sermon writers and hearthrug philosophers. They used to muse about the busy little bee and point out that there in the hive you have the thrift, the industry, the cooperation, the division of labour, the highly developed system of communication and the willingness to die for the queen which had made London the greatest city in the world.

After Darwin however most serious scientific thinkers became far more rigorous and dismissed this kind of talk as the merest literary fantasy. Every creature had now been neatly slotted into its own order, phylum and genus of the family tree of life. They knew it was impossible for man to have inherited anything from the birds, or the rodents, or the insects, because they are nowhere in the line of succession. And for a long time this line of succession was treated as the factor most meriting study and research. It was established that any resemblance between a bird and a bat, or between a whale and a fish, was quite superficial, since the bat and the whale are both, in fact, mammals heavily disguised.

Today the focus of attention has swung in a different direction. Less time is spent on cutting up dead animals and classifying them, and more is devoted to watching the behaviour of live ones and wondering what they are up to. One result is that there is less insistence on isolating our biological thinking into tight taxological compartments. Creatures who behave in the same way, however diverse their origins, tend to encounter the same problems and often solve them in similar ways. Thus a whale's resemblance to a fish may be superficial but it is by no means insignificant or accidental, and there is nothing naïve in thinking that a study of sea otters may cast light on our thinking about penguins, and vice versa.

Let us therefore, if only for the intellectual exercise, consider the most fundamental behavioural modification affecting our species today : the accelerating tendency to agglomerate spontaneously into clumps of many hundreds of thousands of individuals and construct stationary habitats for them; and let us remember that this sort of behavioural change is rare but not unique.

There are twenty thousand species of bees known to science, and ninety percent of them are as solitary as cats. There was probably a time when they were all as solitary as cats. The evidence for this assumption is two-fold. In the first place gregarious bees retain vestigial traces of sex organs appropriate to solitary insects who pair two by two. In the second place there is a great range of intermediate stages between the solitary bee and the social bee. There are bees which lay eggs and forget them; bees which lay eggs, leave food for the larvae, and then forget them; bees which not only provide food but stick around for a while; bees whose daughters also stick around for a while and help to feed the new larvae; bees which are solitary in winter and social in summer. We can't escape the conclusion that the social bee is the end product of a process of behavioural evolution.

Somewhere at some time in the past there must have been the same kind of breakthrough for bees as there was for people – some equivalent of Jericho or Mohenjo-Daro, an evolutionary switch to a new kind of social organisation with greater security and higher living standards.

We cannot know whether it happened for them, as for us,

with dramatic suddenness – five thousand years in evolutionary terms is practically overnight – or whether it took longer. We can't be sure either whether the bees' new lifestyle developed in one place only and diffused gradually around the world, or whether it happened quite independently in Asia, say, and Africa, and South America, as and when conditions became propitious for the change. (We can't even be quite sure about this in the case of human beings.)

What we do know for certain is that, in response presumably to similar environmental stimuli, at least two other quite distinct species made a similar flip over into socialised community life.

Ants are biologically unrelated to bees but they followed a converging route to even higher organisational complexity; and termites – again no relation for they are cousins to the cockroaches – to the greatest complexity of the lot, with workers, slaves, soldiers, masons, skyscrapers twenty foot high, air conditioning, cultivated fungus beds and 'domesticated' representatives of other species valued (like our own cows) for their secretions. Their caste system is carried to far greater lengths even than our own. For example, the worker's job is to feed any termite who demands feeding; but if the suppliant is a young termite who might yet become a queen or winged insect, the worker gives it what food it has in its stomach; while if it is a low-caste wingless adult, as Maeterlinck points out, 'the worker turns head to tail and generously gives it the contents of its intestines.' Even on Animal Farm the business of some being less equal than others never went as far as that.

Like the physical contours of whale and fish, the parallels between the contours of social organisation in hive and city may be superficial but are in no way attributable to blind coincidence. The ecological factor which triggered this striking development was precisely the same in both cases. It was a sudden, explosively successful, mutual aid association between a particular kind of animal and a particular kind of plant.

At one stage in the history of the earth, as the pollen record shows, there was a great leap forward in the number and variety of flowering plants. It was accompanied by a simultaneous leap forward in the population of pollinating insects, bees above all, who were at the same time cashing in on this bonanza and assisting its progress – being indeed indispensable to its progress.

There are many cases of animal species developing a special association with a plant – boll weevils and cotton plants, cabbage whites and brassicas, colorado beetles and potatoes, squirrels and nuts, koalas and eucalyptus trees – but in almost all cases the balance of advantage is markedly one sided, usually in favour of the animal. (Occasionally, as with *Homo sapiens* and the ring-worm fungus, it can go the other wav.) In the case of the flowers and the bees, the rapid upward growth spiral took place because the benefit was mutual.

One other precondition favoured the emergence of the hive. The vegetable product which was fuelling the bees' population explosion was not only a very high energy food; it could under favourable conditions be stored for long periods without deteriorating, which made it particularly precious, especially in temperate zones where so many kinds of vegetable sustenance became inaccessible for long periods of every year. It was advantageous to store and to hoard it, a process which when adopted inevitably converted the nomadic insect into an insect anchored to a fixed habitation, and since it was so precious to their enemies as well as themselves it was advantageous for the bees to build a citadel around it and band together in increasingly complex ways to defend it.

Any account you will read anywhere of the genesis of human civilisation offers an exact echo of this evolutionary happening. The association in this case was between on the one hand a species of hairless biped, which had shown considerable persistence and stamina in overcoming vicissitudes but was still as far as numbers went a very long way from being an evolutionary success, and on the other hand the seeds of certain kinds of grass.

Some experts believe the breakthrough occurred uniquely in the Middle East with man-plus-wheat, and spread from there around the world; others maintain it happened elsewhere quite spontaneously with, for example, man-plus-rice; but this does

not affect the nature of the happening. The population of the
bipeds and the food grains exploded together, as the people
tended the grasses and extended their habitat and cut down the
trees which would overshadow them and declared war on all
their enemies from weeds to drought.

Also, the people had the same luck as the bees in that the
vegetable product to which they had allied themselves was a
high energy food and capable of being stored. They found it
necessary to construct containers for it, to establish sedentary
communities around it, and to be prepared to defend them
against marauders. Their social organisation, hitherto not
greatly differing from the primate model, began to undergo
very rapid mutation and in the short space of four or five
thousand years it has altered and is continuing to alter out of
all recognition.

For the greater part of that period one further parallel could
have been drawn. All the non-human 'urban' communities are
subject to some limitation of size. The most ambitious, namely
the termite hill, may sometimes grow until it accommodates a
million inhabitants: it will never grow to accommodate two
millions. The limitations are doubtless due in the last resort to
economic factors such as the available food supply and the
problems of transportation, ventilation and servicing, but the
necessity for solving the problem of overpopulation in a prosperous season has led to the evolution of elegant and elaborate
behavioural solutions like the swarming of bees, leading to the
foundation of new colonies at an appropriate distance from
the mother hive.

For a long stretch of human history similar limitations on the
growth of urban communities were imposed by similar economic factors. During the magic period when civilisation was
in its first bloom and producing some of its most miraculous
by-products – writing, mathematics, astronomy, sculpture,
drama, architecture, politics – new cities were constantly being 'hived off' from parent settlements and alighting and pros-
pering in some other river valley, or further down the coastline, or on an off-shore island, or across the sea in Africa. It
was thought worthwhile to construct a city wall that would

last for generations, on the unspoken assumption that a city once founded would grow like a baby to its appropriate size, and then stop.

Most of them did. One or two Imperial cities like Babylon and Rome managed to buck the system for a while and exceed these decent proportions; but after Rome had exploded and Europe had recovered from the shock the medieval cities that covered the Continent once again conformed roughly to the old norm. Arnold Toynbee postulated that the size of such a city and the area of its hinterland were determined by how far a farmer and his horse could travel into town with his produce and hope to get back the same night, and by the number of citizens that radius of land could support. This would vary slightly, but not radically, with the climate, the soil, and the local staple products. The French historian Elisée Reclus plotted out in great detail the distribution of European cities in the middle ages and concluded that just such a network did in fact exist and its distribution was remarkably even all over the Continent.

It would be fanciful to suggest that this technological stage lasted long enough to plant in the human mind any kind of instinctive apprehension of what constitutes the 'right' size for a city and at what point it becomes 'too big'. Some such innate alarm signal must be programmed into the biology of bees to warn them when to swarm; but any human estimate of the optimum size for our own aggregations is certainly based on personal and recorded experience – in other words on what we and our predecessors have become accustomed to.

This doesn't detract much from a rather remarkable consensus over the centuries about what that optimum size actually is, as assessed by men who in widely different ages were sufficiently sensitive to this social factor to sit down and think hard about it. If we begin with Plato as one of the archetypal town planners, in his ideal city he limited the number of free citizens to 5040. It has been calculated that by adding proportionate numbers of disfranchised classes such as artisans, merchants, children, etc, the total would be somewhere around 30,000.

Over a thousand years later Leonardo da Vinci independently drew up his own plan for an ideal city complete with municipal gardens and a pedestrian precinct. He decided that if it were to be neither too big nor too small it ought to accommodate 30,000 people. Much later again in 1898 a small shopkeeper's son called Ebenezer Howard, founder of the Garden Cities movement, made his own urban blueprint. Howard was not guided in this matter by Plato, for he would not have known how many Greeks were needed to service 5,040 free men, nor by Leonardo whose notebooks were not at that time available in English. He simply sat down and thought hard and decided there could be only one right and proper size for a city – it should cover a thousand acres and accommodate 32,000 people.

And moving from theory to practice, the size of the inland medieval European cities referred to above remained steady over hundreds of years, showing, with only three or four exceptions, a population range of somewhere between 25,000 and 35,000 inhabitants. It might have been expected that if some people, like some insects, had evolved a newly gregarious lifestyle then the size of the human hive was likely to stabilise at around the 30,000 mark, which typified our Mark One civilisation.

We know that it didn't in fact get a chance to stabilise at anything, because the graph of our population growth gave another lurch and moved into an entirely new scale of expansion. Carlo M. Cipolla is a sober economic historian and no more given than others of his kind to highly coloured imagery, but he objectively describes the change in the graph from about 1750 as 'bacillus-like', that is 'like the growth curve of the micro-population in a body suddenly stricken by some infectious disease'.

Some of the reasons for this will be discussed in a later chapter, but one result was that from this point onward the process of 'hiving off' ceased to operate effectively. It was as if a mutant strain of termites had begun to build constructions covering an incredible quarter of an acre . . . then a more incredible half an acre . . . and went on growing.

It would obviously be absurd to pursue the insect parallel

very far, but some of the concepts it throws up are interesting ones. For example, one characteristic of insect and termite societies is that the members do not react to one another as individuals: they react merely to one another's *function* in the hive. Recently, sociologists have pinpointed the same tendency as one of the most distinctive characteristics of urban as opposed to 'folk' societies – more and more interpersonal transactions are conducted on the level of one person's job, role, or uniform (salesman, policeman, lawyer, taxi-driver, nurse, PRO, bank clerk, etc) reacting with another person's job, role or uniform. This behaviour pattern vastly increases efficiency: functions keep the life of the city rolling, and they will roll more smoothly if interviews and phone calls are not cluttered up with inessentials, such as what kind of people inhabit the respective roles and what they are currently thinking or feeling. 'I don't want to know' is a supremely urban response.

On the other hand there are other projections of the insect model which would lead straight to the realms of Amazing Science Fiction; imagine, for example, that the females in the hive have successfully established their right to work, and liberated themselves from the burden of child-bearing. Could the net result be that all the males hang around doing nothing whatever except eating and sleeping and living for the day when they will be allowed to get together and chase after the only young female who hasn't been desexed?

There are, in fact, only two valid conclusions to be drawn from the insect comparison, but I think they are important ones. First we should be quite unjustified in assuming that for any biological species there is a pattern of social organisation which is immutably the 'natural' one, and that any departure from it must be regarded as unnatural and bound to give rise to pathological symptoms. The history of evolution proves that even for creatures far less flexible and adaptable than ourselves the 'natural' order can change quite radically and the change may prove to be adaptive.

Second, when an animal population finds it economically possible to live at close quarters together in large numbers, it frequently adopts this course with enthusiasm. Take breeding populations of seals or seagulls: in these cases it is not short-age of accommodation which crowds them together, for desir-able residences on nearby cliffs and beaches may be completely ignored. Constant squabbling and bickering goes on in the overcrowded colonies, but never a seal or a seagull pulls up stakes and settles down half a mile off in search of peace and quiet.

In fact a dispassionate observation of human behaviour at work or at play would suggest that the urge to escape from large aggregations of one's own kind is far less common than the urge to join them. Not that anyone who pulls up his roots and heads for the city is going to admit for a moment that his individual decision has anything to do with any centripetal migrationary urge affecting the human race. He will explain he is going there to look for work, or for the mental stimulus, or to get away from home, or to make money, or (like James Thurber's archetypal provincial young ladies) for 'concerts, new plays and the opera'. But then equally, of course, very few people indeed are capable of responding to any irrational urges without rationalising them. A man who has been mesmerised and successfully given a post-hypnotic instruction to open a window at 4p.m. never says: 'I don't know why. Something came over me'. Instead he starts fidgeting at 3.58 and com-plains irritably that the room has got terribly stuffy all of a sudden.

Over most of the world it is only too easy to demonstrate that the people who are trekking to the cities are driven by the hard spurs of poverty and hunger. Yet even the young men and women arriving at the squalid shanty towns of the Third World would probably recognise the sensation that Jonathan Raban was describing in his book *Soft City* when he wrote:

> When I finally arrived in London to stay I felt twice life-size . . . one might see or hear anything in that immense ambiguous ripple of population and power. For me it pro-mised release and a libidinous surge of adrenalin. I wanted London as I'd once lain awake wanting a glossy enamel split-cane trout rod. . . .

and as James Boswell had craved for it until the day he could write 'I was all in a flutter at having at last got to the place I was so madly fond of', and as Chekhovian young ladies had yearned and languished, love-sick for Moscow. The sensation is almost as universally recognisable as that of falling in love, and the language often very similar. It certainly bears no resemblance to the feelings of a captive specimen being ushered into a cage.

There must therefore be some reason for the persistent and arbitrary selection by ethnologists in recent years of zoological parallels which imply that life at metropolitan densities violates the deepest instincts of human beings, and if they continue to endure it, it must be because they are in some subtle fashion *constrained* to do so. There must also be some reason why most of their readers accept this hypothesis without question.

It is very hard to see what the nature of this constraint can be, other than the fact that people find the balance of advantage for themselves lies with being in or near the city rather than away from it – the fact in other words that they are *better off there*.

To say 'I hate it but I was forced to come to find work' is another way of saying 'I am better off here'. To say 'It's becoming intolerable and I only wish to God I could afford to get out' means 'I wish I could live in pleasanter surroundings without having to take a drop in income or settle for a lower paid, less interesting, more laborious job with fewer prospects.'

It is no harder to walk out of a city than to walk into one, yet all over the world at accelerating speed people are pumping themselves into cities and conurbations. They complain bitterly about the noise, the pollution, the squalor, the violence, the corruption, the inequality, the prices, the nervous tension, the chaos and the lack of decent living accommodation. But they stay, and thousands of books, articles and reports fall from the presses about the urban dilemma and urban stresses and the desperation of the people 'pent up' in the cities, and how to find solutions to their problems and their plight. If we witnessed this behaviour in any other species we would see at once there were only two possible explanations. Either they were being compelled by some mysterious behavioural mechanism which had gone wrong (which happens sometimes but is very rare), or else they were fleeing into these unhappy conditions from still unhappier ones, as they would flee from a forest fire. In other words that the real problem was located in the places they had come from.

Barbara Ward some years ago wrote that 'all over the world, often long in advance of effective industrialisation, the unskilled workers are streaming away from subsistence agriculture to exchange the squalor of rural poverty for the *even deeper miseries* (my italics) of the shanty towns that year by year grow inexorably on the fringes of the developing cities'. But 'even deeper miseries' is an outsider's judgement. Sometimes the shanty dwellers themselves will say 'I was happy in the village' just as New Yorkers will sing nostalgic songs like 'I remember the corn fields. . . .'

But the cast iron test was applied when the International Development Research Centre asked newcomers in the most appalling shanty areas of Bandung, Seoul, Manila, Caracas, Kuala Lumpur, Lima, Istanbul and Lagos whether they would be willing to return home. Between 70.7 percent and 81.9 percent said no.

Sometimes again, if questioned further, they will say that they themselves would have been content to stay in the country or even willing to return to it, but that the city was the only place that offered a future for their children. This only means that while the place they came from was short of food, it was shorter still on hope; and man cannot live by bread alone.

If this is the true position, then to concentrate so much mental energy on coping with urban problems is like a man in a flooded bathroom working like crazy at mopping up the water, wondering why he is having so little success, and failing to observe that he has neglected to turn off the tap.

However, we are in danger here of straying rather prematurely into the terrain of the economist. The evolutionary question confronting us is an apparently simple one to formulate. It is: are we to regard ourselves as cast ineluctably in the social mould of the higher anthropoids, programmed for living most happily in small groups and at low densities, and liable to various psychic stresses and breakdowns if those densities are exceeded? Or are we perhaps in the midst of a process of behavioural evolution into a new kind of primate for which the crowd is the preferred and life-enhancing environment? After all, the social insects have travelled so far along this path that a bee prevented from returning at frequent intervals to breathe the air of the hive will promptly sicken and die, far more rapidly than one of Barnett's overcrowded rats.

The question may be simple, but answering it runs into the snag that bedevils all debates about human behaviour – the near impossibility of distinguishing the innate elements in it from the cultural ones. Let us take two examples – crowd behaviour, and the birth rate.

The mere fact that half the human race does now in practice gravitate towards densely packed settlements and assemble in crowds seems purely a matter of culture and economics. They are forced to behave in this way because of new methods of production and political organisation. The reasons are all well documented and understood. And yet, if the word economics means anything at all, then the reasons behind the hive and the termite hill were economic also, but the economics fed back into the biology with dramatic and sometimes bizarre results.

In the case of our own species, the reasons for choosing to attend, for example, a Cup Final or a Nuremburg Rally or a Mafeking Night or a ticker-tape parade are entirely explicable in terms of transmitted cultural behaviour patterns. But the psychic charge sometimes generated in such crowds once they are assembled can appear as powerful, as irrational, as uncontrollable, as the most basic and deep-seated of human instincts like sex and fear and rage. People talk airily about 'the instincts of the herd'; but the anthropoids are not herd animals. The situation of being hemmed in shoulder to shoulder with

milling multitudes of its own kind might be expected to com-
municate a surge of well-being to the nerves of a buffalo, but
it would drive a gorilla or an orang outang (as well as some
people) demented with panic.

Urban populations have learned not merely to tolerate such
situations. Their behaviour on arbitrary occasions such as (in
some cultures) New Year's Eve, suggests that this massing
together not only enhances their enjoyment of the event but
itself *constitutes* the enjoyment: there is no other rewarding
element in the situation. It is hard to reconcile this with the
zoo theory of individuals wretchedly caged in together and
longing to get the hell out. It would rather suggest that at least
part of the species has taken a few steps along the bees'
road.

When we consider the differential fertility of urban and rural
populations, the same ambiguity arises. On the one hand, re-
productive behaviour in any species is surely just about as biological as you can get: on the other hand, of all the phenomena known to urban sociology, none is so confidently explained
away as 'culturally conditioned'.

The existence of this differential has been known for a long
time. Most people are familiar with journalistic references to
'our teeming cities' but it is also widely recognised that
the term is misleading inasmuch as people in cities 'teem'
(i.e. bring forth young) much less prolifically than their rural
cousins.

This statement is not just a blunt-edged assertion that a dirt
farmer's wife is more likely to have ten children than is the
personal private secretary of a Madison Avenue tycoon. There
is a very close correlation indeed between the size of the town
or city you live in and the number of children you are likely
to produce. The following table shows relationships between
fertility and size of community in the United States, on the
basis of figures drawn from a 1950 census report. The fertility
ratio represents the number of children under five years old
per hundred married women of childbearing age.

* Source: Cities and Society (Hatt and Reiss) p 43.

Size of Community	Fertility Ratio
Urbanised areas	
3,000,000+	56
1,000,000 to 3,000,000	61
250,000 to 1,000,000	62
50,000 to 250,000	63
Outside Urbanised areas	
25,000+	64
10,000 to 25,000	63
2,500 to 10,000	66
1,000 to 2,500	69
Under 1,000	70
Rural Non-Farm	78
Farm	83

Similarly, if you take an individual city and draw concentric rings around it you will get an equally smooth descent in the fertility rate as you move outward from the centre in any direction.

Nobody knows quite why this occurs. All kinds of reasonable and plausible explanations readily occur to the layman, but most of them evaporate when rigorous tests are applied.

It seems to have nothing to do with sexual behaviour. This is one department where town and country have always suspected each other of excesses. The country has imagined the city as a hotbed of vice and licentiousness and nameless orgies, while the city has reserved the term 'country matters' for the indulgence of coarse and uninhibited lust. It seems to be a natural human propensity to make these assumptions about any communities you are not very familiar with. The upper and lower classes have often entertained the same mutual suspicions, and neighbouring nations do the same (the English used to call syphilis 'the French disease' at a time when the French termed it 'la maladie Anglaise').

For a more objective assessment of the situation, one of the few documents available is the comment on American statistics by Kinsey et al. in their article 'Rural/Urban Background and Sexual Outlet'. They wrote:

An examination of figure one will show that the differences between the total outlet of the rural males and the total outlet of the urban males was never very great. In general the differences would not be particularly significant if they did not all lie in the same direction which is almost without exception in the direction of a lower frequency of total sexual outlet for the rural males.

So the difference appears to be one of infertility rather than impotence. It could be a biological phenomenon. There have been many reports about the stresses and social breakdowns experienced by the rats in the overcrowding experiments. But less publicity has been given to what happens in the long term if rats are kept in overcrowded conditions. What happens is that the birth rate goes down. One of the mechanisms brought into play is neat if rather eerie. It has been found that some of the female rats who conceived under conditions of overcrowding apparently received some kind of biological signal that yet another litter of baby rats was not really what the situation required. What happened then was that the process of gestation went into reverse like a film running backwards and the growing foetuses were reabsorbed into the womb, rather in the way a tadpole, instead of letting his superfluous tail drop off as lizards sometimes do, thriftily dismantles it and reabsorbs the material for recycling into legs.

By whatever means, C. H. Waddington states about all the overcrowding experiments:

Eventually we find in such experiments that the rate of increase of the population slows down and finally ceases altogether when the population attains a steady size which it can usually maintain indefinitely thereafter.

I am not for a moment suggesting that urban women possess even subconsciously the power of reversing the process of gestation. All I am asserting is that most of the popular *cultural* explanations of their fertility differential fail to hold up under examination.

They usually run as follows: sociologists will explain that at the rural end of the graph farmers need a lot of sons to help them work the land; farmers' wives can bring up their children cheaply on home grown produce: they can turn them out to play without fear of traffic so that they are not whining under foot all day; a farmer's wife can't get a paid job anyway because there are no local job opportunities for women; she is probably more conservative in outlook and perhaps less well educated than city women, which means she may resist the idea of contraception or if she favours it may find the appliances less readily available in remote country districts, or even be less efficient in using them.

On the other hand it is pointed out that women in the cities are more liberated and many of them have fascinating careers and/or are much better off, with nice clothes and nice apartments they don't want to see messed up by sticky fingers; they tend to have higher cultural attainments and have more alternative sources of pleasure to spend their money on so they don't want to squander it on diapers and school fees; or if they are poor they may live in high-rise blocks and everybody knows it's harder bringing up children in high-rise blocks. These explanations were all so simple and obvious that hardly anybody bothered to verify any of them.

But there was a man called Nathan Keyfitz who couldn't help wondering whether there was a way of allowing for all these variables and finding out what the graph would look like then. He went to Quebec and did a survey. He cut out all that contraceptive stuff by confining himself to French-speaking couples composed of Roman Catholic wife and Roman Catholic husband. He eliminated the career variable and the running-out-to-play variable and the cheap-home-grown food variable by confining his survey to farmers and their wives and *nobody else*. He cross-checked on the highly popular and prevalent 'more money means less children' theory by selecting two groups of such farmers, one prosperous group and one much less prosperous group, and analysing these groups separately; he did the same with groups where the wives had more than seven years' schooling and groups where they had less, and so on with a few other such variables; and he noted where they lived.

Finally in the *American Journal of Sociology*, Volume 58, (March 1953) he published his results. It appears that rich Catholic farmers' wives near the city have less children than rich Catholic farmers' wives far from the city. The same goes for poor Catholic farmers' wives and well educated ones and less well educated ones and ones who have married young and ones who have not married young and ones who have had English-speaking neighbours (who might be conducting insidious Protestant propaganda) and ones who have not. Whatever factors you eliminate, *still* fertility rises ineluctably with distance from the city.

As Sherlock Holmes would point out, once you have eliminated all the likely explanations the biological one, however far fetched, still remains in the ring. There may be some half-atrophied hormonal mechanism trying to raise a last ditch protest to the effect that 'I am not a bee nor a termite. I am a primate, and there are a lot too many of us here.'

Alternatively, there is one other possible explanation which Keyfitz did *not* eliminate, and I would like to proffer it here because lately some people have been advocating unrestrained urbanisation as the best cure for the population explosion. Rural people are philoprogenitive, the argument runs: you may tell them about contraception but they reply they do not wish to stop after the second child. Therefore the solution is to pack them into cities and in one or at least two generations the urge begins to wear off.

What we do know is that the birthrate has a strong tendency (in human beings and in other species) to react to the numbers of offspring *remaining extant* in a community. If you steal a bird's eggs, it will lay another clutch. Historical records show that after disasters such as plagues, the number of births rises as if to restore the status quo. Where poverty is acute and infant mortality high, parents tend to produce more children, thus ensuring that at least one or two will survive to maturity and still be around when they are too old to work the land themselves. Conversely wherever infant mortality is reduced, the birth rate soon begins to drop. Whether this result is achieved by conscious choice, or as instinctively as the robbed bird's second clutch of eggs, is irrelevant to my present argument which is as follows.

In rural areas which are undergoing chronic depopulation as the young drift away to the cities, the demographic effect is not dissimilar to that of persistent plague – i.e. the whole of the communal experience suggests that a woman producing six or seven sons will be lucky if one of the bunch is still around at the age of twenty-five. It may be true that the others have not gone to Heaven, merely hopped on a train to the nearest shanty-town, but the effect on the age distribution of the parent community will be the same, and the effect on the birth rate may well be the same also.

So the hidden factor behind Keyfitz's statistics might be that the areas of high fertility were merely the areas suffering greatest population loss through out-migration (which are usually in practice the areas farthest from the city). It would be worth checking up on. If it is true, then the quickest way to reduce the desired size of family in the world's rural hinterlands is not to speed up the rate of urbanisation, but to slow it down.

Coming back to the central question of whether urbanisation is capable of bringing about an actual modification in the species, I would suggest the answer is yes. There are for instance subspecies of birds, virtually impossible to distinguish anatomically, but separately classified because they choose a different diet and sing a different song. No doubt if they go on doing that long enough, like Darwin's finches on their separate islands, they will come to differ in other ways as well, just as the social bee differs anatomically from the solitary one.

By this time anyone who dislikes the insect parallel will have lost all patience and be itching to make the following interjection, so I will make it for him:

It is a total absurdity and thoroughly unscientific to attempt to make this comparison, on the following grounds. First, the social bees and the solitary bees remain entirely separate : there is no interbreeding and no exchange of genetic material. This is nowhere true of people. Second, the modification to the social form of organisation in the case of insects took place very gradually, probably over millions of years, whereas human behaviour can become 'urbanised' in the space of one generation. Third, in insect species the modification is irreversible, whereas in human beings if conditions change it can be reversed as rapidly as it was acquired. Can you show me any gregarious insect which shares a common genetic pool with a solitary form? which adopted its gregarious behaviour in the space of a single generation? which is capable of abandoning this adaptive behaviour, once it has been acquired, without miserably perishing?

The answer, as of course you have shrewdly guessed, is yes. The insect is the locust. One of the species involved is *Locusta migratoria*, a black and russet species which unites in springtime into coherent swarms which move off *en masse*, darkening the whole sky with their wings and covering over a thousand miles in less than a month. Even the crawling larvae they leave behind are stirred by the same impulse and advance steadily in massed columns. The other species is the innocuous *Locusta danica*, easily distinguished by its green colour and differently shaped thorax. It is solitary and sedentary in its habits and does no harm to anybody.

It was purely by accident that the Russian entomologist B. P. Uvarov discovered that these two species are genetically identical. (At first he couldn't believe it. He charged his blameless assistant with mixing up the eggs in the different cages, and got quite cross about it.)

Whenever specimens of *Locusta danica* find themselves in larger numbers or closer proximity than normal, the larvae that hatch out from the eggs they lay are the larvae of *Locusta migratoria*. In their adult form they will differ from their parents in both colour and shape; above all there will be a most violent and menacing change in their behaviour. In other words this species has proved to be socially divalent – it is capable of two different kinds of social organisation according to the situation in which it finds itself.

All this corresponds tolerably closely to what sociologists and psychologists have been reporting over the past few decades about human society, namely that we also are socially divalent. There are 'folk' communities on the one hand and urban communities on the other. They differ markedly and consistently in attitudes and behaviour and psychological characteristics (we shall be examining these differences in more detail in the next chapter), and the trigger that converts the first into the second is the factor of population density. It is true that you cannot identify the urban species by its black and russet colouring or its differently shaped thorax, and there is no definite threshold at which an individual or a society flips over from one form to the other. The differences manifest themselves rather along a spectrum or continuum of change.

Regard all this if you like as not much more than a metaphor. It is actually a little more than that, because throughout the living world there are patterns that tend to recur and we are never totally immune to them. Dense aggregations of population represent one conditioning factor as palpable as a very cold environment, or a very arid one, or a marine one, and no species can entirely avoid being moulded by that factor.

So we may have to drop the idea that there is something 'normal' and 'natural' and 'human' about folk-type societies and 'unnatural' about urban ones. *Migratoria* is quite as natural a phenomenon as *danica*.

It is more probable still (and this is no metaphor, but a statement in literal earnest) that we shall have to drop the idea that we can continue to aggregate in larger and larger conurbations and yet at the same time dictate, or even influence much, the kinds of human beings that will inhabit them.

B

3 Urban psychology: Portrait of a citizen

One of the earliest of urban sociologists was the anonymous author of the popular fable about a town mouse and a country mouse.

This tale encapsulated the conviction that urban people and rural people differ from one another in their pattern of behaviour as much as the black locust differs from the green locust, as much as young and old differ from one another, or male and female, or rich and poor.

This is confirmed by the experience of opinion pollsters who know that if they want a representative cross-section of the opinion of the nation it is no use interviewing only the right percentages of each age group, of the two sexes, and of the various income brackets. Their results can still go hay-wire if they don't also take account of the *fourth* great psycho-logical divide and correct the urban/rural balance also. Then it usually comes out right.

People throughout history have 'known' about this difference in the same way that they have 'known' that a hungry dog will salivate at the sight of food; but the dog's dribble only entered officially into the domain of science when Pavlov weighed and measured it and asked himself: Where? How much? How quickly? Under what conditions? In response to what stimuli? and so on.

One of the aims of that field of academic endeavour known as Urban Studies has been to find ways of measuring the psycho-social differences between town mouse and country mouse, and it is a far more complex problem than weighing a dog's saliva.

One way of trying to quantify it is to visit a representative district in city or hinterland and question the people patiently and politely, asking them things like: 'When did you last see your father? Sister-in-law? Cousin? How often in the last year? Month? Week?' and so on. It is then possible to add up all the answers, tabulate them, give them to a computer and in the end statistically confirm what everyone already thinks he knows, namely that city people tend to have less truck with their relatives than people in small towns and villages.

Nobody pretends this is a shattering revelation. But if this kind of thing is done persistently and scrupulously and the process is repeated with other aspects of the city's lifestyle, it may be possible in the end to devise a kind of working tool for measuring degrees of urbanism in a community as a thermometer measures degrees of heat.

The object is not to arrive at a neat and cast-iron criterion of the urban personality, for which any one of us might or might not qualify. This would be as impossible as to get an agreed definition of the precise day or week in his life at which a man becomes old, or the exact number of pounds or dollars which will suffice to make him rich. All these are adjustable conceptions varying widely in different cultures.

What sociologists prefer to talk about is the sliding scale of behavioural characteristics which they have called the 'folk-urban continuum'. It is not a precision instrument, and some people still dispute whether such a continuum is a valid concept. But these researches have been going on for a long time now and in all parts of the world, and the surprising thing is not how much the results vary but how little.

Louis Wirth, one of the most influential pioneers in this field, when discussing 'Urbanism as a way of life' was determined to lift the subject out of the morass of prejudice and mutual suspicion and ignorance which begets such stereotypes as 'country people are thick-witted and parsimonious' . . . 'city people are greedy and superficial'. He succeeded in writing a classic paper on the subject published in the *American Journal of Sociology* as long ago as 1938 to which he could append the words: 'All these phenomena can be substantially verified through objective indices.' It was the first really scientific description of *Homo gregarius*.

If it is an accurate one, it is a very important document. The folk-urban continuum in some ways, as we have seen, resembles the continuum between, for example, the young and the old. Their standpoints are different, their opinions on various topics are liable to differ in predictable ways, and there is a continuing and creative tension between their views of life, so that they constantly remind one another that there are people (however misguided) who see things in a different perspective. In the case of most of these major dichotomies this will presumably always be the case. It is very difficult to imagine a world in which everyone will be over fifty or everyone will be male. However, it is not only easier to imagine a world where virtually everyone has become urbanised: it is a consummation which a majority of urban theorists firmly believe we are approaching at a rate of knots. If we ever reach that point, there is great danger that we shall very quickly lose the habit of occasionally admitting 'I feel this to be the case because I lead this sort of life', and replace it by the certainty 'Everyone feels this to be the case because it is true'.

You may feel that that prospect is a long way off, and all the business of measuring objectively the urban psyche quite unnecessary. After all, many people now living in cities were themselves born in the country. They remember it with nostalgia, and feel themselves fully capable of interpreting its point of view; and besides, there is a vast literary heritage on the subject of the rural life.

There is indeed. Ah, that literary heritage! The key factor that has moulded it is the fact that publishing is an urban occupation and has been so ever since printing was invented, and long before that. People in cities buy most of the books, and when they read books about rural life they like them to be quaint and happy and picturesque, about simple people and cute animals and lovely landscapes, not about problems and desperations.

This preference goes right back to the pastoral tradition springing from Virgil's Eclogues, and from 'Beatus Ille', the second Epode of the highly urbane Roman poet, Horace:

> Happy the man whose wish and care
> A few paternal acres bound . . .!

and it carries on down through the lyrical traditions of all Western culture. There are thousands of poems about happy piping shepherd boys for every sullen realist who protests with Crabbe :

> No longer truth, though shown in verse, disdain
> But own the village life a life of pain.

It still holds in prose and in the twentieth century, with modern pastoral best-sellers from *The egg and I* to the tales of a Yorkshire veterinary surgeon. There are thousands of them for every *Grapes of Wrath*.

For there is a basic and universal dilemma blocking the prospect of anyone who actually labours in one of the far-flung places that are being drained of hope actually writing a book and telling it like it is.

The dilemma lies in the fact that people would instinctively feel there was something phony about a guy who lived out in the sticks and wrote a book complaining about it. If he is bright enough to write a book then what's he complaining about and where's his dilemma? He doesn't have to stay in that dump, does he? Why doesn't he move into town like everybody else? (It is, of course, axiomatic that nobody 'has to' stay in the country : it is only in cities that they get 'trapped'.)

Very often the guy doesn't stay in the dump : he moves to town and writes of what he remembers. He is influenced by the fact that he is writing of the time when he was young and lusty; the time of childhood and first love; he is influenced by the fact that he is currently suffering the urban inconveniences of noise, pollution, anomie, etc; he is influenced by the fact that his neighbours who never knew such a life exclaim how lucky he was and how wonderful it must have been, and the fact that these people constitute his potential market. He soon contracts the 'I was happy in the village' syndrome and possibly even talks of going back there – if and when he has achieved a high enough city-derived income to render it tolerable.

Raymond Williams in his book on *The Country and the City* cries out at one point: 'It is time this bluff was called.' He quotes a classic example from the works of Stephen Duck, the English 'thresher poet', to show the inexorable shift of perspective brought about by urban contacts and literary success. While still living in the country, Duck wrote:

Let those who feast at Ease on dainty Faire
Pity the Reapers who their Feasts prepare :
For Toils scarce ever ceasing press us now;
Rest never does but on the Sabbath show :
And barely that our Masters will allow.
Think what a painful life we daily lead. . . .

Having been taken up by Persons of Distinction and being established at Kew he began to muse :

Contented Poverty's no dismal Thing
Free from the Cares unwieldy Riches bring . . .
The poor man's labour relishes his Meat;
His Morsel's pleasant and his Rest is sweet . . .

And a few years later he was carolling away like another Horace :

Of blissful Groves I sing and flowering Plains :
Ye Silvan Nymphs assist my rural strains . . .
No plundering Armies rob our fruitful Plain
But blessed with Peace and Plenty smiles the Swain.

If you had asked Stephen Duck to explain the discrepancy between his first poems, which were cries of agony, and his last ones, he would doubtless have explained that he had become wiser, better educated, and able to take a less cramped and distorted view of life. The main thing that had happened was that he had been in the most literal sense of the word 'civilised', i.e. 'turned into or made to resemble a city dweller'.

Because of this universal human frailty it might be best not to place too much reliance on memories or memoirs which paint the contrasting portraits of Folk man and Urban man. Safer to turn to the social scientists, like Louis Wirth and his many successors, with their psychometric statistics and their objective indices.

What then do they report? First the good news: as compared with folk communities, the city people now moving into the human majority tend to be more rational, more sophisticated, more tolerant, more secular, more reserved, and more interdependent. They are also more liable to judge by appearances, and to be ambitious, competitive, and cash-oriented.

There are equally well marked tendencies on the darker side. They are more predatory, more neurotic, more criminal, more likely to develop schizoid personalities and to conduct only fragmented relationships, and to suffer from that peculiarly urban malaise known as 'anomie' – a condition of apathy and hopeless disorientation caused by the breakdown of familiar and universally recognised rules of conduct.

What I propose to do in this chapter is to consider these traits one at a time and try to see whether, and if so why, they are natural and indeed *inevitable* accompaniments of urban life, in any country and under any political or economic system.

Most of the good things in the list arise from the fact that the city is a liberating place. There was a well known saying in the middle ages originating in what is now Germany: 'City air makes free'. It had in those days a precise legal connotation. When a city was granted freedom it could mean a Royal Decree promising exemption to its citizens from all feudal tolls and taxes. A peasant who left his land and arrived inside the city wall was, as Fernand Braudel points out,

> immediately another man, he was free. . . . If the town had adopted him he could snap his fingers when his lord called for him. It was like crossing one of the still serious frontiers in the world today.

This is no longer true in a legal sense, but in a psychological sense the feeling of liberation often remains. Anyone arriving in a great city from his native village for the first time breathes in great lungfuls of that free air. Suddenly no one is peering from behind the curtains, no one is going to tell your mother tomorrow morning 'I saw your Johnny coming out of a pub and he had a woman with him'. No one is taking any notice of you at all. If their eyes do rest on you in passing they are unlikely to register surprise, disapproval or curiosity. They will register nothing. It is the next best thing to realising that fantasy, dear to the heart of childhood, of becoming the Invisible Man.

And when you do make contact with one or two of the millions of strangers you discover that you have been disburdened of a lifetime's load of secondary identities and oft-told tales. You are no longer Simon Green's youngest, the one that set the marquee on fire that time, the one they still call Pudd'n because he used to be such a fat baby. However redoubtable a fellow Simon Green was, London has never heard of him. There are no visible signs and symbols branding you the youngest in a place where the eldest has never trod. All your past follies have been erased and if you like to mention casually 'My friends call me Slim', it's hardly a lie really, only a creative statement that will be a truth by tomorrow. You are free up to a point to invent yourself.

You may object that you can liquefy your identity in this way merely by moving from any one place to any other place. True, but if you move to another village and stay there, the effect soon wears off. Impressions or items of information about you picked up by different people are liable to trickle into a common pool of knowledge until they have built up a three-dimensional picture of you which before very long sets hard.

In the city very often this simply fails to happen. The people you work with in the office eight miles away will never meet the Australian couple in the flat above you or your drinking pals down at the local. None of them will discuss you with the garage man or the girl who always gets on the same train at the next stop. One group may see you as a sober and ambitious youth who will go far, another as a bit of a rebel and a lady's man. You may chat for a few minutes every day with a waitress who's got hold of the idea that you are a financial wizard, so why disabuse her? and for a few minutes every week with the landlady, who knows you are a feckless young idiot without enough sense to come in out of the rain.

This is what Wirth describes as the 'segmentalism of human relationships'. It can lead to a certain fuzziness about one's own identity. (Walter Mitty, a figure who has attained an almost mythic significance in the twentieth century consciousness, was of course a New Yorker.) But there is no need to regard this as in any way pathological. It is more like a continuation into adult life of the child's play that takes the form of 'Now this time I'll be John Wayne and I've been wounded and you must be the baddie and you don't know I've got a gun' . . . and so on.

It may be argued that it's all very well for children (and actors) to keep trying personalities on for size, but that it behoves the rest of us to mature and settle down and make our personalities hold still long enough to acquire a little weight and solidity. I'm not altogether sure about that. The strength of this unsolidified behaviour pattern is that it preserves above all things a flexibility of role playing, and in a world that's changing as rapidly as ours flexibility may be of more value to survival than solidity. To take two obvious examples, those people who had by the nineteen-sixties committed themselves to solidly integrated 'masculine' roles or 'white man's burden' roles are now going through a more traumatic time than people who hadn't, because they are becoming less relevant and that hurts. As Eric Berne has pointed out, there's nothing more shattering than achieving real expertise in conducting a well recognised kind of personal relationship and then suddenly finding nobody's willing to play that game with you any longer.

In fact, this particular urban trait is only bad medicine for beginners, for the people who try to play all their segmentalised roles for real and get upset when acquaintances from two different milieux happen to meet and compare notes and discover that Johnny Green is two different guys. The myth figure here is Billy Liar, playing urban-type games against a small-town social background with disastrous consequences.

The more sophisticated urbanites stopped worrying about all of that ages ago. 'Oh look there's Paul! He's the one that *will* always talk to me about ghastly Utrillo. Excuse me while I put my art-lover's face on. . . . Paul this is Ellen, a dear soul, but refuses to believe I'm interested in anything but cooking and bridge. That's because she's never seen the other side of me'. . . . and so on, serenely assuming that we all know that everyone of us has as many faces as a Happy Families pack and more sides than a dodecahedron.

Anyone from the other end of the folk-urban continuum is apt to find that kind of talk brittle and false and decadent. False by the sternest standards such a character certainly is, because either she is interested in Utrillo or she is not, and if she is not it would have been more honest and straightforward to have yawned in Paul's face the first time he brought the subject up. But the word 'politeness' comes from the Greek 'polis' meaning a city. Cities would be intolerable places without it and it isn't always compatible with the truth, the whole truth, and nothing but the truth. The behaviour the lady is displaying denotes a high degree of adaptation to a very complex and exacting environment. If the world is really to become hundred-percent urban all our children will have to learn it on the way to Ecumenopolis.

Equally highly adaptive is the Invisible Man routine – the ability to walk along a city street and pass a thousand people and (provided you don't walk smack into them) behave as if the people weren't there. They adopt this protective blindness not because they are in a hurry or preoccupied with gazing into shop windows. They may be standing in a lift together where hurry gets you nowhere and there's nothing to look at but the closed door, but they will still do their best to ignore one another's presence, and the more strangers that enter the lift the greater the likelihood that they will all line up facing one way, mathematically spaced to minimise the danger of touching one another and with their gazes as parallel as compass needles.

A lift full of dogs would never line up like that. We should consider it highly comical if they did. I doubt whether Eskimos or Bushmen would do it either. But a really experienced commuter can stand in a tube train if necessary for twenty minutes or half an hour with somebody's elbow sticking into his ear, somebody breathing down the back of his neck and somebody else's hair tickling his chin. Yet his mental faculties are withdrawn like a snail's horns so far into his interior that the legs and elbows and torsos have no more effect on him than the briefcases and umbrellas. Only if one of his fellow travellers so far infringes the rules as to stare directly into his eyes does he feel that his privacy has been invaded. When he emerges on to the pavement his eyes maintain an opaque look as if the soul behind them had hung out a sign 'Out to Lunch'. Some psychologists explain it by saying that if anyone tried to treat each of the city's millions as a savage treats the odd strangers he encounters – girding up his emotional loins and secreting the appropriate amount of adrenalin ready to react to hostility or friendliness as the situation requires – the attempt would very quickly blow his mind and he would run raving mad. Even ignoring other people is a constant drain on psychic energy, like the mental effort to shut out noise.

This acquisition of a retractable psyche is one manifestation of what Wirth calls urban 'reserve'. Visitors fresh in from the country or the provinces are more likely to find other words for it, ranging from 'stand-offish' and 'toffy-nosed' to 'bloody rude', and sociologist Georg Simmel would agree that they've got something there. He wrote in an article on 'The Metropolis and Mental Life':

> The inner aspect of this outer reserve is not only indifference but more often than we are aware it is a slight aversion, a mutual strangeness and repulsion which will break into hatred and fight at the moment of a close contact.

At its most civilised, though, the subconscious aversion doesn't break into hatred and fight. It breaks into words – debate, discussion, argument, oratory – or it breaks into laughter, or satire, or that hard to define and ineffably urban type of verbal gymnastics known as wit, which is typically the city's safety valve for the city's malaise. It is the source of some of literature's pure gold from Menander and Horace through Swift and Wilde to Noel Coward and Dorothy Parker.

Nobody who stayed in the sticks ever made an epigram sparkle so brilliantly or trained his ideas to jump so lightly through so many marvellous hoops. The strength of these people is in the intelligence and honesty that drives them to cut through the phonier kinds of *politesse*, bring the 'slight aversion' and 'mutual repulsion' of city life out into the light, release the laughter that always greets the breaking of small taboos, and sublimate the latent hostility into verbal crackerjacks. At their best they can light up areas of the inside of your head like neon signs. All homage to them.

But let me by way of digression make just one point. All the mass media are in the hands of metropolitans. They are all rightly aware that the writers who give vent to some of these suppressed urban repulsions are honester and therefore better than the ones who feel the repulsions and cover them up. Therefore they favourably incline towards those who fearlessly bring to stage and screen and paperbacks some of the darker and sourer truths about human beings, revealing that they are often greedy, cowardly, lecherous and cruel (which is true).

Increasingly they look askance at contributors making the opposite point that human beings are often tender, brave, patient and loyal (which is equally true). Anyone claiming to see people in this light is felt to be either ill informed about human depravity or stupid or 'sentimental' (which usually translates as 'holding a less jaundiced view of life than I do') or else downright hypocritical. Even in America, which has great underground reserves of sentiment, anyone wishing to write a story about a heroic hero and with a happy ending will be well advised to cast him as a seagull or a rabbit, since metropolitans do not feel an above-average level of aversion towards seagulls.

If world population were to continue its present implosive migration, this sardonic view of life and humanity might well prevail. My only point is that it is just as subjective as the converse, and that the black locust's view of life, though it may win out by sheer weight of numbers, has no more God-given right to be considered 'true' than the green locust's.

Returning to the urban tendency to insulate one's self against human contact, it doesn't at first sight seem a quality to celebrate. It has one beautiful by-product though: its name is tolerance.

Anyone growing up in a village or small town who turns out to have an urge to be different from his fellows will be greeted with a low social buzz of concern and apprehension: 'Well I never did hear in all my born days. . . . It was always good enough for his father, tell him. . . . The sooner you knock all that nonsense out of him the better, no good will come of it' . . . and the pressure will be on to bring him back into line. A lot of it will be loving pressure, because they care about him and their experience of life has been so homogeneous they can't believe they can all be wrong about the right road to happiness. Some of it will be resentful because they see his nonconformity as a criticism of themselves. Only a very little of it will be the mindless hatred of the child who while beating to death a small creature found under a stone mutters 'I'll l'arn ye to be a toad!' The odds are that the pressure will induce him either to become more like everyone else or else to light out at the earliest opportunity for the nearest city.

There he'll be more able to do his own thing. As long as he can contrive to do it without causing grave inconvenience to anyone else, the opaque eyes will look right through him and just let him get on with it. That sounds a cold and lonely thing and so it can be, but at worst it may be better than having his individual spark snuffed out altogether. And at best there is a good chance that among a million people he can find maybe half a dozen of his own kind with whom he can go jingling shaven headed down the street, or share a garret and action-paint, go into training for Mr Universe, set up an experimental street theatre, go to a gay night club or try out a new way of making an entrepreneurial fortune or starting a revolution or a Vegan lunch counter or a religion or a small magazine. City centres may be short of vegetation but in Mao's non-botanical sense we must vote them the places most likely to 'let a hundred flowers grow'. It is true that many of the most exotic seeds are blown in from outside, but the cities provide the humus.

Of all the facets of urban adaptive behaviour, the most creative is what Wirth calls 'rationality'. There is undoubtedly something new and different about the quality of thinking which emerged when men first began to leave the land and congregate in cities. It was absent in Homer; it was present in Socrates. It may have had something to do with the greater number and variety of stimuli to which urban children were subjected. It may have been a spin-off from the new and more complex tasks they were engaged on; it may have arisen because a higher frequency of human interaction led to a lot more verbalisation and argument; it was probably helped by the fact that a high proportion of the hinterland's more lively and enquiring minds were creamed off into the city and honed one another to new keenness of attainment, as diamond cuts diamond.

For whatever combination of reasons urbanised people tend to think more quickly, more articulately and more logically. They are better placed to absorb a share of whatever knowledge and skills are available. If you asked a citizen about this almost anywhere in the Third World, he would not pussyfoot around the question but define the difference quite straightforwardly by pointing out that his compatriots in the hinterland are compared to himself superstitious, ignorant and stupid.

In the West the distinction is nowadays not so clear, because education on the urban model is universal. It probably remains true though that the longer people live in the city, the more acutely they become aware of intelligence as the number one survival factor. 'It's up here you want it' says the urban conventional wisdom, winking shrewdly and tapping its temple. Rural wisdom is more inclined to believe that you want it down there, in the green fingers and the powerful back muscles and the patient plod. 'There is no better fertilizer than the farmer's feet.'

Indeed the English language and probably many others is littered with evidence that in our rural past the intellect was highly suspect. Words of praise introduced into the language to denote approval of mental agility – 'artful' (meaning skilled), 'sly' (cognate with sleight) 'crafty' (good at one's job), 'cunning' (possessing knowledge) – were all inexorably downgraded by the folk to mean untrustworthy. It isn't yet happening to 'intelligent' which means either that it's a word the folk don't use much, or else that the folk themselves have become urbanised.

Some sociologists consider that the link between urbanism and reason had something to do with money. 'Money economy and the dominance of the intellect' says Georg Simmel 'are intrinsically connected'. But he also links this with the defensive crust the urbanites developed against the intrusive claims of all those other people :

> The reaction to metropolitan phenomena is shifted to that organ which is least sensitive and quite remote from the depth of the personality. A metropolitan type of man . . . reacts with his head instead of his heart.

Wirth prefers to link it with the heterogeneous nature of city life. 'The juxtaposition of divergent personalities and modes of life tends to produce a relativistic perspective and a sense of toleration of difference which may be regarded as pre-requisites for rationality.' When your environment keeps changing, you are more likely to conclude that the view of the world you gleaned at your mother's knee cannot be piously clung to because it doesn't apply any longer. You have to start from scratch and work one out for yourself. You become, say the sociologists, 'secularised', and that is the beginning if not of wisdom at least of ratiocination.

We need to get a more precise idea about the nature of the link between rationality and urbanism. If it were anything like the link between smoking and lung cancer, we should have good grounds for encouraging urbanism to continue unchecked. We might expect that as cities grew larger and their problems more complex and intractable, the supply of human logic and understanding would increase *pro rata* and enable mankind to solve them.

But this does not seem to be the case. There is no evidence to suggest that the greater the conurbation the mightier the intellects or the more outstanding the discoveries. Euclid lived in a 'city', but it was a city that would rate by today's standards as a small town.

There is a slight danger that *too many* good minds working too closely together in any intellectual field may sometimes tend to reinforce one another's basic assumptions even when they are mistaken, and harden them into orthodoxy, and construct hierarchies to defend them, like the medieval Church. Many of the real revolutions in scientific thought have come from places like Pythagoras's off-shore island, from Darwin's country house at Down or Wallace's bed of fever in the Moluccas, from Newton living quietly at Woolsthorpe to escape the plague, or from the monastery at Brno where Mendel worked quite cut off from the intellectual life of that city and discouraged by the monks who burned all his papers when he died.

So we need not fear that if the cities now collapsed, rational thinking would collapse with them. When America was invaded by the first white settlers, they took with them such city-born disciplines as mathematics and the physical sciences and navigation and inductive reasoning and applied them successfully to the problems of the wilderness. That could happen again. Indeed where fears are being expressed in this connection, it is not that cities have too absolute a monopoly of reason, but that they are beginning to part company with it.

Doctor Jacob Bronowski towards the end of his life was disturbed by (but as far as I know did not try to account for) the fact that where urban civilisation has reached in material terms its highest points of development, people are lately showing signs of becoming hostile to rationality and kicking away the ladder by which they climbed. He stood before the TV cameras in his California home and said:

I am infinitely saddened to find myself suddenly surrounded in the West by a sense of terrible loss of nerve, a retreat from knowledge into – into what? Into Zen Buddhism; into extra-sensory perception and mystery. . . . We are being weighed in the balance at this moment. We have not been given any guarantee that Assyria and Egypt and Rome were not given. . . .

If I didn't think he had slightly misinterpreted its significance I would share his sadness about this. Reason is the last thing we can afford to jettison. Admittedly it never made anyone a nobler or a kinder person. It is only a tool and can be used by the greedy and tyrannous as effectively as by the compassionate. But it is a beautiful tool. To turn against it would be like a man cutting off his right hand because he had noticed that hands can be used for strangling people as well as caressing them. It is sad too that the revulsion against it is commonest among the warm hearted young, because it will be a poor world if all the nasties are shining the torch of intellect along their forward path while the pure in heart grope their way with their eyes closed to everything except sensations of bliss and a vision of the Infinite.

However, I don't really believe that the reaction towards Zen and the rest of it is as negative as Bronowski feared. We have to bear in mind that the converse of urban rationality is not necessarily stupidity. It may be simply a different mode of response to a different set of problems. Professor Robert E. Ornstein of California University Medical Center is one of several people who have been conducting research on the two sides of the brain. He has demonstrated how the left side is predominantly used for analytical thinking – logic, mathematics and language – and the right side for orientation, body awareness, artistic and creative endeavours. He reports that it 'processes information more diffusely and in a simultaneous rather than sequential fashion'.

The thing is that many urbanites tend to be such compulsive verbalisers that they don't recognise the second process as being thought at all. Possibly it is the right side, semiatrophying in modern urban conditions, that the antirationalists are trying to resuscitate. Sometimes they fall right over backwards in the attempt, but the attempt itself need not denote 'a loss of nerve'.

Their intention is to learn to exercise underemployed human mental faculties in the way that Bronowski might have taken a walk to exercise underemployed limbs after too long a spell at his desk. It doesn't mean – at least I hope it doesn't – that they are resolved never again to go back to the drawing board and put two and two together.

So far we have tended to concentrate on the more benign aspects of the urban character and experience such as liberty, tolerance and mental agility. The rest of the Wirthian portrait is painted in more sombre shades.

Take for instance the factor of interdependence. When something suddenly goes wrong a countryman is likely to ask himself 'Now what can I do about this?' but a city man is far more likely to wonder 'Who can I get hold of to deal with this?' It is a natural reaction to the situations they find themselves in. A healthy hill farmer in a poor country may live out his whole life without calling upon the personal services of more than half a dozen people outside his own family.

Compared to this the network of needs of a city office worker is like the life-support system of an astronaut with the whole of Cape Kennedy keyed up to monitor him. A whole army of people stands ready to facilitate the transport of such people from their houses to their desks – bus and train drivers, garage hands, road menders, ticket collectors, taxi drivers, conductors, traffic controllers, painters of white and yellow lines, meter maids, parking lot attendants, lift men. No one expects them to survive the rigours of the day without the ministrations of restaurateurs, cooks, waitresses, canteen staff, dishwashers, cafe cashiers. At work they need to be serviced by telephone operators, secretaries, night cleaners, tea women, office boys, auditors, window cleaners, stenographers and typewriter maintenance men. Their home lives would be untenable if they could not rely at need on the electrician, the decorator, the refuse collector, the dry cleaner, the sewer man, the accountant, the plumber, the laundry man, the gas man, the milkman, the bank manager, the delicatessen, the hairdresser, the delivery man, the chiropodist, the bar maid and of course increasingly the psychiatrist.

Up to a point this specialisation is the glory and splendour of urban civilisation, and a source of much of its created wealth. But it has proved to be subject to a very stringent law of diminishing returns. As the economic networks of megalopolitan life become every year more complex and more intricately geared, city dwellers are more and more frequently reminded that a chain is only as strong as its weakest link.

If one of these links snaps – an unscheduled go-slow, say, by the Associated Society of Locomotive Engineers and Firemen – *Homo gregarius* is left in a state of angry helplessness, especially when he thinks of all the other human links further along the chain who are relying on his own services and will now be experiencing the same frustration as himself and probably, if unjustly, blaming it on him. It is in this kind of situation that urban gentlemen get into the headlines by rushing up the platform and buffeting the engine driver with umbrellas ('A new type of terror' cries the *Daily Express*, 'has hit London's trains and buses. Today the alert is for the bowler hat and brolly brigade – bully boy businessmen who attack uniformed workers. . . .')

The larger the city, the more often the interdependence erupts as a crisis of frustration, and the greater the permanent residue of subliminal anxiety it leaves behind. 'Will I be able to get a taxi this time?. . . . Can I rely on Carson?. . . . What if the telephone lines to LA are blocked?. . . I wonder if his secretary gave him the message?. . . . I'm going to be late, where the hell is that waiter?. . . . If Brown goes bankrupt where does that leave me?. . . .'

Of some relevance here are the ingenious experiments conducted with rats by Jay M. Weiss (*Scientific American*, Volume 226, No.6). Two rats in adjoining cages were subjected to recurring mild electric shocks preceded by ten seconds of bleeping as a warning. The shock could easily be averted *for both* if Rat A during the warning period jumped on to a platform at the back of its cage, thus depressing a lever. The second cage contained no such platform. Rat A, who could act for himself to prevent the shocks, was not much affected by the situation even though he carried more 'responsibility': he gained weight at eighty percent of the normal rate. Rat B, the dependent one, who could do nothing but sit and fume and hope that Rat A would have enough sense to take appropriate action, gained weight at only thirty percent of the normal rate and rapidly developed severe stomach ulcers. Small wonder that city life is so rough on the duodenum.

This may be one of the major factors conducive to urban/ rural personality differences. Whatever the cause, the differences manifest themselves quite early in life.

An investigation was conducted in Miami County in 1946 into the personality adjustment of rural and urban children respectively at the third and sixth grade level. It involved 1,229 children and the standardised personality test was cross-checked by assessments of teachers and others.

The results suggested that rural children, from farm or village, as compared to urban ones, were more self-reliant, were 'especially favoured in the possession of a sense of personal worth', had a greater 'sense of belonging' in their relations with other people and groups, were freer from withdrawing tendencies and nervous symptoms, were better adjusted to the school situation than city children, mingled more happily with their neighbours, took more pride in their neighbourhood, and had greater social skills. 'Since farm children', wrote A. R. Magnus, 'are thought of as being rather isolated from many social contacts it was surprising to find that they showed decided superiority over urban children in being socially skilful or socially effective, as measured by test results.' The only plus factor on which the farm children did not score higher than the urban ones was in the 'sense of personal freedom'— and on that score the village (non-farm) children scored higher than either farm or city ones.

The outcome of this research was in line with Wirth's contention that urban life is conducive to a mercenary and 'predatory' kind of human relationship. The mechanism behind it is this. There are still very large areas of the world where cash transactions hardly figure at all. In such stable societies as these a man who wants something done for him – help with his harvest, the loan of a tool, his wounds bound up – soon learns that the best way of being treated right is to build up over the years a reputation for being a man who treats other people right. This was how the world wagged when most of the great religions were founded, and in those conditions the ethic of the golden rule (which figures in one form or another in so many of them) was not just a noble sentiment. It was also a chunk of hard-headed rustic common sense: 'Do as you would be done by, because you can be fairly sure that in your hour of need you will be done by as you did.'

For urbanites it may remain a noble sentiment but it gets no pay-off. They move around too much. You don't get better service from the waiter in WC2 because you helped a blind man across the street in Shepherds Bush, or because you used to be a great comfort to your old mother back in Stoke-on-Trent. Eighty percent of your daily social interactions will be with people who have got to know you only slightly, or quite recently, or who only know 'one side' of you, or don't know you at all. In most of these you will be done by not as you did, but according to what you can pay. The canny bit of advice is no longer Jesus's but Iago's: 'Put money in thy purse.'

It isn't that city people don't feel, quite often, the human impulse to help one another, even though they have less reason to think that the bread they cast on the waters will come back to them in a society where the waters are so much more turbulent. There is another reason why so often they fail to act on the impulse, as was illustrated by John M. Daley and C. Daniel Bateson of Princeton University who conducted an experiment with the students of a theological college (*Journal of Personality and Social Psychology*, Volume 27, No.1). The students were interviewed singly and each was asked to prepare a short talk and later told to go to another room to record it. In the case of half the students the talk was to be about the Good Samaritan, and the experimentor read out the parable to them before they left.

On the way to the recording room each student passed a 'victim' sitting slumped in a doorway coughing and groaning. An account was kept of those who stopped to ask if they could

help and those who passed by on the other side. Alas for the
Gospels, the fact of having just heard and pondered on the
story of the Good Samaritan made no difference to the score.
But if the word of the Lord had little effect, there were two
other little words that had a great deal. To half of the students
in each set, after telling them to go to the recording room the
experimentor added: 'Hurry up'. Most of them obediently
hurried, and for those the putative victim slumped and groaned
in vain. No doubt the passers-by all told themselves that it was
a populous corridor and there'd be another Samaritan along in
a minute. Such a victim would groan in vain longer on a city
street than on a village one and partly for the same reason –
far more of the urban passers-by would be convinced that it
was absolutely vital for them to reach point X within Y
minutes and that in point of fact they were late already.

Whether or not it is really vital for them to reach point X
seems to be immaterial. Researches in fifteen cities of Europe,
Asia, and North America, conducted by the Department of
Psychology at Princeton University and the Max Planck Institute at Munich, established that while people in towns of
1500 inhabitants or less have an average walking pace of less
than a metre per second, inhabitants of Prague, Munich and
New York hurry along at almost twice that speed. The correlation holds for all intermediate community sizes, and the
conclusion seems inescapable that when all variables have been
eliminated, urban stress and high walking speeds are inextri-
cably connected.

The urban predilection for 'judging by appearances' is part
of the same process. If your experience of most of the people
you encounter is too fleeting for you to learn much about
their past deeds, reliability, compassion, competence, mental
stability, etc, you have to develop the knack of 'placing' them
roughly before you can successfully handle the interaction by
taking short cuts, and the shortest cut of all is the optical sizing
up. You assess them by their appearance, their clothes, their
manner, their immediate surroundings, and their possessions.

People hoping to come well out of this scrutiny acquire
status symbols, in lieu of carrying little placards reading 'Re-

spect me, I am important', and the bigger the city, the more thing-oriented as opposed to people-oriented it becomes. A good index of psychological urbanisation would be to put to the subject the old dilemma of the overloaded raft and ask him whether he would choose to jettison the old woman or the famous painting, and record not only his answer but how long it took him to decide.

At this point we are driven to ask some very tough and fundamental questions such as : Ought we now to come to terms with the possibility that neighbour-loving ethics were simply a useful cultural adaptation to the pre-urban stage of our economic history? Have we got any reason, outside the precepts of revealed religion, to go on supposing that Christ's precept is more valuable than Iago's? and for those who have thrown Christ overboard anyway, is there any reason to suppose that the ethics of Marx and Lenin will be any more immune to galloping urbanism? The exhortation 'Have solidarity with thy fellow workers' may differ in many ways from the exaltation 'Love thy neighbour', but it is just as vulnerable to the erosive effect of daily perceiving that in modern urban conditions it is demonstrably no longer the most effective way of looking after Number One, or Number One's immediate family either.

Most of us still pay at least lip service to the old rules and deplore the increase in predatoriness – especially when we become the victims of it. What society is still vainly seeking is an urban substitute for the controlling power exercised by public opinion in small stable communities. In the West it is trying, by immensely cumbersome machinery, to replace the twitching curtains of the nosy neighbours by the activities of the muck-raking journalist. The long drawn out agonies of Watergate were a touchstone of the clumsiness of this substitute. It was like watching a fight to the death between two dinosaurs swimming in treacle.

The State can of course, and usually does, take legislative action and introduce deterrents, saying in effect 'Thou shalt do as thou wouldst be done by or else'; but for those who have ceased to believe in the exhortations this results only in the introduction of yet another and overriding commandment: 'Thou shalt not get caught.' One correlation seems to hold true all over the world and in all types of economy: the crime rate is higher in town than in the country, higher in the city than in the towns, and higher in big cities than in little ones.

Bertold Brecht in his study of the gangster/dictator Arturo Ui pinpoints the hunger behind his rise to power: 'I want respect.' Don't we all. But the further society moves towards the urban extreme of the continuum, the more everybody treats respect as a saleable commodity. And where that climate of opinion prevails, you will get crime and you will get corruption.

It is open to anyone to decide that this is a price well worth paying for the freedom, variety, amenities, excitement, tolerance, social and financial opportunities, and intellectual stimulus of metropolitan life. (Though the freedom, it is true, might shrink a little as the crime proliferates. One section of the rich and presumably honest citizens of New York, having despaired of putting all the criminals behind bars, are taking the alternative option of leaving the city to the muggers and interning themselves and their nearest and dearest inside electric-fenced reservations. Some of the Red Indians must be laughing.)

What we *cannot* reasonably assume (as most people did assume until this last decade) is that the rising incidence of crime, corruption, distrust and alienation are accidental blemishes that have somehow crept into the cities and can be eradicated by homilies in the Press or clean-up drives from City Hall. They are not accidental, they are integral.

This is a depressing conclusion. Naturally, many of the most humane and positive thinkers in the field – especially those who were brought up in cities and loved them – strenuously resisted and searched eagerly for evidence to the contrary. Regularly over the years sociologists in various countries have raised cries of *Eureka!* and announced that they have found a little urban enclave, more often than not poor and densely overcrowded, where the environment and the economy are urban but the society retains a large number of 'folk' characteristics.

Boston in Massachussets is one happy hunting ground for such discoverers. Jane Jacobs in her book *The Death and Life of American Cities* came out strong for Boston North End; while Herbert Gans wrote his book *The Urban Villagers* about Boston West. Probably the best known among similar English studies is Michael Young and Peter Wilmott's *Family and Kinship in East London*. This was about Bethnal Green, which thereafter attracted so many sociologists eager to study its folksy lifestyle before it vanished that the native population was in some danger of being outnumbered by researchers. Similar phenomena have been reported from Delhi, Cairo, Mexico City and many other places.

In urban areas like these the 'When did you see your father?' count reveals that family ties remain strong, and extended family ties are kept alive. So are neighbouring, mutual supportiveness, mutual dropping in, and mutual criticism. The tribal consensus on the right way to behave is strong and specific and vented as loudly on your neighbours' children if they step out of line as on your own. The inhabitants tend to be less thing-oriented and more people-oriented than in other urban areas. If you question them in general terms about their neighbourhoods, their first answers are more likely to be about the society – 'people around here are very friendly' – than about any physical or economic aspect.

The common factors seem to be (1) that such areas consist of people who arrived in the city in sizeable numbers at the same time and settled close together so that instead of merging into the urban melting pot they could continue to operate their own social patterns; (2) they were people who had some cohesive factor – religion, tribal or ethnic origin, language, colour – to keep them distinct and self-respecting long enough to get their own kind of pattern functioning in a new place; (3) they were left alone for a few generations to settle in.

In such cases, as with the Huguenot weavers in Bethnal Green, the Italians in Boston North End, the Russian Jews in Whitechapel, or the suburban enclaves in some African and Indian cities, they established something like a successful graft or transplant, which while drawing nourishment from the surrounding tissues of its new environment yet continues to obey the laws of its own nature.

Some sociologists such as R. Pahl take the existence of urban villages as tending to disprove Wirth's theory of Urbanism, since these communities are sometimes found in the centres of cities, the very last place where Wirthian logic would lead us to expect them.

It seems far more likely that they are rather tough gobbets which the city is taking longer than usual to digest and process into its own likeness. For example, it was believed for quite a while that the social structure of the family life of Chinese American immigrants was so durable that the young men in the various Chinatowns would remain proof against the contagion of delinquency well into the forseeable future. Unfortunately that future proved shorter than any of the hopes or prophesies.

In the case of the longest established and therefore more centrally placed of the urban villages, the third proviso – that they be left alone – is precisely what the urban dynamic is incapable of fulfilling. Almost every day somewhere in the world one of these communities is being uprooted by the bulldozers and road makers and office-block builders of the growing cities and dispersed, or resettled among strangers in 'improved' accommodation with built-in broom cupboards or whatever. Every time, it raises a scream like a mandrake. But nobody can afford to listen and nobody can ever put Humpty Dumpty together again.

No one can get any pleasure out of thus throwing cold water on the views of these optimists. God knows there are few enough of them around. They are the heirs of a thousand years of Utopian thinking and they still believe that with patience, ingenuity and goodwill we can isolate a few minor causes of present-day urban snarl-up and thereby get the bugs out of the system once and for all.

Perhaps, they say, we can do it by improving the architecture. Break up the long straight blocks with cross-streets; pull down the high-rise housing; give the people little areas of defensible space, walkways, more light, parks more strategically placed. All this in itself is very good. It is a rare and splendid thing to hear such a man as Richard Seifert, once Britain's leading advocate and architect of tower block housing, having the grace and humility to admit : 'I was wrong.'

And yet if the snarl-ups in contemporary cities are not incidental but integral, then the search for palliatives is diverting too many of our best minds away from addressing themselves to the real question. It keeps their attention directed inwards towards their own metropolitan parish pumps as if the answer could be found there. It cannot. Beyond a certain point as a city grows in size and complexity, the initial advantages of urban living – convenience, freedom, tolerance, mobility, politeness – begin to go into reverse, while the disadvantages – noise, overcrowding, tension, hostility, neurosis, crime, and fear – go on increasing.

Rather a long time ago there used to be an English school of urban theorists who were prepared to draw a conclusion from all that, simple enough to be expressed in words of one syllable: 'The place is too big.' That proposition has gone out of fashion. There are people in various countries and of various economic persuasions who argue that a city can never be too big – the bigger the better. There are others who think it pointless to say that a conurbation is growing too big when no one has yet found any method of preventing or limiting its growth.

One of the most prolific writers on the subject is Doxiadis, a high-powered Greek ekistician, who believes we are destined to end up one city which he calls Ecumenopolis which will stretch right around the world, with intervals for the oceans. He is far from being the only one who believes this, but he is the one who predicts it with the broadest smile.

Yet even Doxiadis betrays a certain apprehension and helplessness in his choice of verbs. The eventual emergence of Ecumenopolis is, he writes, 'an inevitability which we must accept . . . determined by many biological and social forces which we do not understand properly, let alone dare countermand.'

'Dare'? Not 'dare'?? They used to breed their prophets less spineless in the old days. When Karl Marx foresaw, and disapproved of, the prospect of the rich continuing to grow ever richer and the poor ever more destitute, he asked the right questions : 'Is this the kind of future men desire? If not, why is it happening?' I think he failed to get a complete answer, but at least he had the guts to shake a pygmy fist at the heavens and declare : 'The point is, to change it.'

4   Urban genesis: How it began

Unlike any other species that may have undergone a be-havioural shift towards dense complex social units, we have the mental capacity to try to understand what is happening to us, rather than merely be swept along by it. We can be made aware of the psycho-social changes in ourselves that are accompanying this shift, and we can attempt a conscious judgement about how far we wish to go in that direction.

But the judgement and the wishing will be in vain unless we can get some overall understanding of the forces that have brought the change about, and for that it is best to go back a very long way.

Long before the city came the village. It was a kind of settlement that evolved when some people had begun to set up permanent dwelling-places based on agriculture, but when the number of people involved was not significantly larger than can be found among nomadic tribes of hunter-gatherers. A village in Neolithic times would probably comprise seven or eight households. The largest so far discovered might have included about thirty households and covered an area up to six acres. Remains of such villages have been found preserved in Polish swamps, Swiss Lake bottoms and the mud of the Egyptian Delta.

They are found in such places partly because the mud has preserved the remains but also because it was only on that kind of site that permanent habitations were then possible. Hunters and nomads could not built them, nor food gatherers, because they would never find enough wild food in one place all round the year, and primitive agriculturalists found that if they stayed too long in one place the soil's fertility became exhausted. However, it was possible to occupy permanent sites by the sea, or by some lakes and rivers, because there new food sources were constantly brought to the people in the shape of fish and/or the annual deposits of new fertile silt that came down with the flood water.

Lewis Mumford in his book *The City in History* maintains that the village was created by women. It was all a very long time ago but whatever hard evidence we have been able to piece together seems to support his thesis. He writes:

> It was woman who wielded the digging stick or the hoe: she who tended the garden crop and accomplished those masterpieces of selection and cross-fertilization which turned raw wild species into the prolific and richly nutritious domestic varieties: it was woman who made the first containers, weaving baskets, and coiled the first clay pots. In form the village too is her creation, for whatever else the village might be it was a collective nest for the care and nurture of the young. Here she lengthened the period of child care and playful irresponsibility on which so much of man's higher development depends. . . .

These settlements already displayed some of the characteristics of the later city. There is evidence of continuity; there is evidence of communal effort expended on modifying the environment for communal advantage by the clearing of woodland and the construction of irrigation ditches; there is evidence of foresight and forward planning, at least to the extent of preserving this year's seed for next year's planting or against next year's dearth. For even the most primitive delta hamlet would contain 'a communal granary consisting of woven baskets sunk into the ground'.

But other factors were missing. There is, for example, no evidence of war. The earliest permanent settlements are full of containers but empty of weapons. There is at first little evidence of specialisation: the only craft with a name common to all the European languages, so that it must have been coined before the languages split up, is the carpenter's. And the size was finite, limited by the food resources of the area. Each village was economically self-sufficient and if the population rose too high the tendency was for some of the people to move off and found a daughter village on some other promising site.

The villages continued, essentially unchanged, for thousands of years, and then came the emergence of that quite different and more dynamic entity, the city. Up to that point we have more or less agreement from all the experts.

When the city did finally appear there is far less agreement about the why, and when, and where. Everybody accepts that there was one major spawning ground of cities in the so-called fertile crescent stretching from the Upper Nile to the Lower Euphrates. But it is impossible to be quite sure whether the development emerged spontaneously only once, and only there, so that all the cities in the world are spin-offs and imitations of that one leap forward, or whether under similar conditions, similar institutions evolved quite independently elsewhere – in India, in China, in South America. Thor Heyerdahl's journeys were attempts to establish whether it would have been possible for water-borne spores of civilisation to have crossed the ocean at the relevant date and taken root on the other side.

As for what exactly it was that took place, the most simplistic type of account runs something like this :

At a certain fortunate place or places on the earth's surface several factors co-existed favouring the emergence of civilisation. These included a benevolent climate, a fertile soil, annually revitalised by a silt-bearing river deep enough to be navigable and facilitate the use of water transport, and a human population already made relatively abundant by a few thousand years of the practice of agriculture and a co-operative village-based economy. Given these propitious conditions the people saw that they could now produce far more than they needed to keep themselves alive, and out of this surplus they were able to build and feed the city with its temples and palaces, its stonemasons and priests and jewellers and spinners and weavers and merchants and slaves and seal-cutters and glaziers and officials and clerks. Hence civilisation.

For anyone with an urban mind it may seem the most natural thing in the world for these cultivators to say to one another,

> Well lads, we've got a good crop of barley again this year, this is the chance we've been waiting for. Time to get up and go. Let's all go down to Lagash and build ourselves a ziggurat, and then if we all work hard and put in some over-time we could very probably increase output by forty or fifty percent which means we could release some of our fellow cultivators, him and him and him and him, so that they could go and be glaziers and jewellers and officials and clerks.

But a much more natural reaction would be

> Well lads, we've got a good crop of barley again this year; the women can make twice as much beer and we can all spend twice as much time lying around drinking it and we can all get twice as sloshed. And next year if the crops are going to go on being as heavy as this, we could easily get by on less acreage. Or better still you and me, and him and him, can retire early and let our sons get on with it. There's no sense in everybody wearing themselves out.

Many if not most readers in the northern hemisphere – where even the most remote are liable to have been brain-washed by doses of urban-inspired education – may feel that this is contrary to the way human beings behave. A spokesman of British Trade Unionism, when someone rather irritably asked him what exactly it was the unions were after, gave a succinct answer: 'More'. He meant more money. as a way of obtaining more goods and more services. Nobody has ever questioned that that is also what the employers want, and the share-holders. And if we move East to Russia and China the State wants more, so that it can distribute the increased gross national product, according to socialist principles, among its citizens who are presumed also to want one thing, namely 'More'. Different countries may vary in the amount of stress they place on 'more for everybody' as opposed to 'more for me'; the fact remains that the promise of ultimately having more consumer goods is sufficient incentive for putting in more work. According to this way of thinking, the offer of more material reward produces more labour according to this nice little graph*:

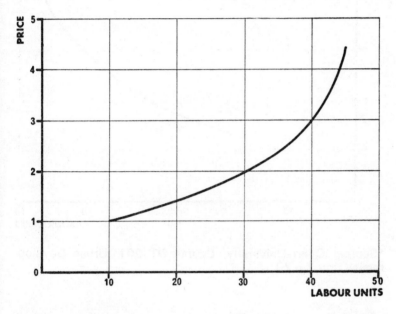

*Source: Open University, Course DT 201 'Urban Development', Unit 1 p.20

Now let us move to the southern hemisphere and look at this even more intriguing little graph*, which employers often encounter in places like South Africa, where a large proportion of the native labour force has never been processed into urban ways of thinking:

This is known as a 'backward sloping supply curve' and it means that above a certain point, the more money you offer for labour the less labour you get. If you asked these workers what they wanted, their answer wouldn't be 'More', as their

c

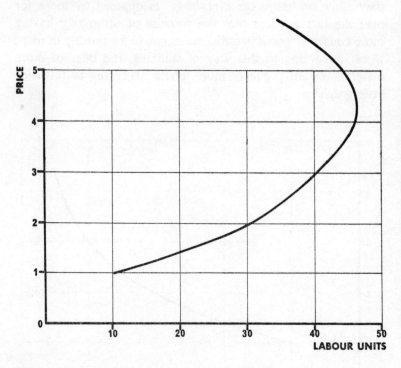

*Source: Open University, Course DT 201 'Urban Development', Unit 1 p.20

actions prove beyond all argument. Their answer would be 'Enough'. If you raised their rewards to the point where they could get 'enough' by working a four-hour day, or a two-day week, they would see no earthly reason why any man in his senses should work longer. In the same way employers in Australia may one day be going great guns with a willing force of Aboriginal labourers and wake up the next morning to find they have all melted away like the morning dew, for no reason in the world other than the feeling that 'that's enough of that'.

I would suggest that before men built Jericho or Ur of the Chaldees, the frame of mind indicated by the second graph was endemic to the whole of the human race. When God – or nature – raised the rewards by providing lusher and easier harvests, this would be likely to lead to relaxation of effort, not to a Great Leap Forward. The really mysterious thing about the first cities is that they can't have been built by urbanites because there weren't any. They were built by the folk. Now why would they do a thing like that?

It is sometimes airily implied that devoting part of the agricultural surplus to building a city is a natural extension of the habit of devoting part of it to buying a plough. All you have in both cases is the principle of division of labour. Once you have accepted the specialisation of the smith and the carpenter, the argument runs, then all the other specialisations must follow as the night the day. This ignores the pertinent fact that if a farmer keeps back some of his corn to buy a plough it is then his plough. If he keeps back some of his corn to feed a city-based clerk or architect, it will not be his accounts the clerk is keeping nor his barns the architect is designing. The economist may not be able to see the difference but the farmer certainly will.

Man in his natural state doesn't like work. The Christian bible recognises this by treating it quite naturally as a punitive *where?* affair, invented by God when he was gravely displeased with humanity's behaviour. Almost any kind of activity can be pleasurable as long as you're indulging in it voluntarily and can stop when you get tired or fed up with it. If you can't it's work. At that point it is natural for pre-urban man to stop doing it unless he has hunger, thirst, cold, fear or some other overriding discomfort to drive him on.

So it is simply not enough to say that cities arose in conditions where an agricultural surplus became possible. A surplus means 'too much', and a possible surplus only becomes an *actual* surplus if people go on working past the 'enough' point. This behaviour comes so naturally to most of us in the urbanised world that we forget it needs explaining, but it does. By far the likeliest explanation is that at some point the beneficiaries of the work became separated from the performers of it. Somebody got the bright idea: 'With crops like that, if he'd only put his back into it he could grow enough for two and the second one could be me.' Predatoriness in some form or other was not only, as in Wirth's model, one of the consequences of urbanism. It was also the genesis of it.

This is how Dr Jacob Bronowski describes the genesis: '. . . that form of theft began ten thousand years ago when the harvesters of wheat accumulated a surplus and the nomads rose out of the desert to rob them of what they themselves could not provide.'

Lewis Mumford puts it this way:

> No longer was it sufficient for the village farmer to produce enough to feed his family and his village: he must now work harder and practice self-denial to support a royal and priestly officialdom with a large surplus. For the new rulers were greedy feeders. . . . The village neighbours, no longer families and equals, were reduced to subjects whose lives were supervised and directed by military and civil officers, governors, viziers, tax gatherers. . . .

V. Gordon Childe envisaged it this way:

> Society persuaded or compelled the farmers to produce a surplus of food stuffs. . . . The artisans, labourers and transport workers may have been 'volunteers' inspired by religious enthusiasm. But the gods, being fictitious, must have had real representatives who must have done much to give concrete form to the imaginary beings and, by interpreting, must have invented their desires.

Other writers believe that ascendancy was not gained by the exploitation of superior force, nor of superstition, but of knowledge. Elliot Smith thought the people who invented and controlled the system of irrigation became kings (although there are tribes in New Mexico and the Philippines, for example, who manage irrigation systems co-operatively and successfully without putting their necks under a royal yoke). And another theory was that whoever studied the heavens and constructed the calendar exploited his monopoly of the knowledge of when the Nile floods were due.

Yet another version (Mumford again) is that as any given

tribe settled down to agriculture, some of their number found the change uncongenial and continued as hunters and that these hunting bands remained separate from the agriculturalists – rather in the way that bachelor bands of some species of monkeys remain separate from the main body of their tribe – and that these hunting bands remained swift, cunning, armed and often hungry while the homesteaders had become patient, plodding and well fed, and had beaten their spears into ploughshares. In such circumstances the hunters would perhaps in the first place offer to keep the wolf or the lion away from the flocks and herds in return for a meal ticket; later, when they saw how easy it was to lean on the settlers, they might begin operating a protection racket by threatening to turn their weapons away from the predators outside the village and direct them against the men inside it.

All this again is an area of speculation which is not germane to the present issue. The essential point is that the urban revolution, as surely as the industrial one, was made possible only by releasing vast, latent, hitherto untapped sources of energy.

In the case of the industrial revolution it was given its major impetus when men learned how to utilise the fossilised energies locked up in coal and oil. In Egypt and Mesopotamia at the dawn of civilisation these forces were unknown. They had harnessed some of the energies of water by building river boats, of the wind by constructing primitive sails, and of the muscles of animals by using them for transport and traction.

But the real increase in applied energy derived from the straightening out of that backward sloping supply curve, ensuring that when a man became fatigued or exhausted with the task he was engaged on he couldn't, or didn't, pack it in; and when a family had produced enough to satisfy its own needs, it would go on working and producing to satisfy someone else's. It was the greatest innovation since the domestication of the horse. It could be described as the domestication of people, and one of its names was slavery.

In as much as it is possible to link social institutions with sex in this way, then where the village had been 'feminine' in its inspiration the city was certainly 'masculine'. The distinction can easily be carried too far and is sometimes elaborated with a lot of dubious Freudian symbolism. But there is a certain amount of truth behind it. It is perhaps significant that in the interval between the appearance of these two types of settlement the women's digging stick had been replaced by the ox-drawn plough, requiring less patience and more strength and supporting a larger population and, according to all the available evidence, operated by men from its inception. They had thus moved from being freeloaders to being producers and no doubt it did wonders for their morale.

On many of the new urban institutions they certainly stamped their mark. As, for example, the hierarchical social structures with their royal or priestly kingpin, the pursuit of pomp and grandeur, and the emphasis on aggression and war. Lewis Mumford put it like this:

> In the cities new ways, rigorous, efficient, often harsh, even sadistic, took the place of ancient customs and comfortable, easy-paced routine. Work itself was detached from other activities and canalised into the 'working day' of unceasing toil under a task master. Struggle, domination, mastery, conquest were the new themes. . . .

However, it would be vastly oversimplifying to imply that the millions of man-hours of additional labour were all elicited by use of the whip and the goad. Men after all are not horses and cattle. They are in some ways far easier to control and manipulate than animals are. (In some Third World countries, in the heyday of the British Empire, there was a tradition that the monkeys only held their tongues because if the white men ever found out they could speak they would immediately set them to work.)

One alternative to force, as has been suggested, was to gain domination over the minds of the people rather than their bodies. It could be done by filling them with a love of (or the fear of) a god or gods and persuading them that the gods wanted them to build temples and to serve and enrich the priesthood. Or it could be done by filling them with partisanship, rivalry, patriotism, the determination that whatever the cost in sweat and blood our side and our king must be richer and more feared and build more splendid monuments than their side and their king.

It could be done by simple or disguised confiscation. If you take away every year a percentage of a man's crop he has to work harder to make up his loss. Initially he will see this as straight theft and you may have to fight him for it, but if he knows it happened to his father and his grandfather and his great grandfather before him he will learn in time to call these confiscations ground rent, or dues, or tithes, or taxes, and the force required to extract them from him can remain latent. The South Africans, faced with the inconvenient conviction of black villagers that a man was entitled to stop working when he had enough for his needs, and aware that slavery had gone out of fashion, resorted to the more 'civilised' alternative of imposing a hut tax.

These methods of harnessing and maximising the supply of applied human energy resulted not only in increasing the total output of available food and artefacts – it also had the effect of sucking vastly disproportionate amounts of this output into a central place, the vicinity of the palace and the temple. All over the Middle East are dotted the tels, lofty mounds of earth and sand where in the earliest days of civilisation, for generation after generation, human beings had been taking things from the surrounding area and from further afield, and sometimes from overseas – food, raw materials and man-made products carried or dragged on foot or on pack animals or on the heads of women or the backs of slaves until even the ground they walked on rose above the level of the countryside around it like the mound of a giant brush turkey. After all, the only point of despatching soldiers and tax gatherers to confiscate corn and wine and timber and cattle and slaves is in order to bring the stuff back home.

But far and away the most cordially received method of getting people to work on after they have fulfilled their needs is to increase their wants, by offering new objects and amenities for which they will trade their labour or their own products.

So after the king and priest, the third key figure in the urban economy is the merchant. Urban historians who are most hooked on cities often write as if he was the only one that mattered. Jane Jacobs suggests the merchant came even before the farmers and begat them, let alone before the captains and the kings. H. Pirenne defined the city as in its purest essence 'a colony of merchants'. Behind this version there is an implicit belief that trading in itself can and does increase the wealth not only of the merchant but of everybody else as well. It is buttressed by the unarguable fact that the great trading cities and the great trading nations have become the fat cats of the world throughout history. There are some elements of truth in it but they need to be carefully defined.

One element of truth is that the mere fact of having some people travelling around carrying things often has the effect of increasing human potential. It may bring together raw materials occurring naturally in places far apart, and their combination may be fruitful. For example there may be copper-bearing ore on one naked rocky island, while the mainland is thickly forested. You have to get the ore and the timber into one place to make the fire to smelt the metal. You then get a big and permanent pay off, because a copper knife is more efficient than a flint one. Of course you don't have to be a merchant to effect this juxtaposition. You may be an itinerant smith (some people believe he was the prototype of the merchant and took to buying and selling unconsidered trifles only as a sideline), or you may be a marauding army. But most of the fetching and carrying is undeniably done in the name of trade; trade is more than juxtaposition, and a merchant is more than a carrier.

The question is whether the merchant in his own right does anything to add to the total supply of wealth; and the answer is that he does, if only by acting as a catalyst.

Suppose that I am a farmer and you are a trapper and I meet you in the village and swap you a bushel of corn for a fur pelt. We both feel better for our transaction, because I will not be so cold and you will not be so hungry. Yet there are still the same number of bushels and pelts in the world. No new wealth has been created. How can that be altered if we happen to live further apart and deploy a middle man to go between us to carry the corn and the furs?

It is altered because the merchant, if he is any good at his job, knows just what the market will bear. He may tell me that there has been a plague of polecats or an outbreak of mange so that good pelts are very scarce and fetching two bushels of corn this year: if my harvest is rich or my children are cold, I will pay it. He will tell you that there has been drought or flood or locusts or weevils and that in offering you a whole bushel of corn for two miserable pelts he is being crazily quixotic, robbing himself, and will end up a beggar.

He feels, with some justification, that nobody is worse off for this. You can easily get hold of an extra pelt – it means only a slightly longer spell of healthful exercise in the open air and you will sleep all the better for it – and as for me, what is a bushel of corn? Next year I can plough one extra furrow, or send my children out to scare the crows off more diligently, or get my wife to be a bit more assiduous in gleaning the last grain. A little bit more latent energy will have been usefully expended by everybody; more goods will have been produced than would have been produced without the merchant's intervention; he himself is a pelt and a bushel to the good, and he takes them back to the city to store or to sell.

Archaeological evidence suggests that he was the latecomer to the urban trio and that in the earliest cities the merchant's quarters, unlike the palace and the temples, were originally outside the city walls. But the king and the priest soon recognised how useful he could be and invited him in, and the market place became the third of the city's architectural landmarks and trade marks. He was invaluable to them in bringing food, raw materials and treasures from distant lands to feed and equip their armies, craftsmen, courtiers, servants, acolytes and retinues, and to deck their persons and concubines and buildings.

It was also very convenient for them that he increased productivity in the surrounding area and magnetised a good deal of the extra wealth into his own pocket, because they could then get their cut by taxing *him*, which saved them a good deal of trouble. Last, but not least, he enabled them to plug in to the unused muscle-power in countries far afield without the bother of sending armies there. Any strong minded foreigner on a distant strand whose eyes could be made to light up at the sight of glittering wampum from the city would lie awake nights working out ways to exhort, coerce, terrify or bribe the local layabouts to stop sitting around in the sun and digesting, and get cracking on mining copper or felling cedar trees.

To call a man a catalyst is not quite the same thing as calling him merely a parasite. The king/priest/merchant consortium was often very tough and very greedy. Countless thousands groaned and died under their lash, and as many starved because of their exactions, but it would surely take a supreme hypocrite to regret that it happened. They were as essential to the rise of civilisation – of alphabets and mathematics and all the arts and all the sciences and everything that flowed from them – as yeast is to the rising of bread, and for a twentieth-century human being who has benefited from those things to wish them back into Limbo would be a kind of self-mutilation, if not a death wish.

All I wish to stress – because we cannot hope to diagnose civilisation's sicknesses if we fail to understand what makes it tick – is that when the wilderness blossomed into splendid new cities – those miracles of multifarious life and splendid monuments where previously there had been only sand and mud and reeds – it was recorded on clay tablets and stone obelisks that their illustrious founders had 'created' them – conjured them forth 'out of nothing'. And this was not true.

This primitive (or possibly sycophantic) mis-statement would not matter except that some economists even today write as though all that wealth was the outcome of a neat and repeatable set of tricks; as if, after an initial phase of sweat and blood and raw exploitation, an urban economy becomes as it were airborne into a rising spiral of self-made prosperity.

A popular example of the kind of feed-back alleged to have kept the spiral rising is the fact that around the cities even the farmers themselves grew fat and prosperous. This, we are told, was partly because the dense concentration of people and their pack animals in the city 'generated' a rich supply of compost and sewage which could be used to fertilise the land around, and this is envisaged in typically benign urban terms as a free gift, a bonus, to the agricultural sector. In fact, of course, they did not generate it at all : they merely processed it. And if a farmer wants to see the organic materials his land supplies return to the land to keep it healthy, there can be few ways of doing this more wasteful in energy terms than having it carried all the way to the city and passed through a donkey, or even a king or priest or philosopher, and then carried all the way back again. At its best the process represented not a gain but only a redistribution, by which the farmers nearest the city wall benefited at the expense of those furthest away.

The nearby farmers smiled and prospered, partly because cities were built in the first place in the most fertile spots; partly because they tended to be retired campaigners or royal favourites on whom tracts of the best land were 'bestowed' by a grateful sovereign, and who had brought home or could afford to buy slaves to help them work it, while the unsmiling evicted villager who had previously tilled it was no longer in evidence; and partly because they had on their doorstep a market composed of citizens too rich to need to haggle long over the price of anything they needed or fancied, and the riches all came in the last analysis from people they were plundering or conning or leaning on.

Nevertheless, it was the most natural thing in the world for such citizens to believe sincerely that they were doing everybody a favour. The conviction has stayed with us down the centuries. Almost the whole of history is one-sided because for the most parts the cities wrote it. We have a vivid picture of Rome in which, at intervals, fresh supplies of slaves turned up on the block and were sold to their new masters. But we know next to nothing about the families into which they were born and from whom they were taken, the methods and circumstances of their capture, or the way of life of whole areas of the world in whose eyes the rise of civilisation must have appeared as malignant as the rise of Nazism to the Jews.

When a man grows affluent and secure he likes to be surrounded by pleasant sights and sounds, and by people who like him: the physical signs of starvation and disease, the sounds of suffering, and the face of resentment are an offence to the eye. If he has slaves in his household they will tend to be sleek and well fed. On the other hand if he has slaves in his fields or on his plantation they will fare worse because he doesn't need to encounter them. And if he buys cheap from a Phoenician merchant because somewhere across the sea some Carthaginian slaves are being driven even harder than his own to satisfy the Roman market, that doesn't even touch the fringes of his consciousness. Even when the suffering is nearer home, people can be highly selective about what they actually see, just as decent sensitive people like Jane Austen in the last century could have their hearts wrung by the sufferings of impoverished gentlefolk who could afford only one maid to do all their work, and yet remain blind to the sufferings of the maid.

The fact is that there was no invisible multiplier at work, and the economic aspect of the lift-off had no element of the miraculous about it. With only minimal assistance from wind and water, every stone and brick and chariot and robe and jar and jewel, every ounce of food and every cup of wine that went into the making of the city was produced, processed and transported by the energy output of human muscle and human sweat. For thousands of years, for every city, and at every stage of its development, the only way to repeat the trick and achieve further economic expansion was somehow to harness additional human beings, near or far, to the task of building and provisioning the cities, or to increase the pressure on those already harnessed.

It is true that there were animals, but with the coming of civilisation, as Bronowski has pointed out, their economic contribution ran into a law of diminishing returns. In pre-urban days the domestication of equids had dramatically reduced the amount of human toil required to keep a village fed, for the ass or the horse – or the ox – pulled the plough instead of the farmer pushing it. But cities mean pomp and splendour. Cities demand speed and mobility and transport. Cities cast jealous eyes on one another's coffers and go to war. And to serve all these purposes the horse came into his own, first as chariot puller and later as steed and status symbol. Like Western pets today, it was often better bred and better fed and housed than fifty percent of men and women, and as the cities grew it was employed more and more for 'civilised' purposes, such as pageantry and war and to save the well-to-do from having to walk and to enable their orders to be carried out more speedily or simply to make them feel good. 'Mounting the horse was a more than human gesture, a symbolic act of dominance over the total creation.' Psychologically it was the equivalent of the modern motor car. Viewed from the land it had largely ceased to be a co-producer and had become simply another mouth to feed.

Professor Raul Prebitsch, writing of our own more recent civilisation explosion, has formulated a Law of Peripheral Neglect which states that in a nation-state the degree of neglect varies as the square of the distance from the centre (that is, the centre of power, not the geographical centre). The formulation may be new but the phenomenon is as old as Ur and Jericho.

To make it apply to the ancient world it would need two small modifications. In the first place, against that background it would be more nakedly obvious that the phenomenon is not a characteristic of nation-states but a characteristic of cities. And secondly, 'neglect' would be an inappropriate term because it presupposes some degree of assumed responsibility which was not being adequately carried out, and the early cities accepted responsibility for nothing and no one outside their walls. The law as amended would read 'In all areas within the economic orbit of a great city, the degree of exploitation varies as the square of the distance from the centre'.

Inside the city were at the top the absolute winners, who toiled not neither did they spin, yet they reaped luxury, privilege and honour; there were also once-free craftsmen working now with finer materials and better tools, but working to other men's orders. And there were slaves who however hard they were driven shared at least some of the excitement and satisfaction of belonging to a great enterprise and seeing the city rise under their hands.

Outside the city, but within the orbit of the city-based economy, there existed as it were concentric rings of people who had put in as much as anyone of the increased labour but got less and less out of it as the distance from the city lengthened. There were nearby farmers who lived well on the overflow of urban affluence; further out there were people who had once eaten what they grew and then sat around in the sun, but now worked much harder and lived no better for it because they were further away from the customers but still within range of the tax-gatherer. They couldn't afford the new metal tools that might have lightened their labour; these were used only by the men directly employed by the temple. In the hinterland, cultivation was still carried on with the old neolithic axes and ploughs. After the invention of money, when land itself became a commodity, tracts of it might be bestowed on soldiers or courtiers who had served the monarch well, and then the people who had previously worked it were pushed off, with the option of becoming tenant farmers or labourers or slaves or beggars.

Further away again there were the miners. Bronze was very expensive, the rich man's metal. His weapons were made of it and his supremacy was secured by his monopoly of it. So over the sea in Cyprus (which gave its name to copper) and still further afield in Portugal's Algarve, men were working harder and digging deeper than ever before to step up the output. According to the theory of the benevolent merchant as the city maker, you might think this would operate as 'trade' and that the tribes who supplied this coveted commodity would themselves grow rich and become the equivalent of our oil millionaires.

Well, the copper went out all right, but archaeologists have found very little sign of anything from Egypt or Mesopotamia that came in in exchange for it. Obviously the civilised people

from the fertile crescent weren't about to stand any nonsense from a lot of shaggy hill dwellers. The Sumerian sign
for 'slave' was 'mountain woman'; the Egyptians sent their
army to knock hell out of the presumably non-cooperative
nomads in the copper-bearing area of Sinai; and they fixed the
price they offered for Nubian gold at nil, by the simple expedient of conquering the whole region and demanding the
gold as the tribute of a vassal state.

In all the regions the traders touched, there were men of
power who were allured by the new treasures displayed to
them, and below them there were men without power who
were made to work harder because in civilised Egypt there
were now goldsmiths and jewellers who could dazzle their
master's eyes. In a place like Byblos, which exported the
cedars of Lebanon, a prosperous independent city grew up with
graceful public buildings, exchanging ambassadors with Egypt
and thinking up new ways of maximising the labour of the
lumberjacks who were busy denuding the land of its trees.

Right out at the periphery, there were the conquered and
the looted, and the ruined and depleted communities of what
were regarded as the enslavable tribes, in the sense in which
Graham Greene somewhere writes of the 'torturable classes'.
Concerning them history is silent. They were the absolute
losers.

However, for the beneficiaries the new order was a splendid
invention. Its advantages were so obvious that it was widely
imitated, and fairly soon it became apparent that 'the chief
enemy of a city is another city'.

That was, of course, inevitable. The basic mainspring of the
system was acquisitiveness, and the powerful and acquisitive
men who founded the cities could not fail to see that it takes
a long time to scratch together a really satisfying store of
desirable objects merely by exploiting helots and craftsmen
and despatching merchants to do a bit of crafty bargaining.
One way of taking a notable short cut was to rub out a neighbouring city where such a collection was already under way,
and carry home the loot.

Before long, as Lewis Mumford points out, 'War had become

one of the reasons for the city's existence'. The conquerors took a literal view of the rubbing out too, as Biblical sources among others reveal: 'And he took the city and slew the people therein; and he beat down the city and served it with salt' – a primitive scorched-earth process. It is rather ironical that the word 'vandalism' derives from the name of a bar-barian, envisaged in most people's minds as an uncouth nomad storming in and defacing buildings and monuments whose beauty he was too boorish to appreciate. Very likely, but the efforts of the vandals and their kind have always been pathetic-ally amateurish compared to the venom of the civilised who perceived the beauty and the splendour all too well and were maddened by it, as Sennacherib was by Babylon. When the looting was over he boasted 'the city and its houses from its foundations to its top I destroyed, I devastated, I burned with fire. The wall and the outer wall, temples and gods, temple towers of bricks and earth, as many as they were I razed and dumped into the Arakhtu Canal. Through the midst of that city I dug canals, I flooded its site with water and the very foundations thereof I destroyed. . . .'

Our own destructiveness – Coventry, Dresden, Hiroshima, Stalingrad – is more efficient still, and more elaborately rationalised these days. But it was only in the last century that Marshal Blücher, upon first clapping eyes on the City of London, uttered the spontaneous exclamation which could have come from any visiting soldier in any city right back through history: 'What a place to plunder!'

And again dotted over the world are the relics of cities which appear to have died without leaving any sign of enemy action or act of God – floods, earthquakes or volcanoes – to explain their downfall. Their bleached bones demonstrate even more dramatically the lesson that Sir Kenneth Clark derived from the fall of Rome: 'This almost incredible episode does tell one something about the nature of civilisation. It shows that how-ever complex and solid it seems, it is actually quite fragile. It can be destroyed'.

It is fragile not necessarily in spite of its complexity, but possibly because of it, in the same way that a space rocket is more vulnerable than a steam engine. For a civilisation to be destroyed it isn't necessary for all its citizens to be wiped out or to starve. Long before that point is reached they can become demoralised. Some of the assumptions on which the system is based may prove to be erroneous. Perhaps some of those that died merely leaned a little too hard on the producers of their wealth, as a man may overload a horse or camel until it collapses under him, and as the farmers of Oklahoma leaned a little too hard on their topsoil and dust-bowled it.

Unfortunately it is too late to diagnose with any certainty the symptoms of most of the ancient civilisations that rose and flourished and died. We can only dig up their colossal monuments and sometimes decipher in their inscriptions the stereotyped paranoid snarl of so many of the archetypal city builders:

> My name is Ozymandias, King of Kings.
> Look on my works, ye mighty, and despair.

PART II

Historical

5 Classical cities: The glory and the grandeur

Civilisation survived the death of a thousand Ozymandiases with no trouble at all. Individual cities might relapse into chaos and anarchy and sink into the sand, but the *idea* of the city seemed imperishable.

Far away on the flood plains of the Punjab flourishing cities appeared. In Mohenjodaro and Harappa by 2500 BC there were highly organised communities with vast granaries, streets of two-storey houses with bathrooms, thriving markets, municipal drainage, glazed pottery, professional metalworkers, wheeled carts and systems of writing and numbering. And when the same phenomenon manifested itself on the flood plains of China's Yellow River the organisation of the economy and, with local variations, the artefacts, showed remarkable similarity to more westerly versions.

The next breakthrough came in the Mediterranean. It was the revelation that in order to have a city you don't necessarily have to have a king, and that, in fact, the greed and vanity and lust for conspicuous consumption of these inflated hominids and their hangers-on were part of the reason why the system in one area after another kept breaking down.

This new version of the city was not developed by some early urban Robespierre ousting a ruler from his seat of power and setting up a parliament. In its most famous form, that of the Greek *polis*, it was invented by the descendants of a bunch of barbarians who invaded Greece after one of the periodic relapses of monarchic urban culture, when most of the area had sunk into illiteracy and more or less lost contact with other and more thriving centres of civilisation. They settled in the little valleys and along the narrow coastal strip, sharing out and fighting over the land, living in the first instance by subsistence agriculture and fishing. Such war chiefs as they had recognised while conducting their invasion ceased to have any function, and lost their hold. The people built villages consisting of peasants plus a few professional craftsmen such as potters and smiths. Whenever the population of such a village grew larger than the land could sustain, their sons emigrated and founded new village settlements on nearby coasts.

When Phoenician merchants began visiting to see whether these newcomers had anything worth trading they offered not the finely wrought products of royal craftsmen, but cheap, unpretentious vases made by hard-working village potters for small returns, and wine and oil from Attic peasants eager to develop and export a sideline. After a while, they began carrying the merchandise in their own ships. Their potters and carpenters turned to mass production and many of their farmers began to specialise henceforth in vines and olives and import their own grain crops from overseas. The population increased rapidly. Many of them became wealthy, and some of the villages grew large enough and complex enough to qualify as cities, without ever having had any king to demand tribute and lick them into shape and have his name carved on their monuments as the only begetter of all this prosperity.

They were not the only republicans around at the time. The Phoenicians, too, had independent younger sons who crossed the seas and settled as colonists. And (as George III discovered) the divinity that doth hedge a king can get sadly diluted once a section of his loyal subjects puts enough salt water between themselves and the throne.

But it was the Greeks who stamped their image indelibly on the vision of the city as an ideal, a way of life, a place where free men could hold their heads up and walk as equals and have leisure to exercise their bodies and develop their minds and discuss loftier matters than pig swill and fowl pest. It was the Greek *polis* that gave us our words for politics and policy and politeness and police, as well as the unwieldier words for those unwieldier structures, the metropolis, the megalopolis and the world-wide Ecumenopolis which we are promised (or threatened with).

In recent years, because the ancient Greeks were at one

time over-idealised and because our own vision of democracy is a more comprehensive one, it has been frequently pointed out that Athenian democracy was not democracy at all since it was based on slavery, and that is, of course, quite true.

However, I am not going to spend time knocking Sophocles and Euripides and Aristotle and Socrates for belonging to a slave-owning society (Socrates was only a stone-cutter anyway), any more than I would waste time knocking Shakespeare, Leonardo, Beethoven and Einstein for belonging as they did to the privileged half of a society based on male domination. It would do all of us good, every so often, to remember and weep for the mute inglorious Miltons and Newtons who were lost to history through being tied to the galley oars, or the hoe and the sickle, or the cradle and the cooking pot, and who thus got ploughed under to provide the compost for the occasional emergent white male genius. But we are, or ought to be, human before we are anything else and if we cannot remember human greatness wherever it has appeared with more of pride than of envy, then we are sunk. The *polis* with all its faults was a better and more promising form of society than any that had gone before.

The more pertinent question is what made it so good? The way the twig is bent the tree will grow, and a good deal of western thinking still leans in the direction it was tilted by the Greeks of the fifth century BC who were intoxicated with the new society they had built up so swiftly from a base of barbarism. Since they had no king to bow down to, and were rapidly running out of reverence for their assorted gods, they found an outlet for some of this dammed-up awe and gratitude by displacing it on to the city itself, as an abstract concept to contemplate and argue about, to identify with, serve, glorify, live and fight and die for. Socrates in the 'Phaedrus' says that the whole natural world outside had nothing whatever to teach him : he could acquire all the wisdom he needed by observing men in the city. 'That', observed Lewis Mumford dryly, 'was a cockney illusion.' It was also a particularly tenacious one. Today the people who subscribe to it could be numbered in hundreds of millions.

And yet on any kind of folk-urban continuum, as we would measure it today, what they had there at the beginning of their astonishing outburst of creativity was not much more than a small town. 'City' to them meant a few thousand people – very few had more than ten. As for Athens, the biggest of them all, estimates vary, but including wives and children, slaves and resident aliens it probably reached 100,000.

The streets were narrow alleyways winding between little one-storey houses, flimsily built of wood and sun-dried clay. Sanitation was primitive or non-existent. Refuse was scavenged by pigs and dogs, or dumped on heaps outside the city together with human sewage. Water supply was a problem. Municipal government was by an urban equivalent of the village meeting at which all free citizens were entitled to contribute their views – one reason perhaps why Aristotle limited the size of the ideal city to the greatest number of people which suffices for the purposes of life 'and can be taken in at a single view'.

The theatre which produced the great Greek tragedies and comedies resembled Leicester Square or Broadway less than it resembled Oberammergau, except that it demanded a constant supply of new plays; for the cast was not recruited from members of Equity but consisted, like any small town drama group, partly of people so keen they couldn't be kept out and partly of the other kind, prodded into cooperating out of good nature and public spirit because the show must go on. The cultural festivals which periodically brought together people from different parts of Greece resembled in many ways the National Eisteddfod which unites for an amateur feast of poetry, music and drama the people of the equally scattered mountain valleys of Wales.

Everyone was expected to pull his weight in running the city. And most of the public offices were filled by drawing lots rather than by eager citizens touting for a little brief authority, or professional bureaucrats: it was the time-honoured system of 'volunteers – you, you and you'. The highest office might thus fall to a prosperous farmer doing his stint as citizen, or to a tanner, lamp-maker or stonemason.

The expenses of the free music and drama were defrayed by the richest citizens. However, the machinery for getting the money out of them was not the urban method of imposing a tax, but the folk method – the steady expectant gaze and subtle hinting of friends and neighbours who have known you from way back and can estimate to a drachma what you are worth, and make it plain that it is about time you took your turn at dipping your hand in your pocket in exchange for a speech of thanks and a round of applause. The money was not too hard to extract because the Greeks had only recently emerged from a state of stringent poverty and had not yet acquired habits of luxury or ostentatious personal display.

Above all, the place had the one essential prerequisite of a folkstyle society – stability and continuity of social relationships. A man of sixty could confidently expect to find the 'men who were boys when I was a boy walking along with me', and wherever in the city they lived it would not be too far away for him to stroll over and have a chat.

From where we stand it is not easy to understand how a place so moderate in size and so corny in lifestyle could have generated such a powerhouse of intellectual, political and artistic excitement. Even in the ancient world, after Athens had become famous, visitors from overseas sometimes exclaimed incredulously on entering the city: 'Is this the place all the fuss has been about?' Was there then in classical Athens some miraculous genetic endowment? A mass hatching of natural genius? Was there a shaft of illumination from outer space? I find all these explanations equally unacceptable.

One reason we find it so incredible is that in our age a place so small and folksy is almost invariably a place low in the rank order: a place from which its most talented children cannot wait to fight their way up and out. If I were to try to imagine a community – a pool of native talent – comparable in extent to Athens at its finest hour, I would need to look no further than the town I was born in (or ten thousand others like it). I am not claiming that anyone visiting Pontypridd immediately feels along their nerves an electrifying zing of intellectual ferment and cries out: 'Aha! The Athens of Glamorgan!' – on the contrary. And yet, if you could count up the people the place has (in the sadly apposite phrase) 'turned out' – all the musicians, educationists, playwrights, singers, novelists, preachers, statesmen, actors, scholars, artists and administrators that have left it in my lifetime to quicken the tempo of life in other places nearer to the pulse of power the list grows long. If the town had been suddenly islanded, it would have had all those far-flung headmasters, town clerks, cabinet ministers, barristers, colonial administrators, bringing their minds and debating skills to bear on how best to make it a great, good place; the writers and artists forming salons on the left bank of the Taff and knocking sparks out of each others' minds; and on Saturday nights instead of wowing them in La Scala and Las Vegas respectively, Geraint Evans and Tom Jones would have been putting on a double bill in the town hall. It would have been quite a place. The only point I am making is that it is seldom or never the lack of good human raw material *in its cradles* that holds a town back.

The mixture that produced the best generations of Athenians was not a repeatable recipe but it was not supernatural either. It had the humanity and vigour of a recent peasant past. It had the self-confidence and leisure bestowed by a rapid access of affluence, the implosive magnetism that comes from being the luckiest, wealthiest and strongest centre of population in its own particular part of the world, and the spur to the imagination that comes of facing new situations and intellectually treading new ground. In the beginning, at least, while richly displaying the increased verbal and mental agility and the receptiveness to new ideas still characteristic of the 'urban' end of the spectrum, it seemed to show few of the less attractive traits – the boredom, materialism, reserve and anomie.

But it went on growing and the freshness did not last. Louis Wirth's syndrome began to set in. At first the high thinking continued, but the plain living became less austere. If not for themselves, then certainly for their beloved city nothing could be too costly or ambitious. But temples and monuments, however ethereally beautiful, have to be built and paid for with smelly sweat and filthy lucre. The people who work on them have to be accommodated and fed (on corn which was by now mostly imported). The citizens began to look on their citizenship as a higher calling than any form of manual labour could be, and gradually began to reserve their energies for this and let other people do the work. And among the people flocking to the city eager to do just that, were not only new-comers and hicks and hobbledehoys who didn't understand about the city and oughtn't to be trusted with any influence over it, but also a rabble of aliens and fast-breeding foreigners. All very well to admit that they were free men – especially since they produced a lot of the exports which financed the city – but it would hardly do to call them citizens. They might get to outvote the natives, and then where would it all end? Hellenic democracy, it was decided, was too precious an ideal to be entrusted to all free men within the city.

So citizenship became a restricted privilege. No traders were admitted, no shopkeepers, no hand workers. Those trades were *banausic* (ignoble). This was a great mistake, because as the city grew some of the traders and shopkeepers and crafts-men enlarged themselves into merchant princes and cosmo-politan bankers who had so much real power that they couldn't have been bothered to participate in the rituals of democracy even if they had been paid to. As the real power of the demo-cratic assembly diminished, the quality of those who did participate deteriorated. They found the job of administration growing more complex and unwieldy and they tended in-creasingly to break up into factions and caucuses and leave the more boring and essential jobs (like keeping the accounts) to educated slaves.

The streets grew wider and the colonnades more splendid and the citizens took increasing pride in their good taste, their eye for beauty, their talent for gracious living. They spent more time in the baths; their tastes in food and wine became more refined and demanding; they began to import and collect as well as to commission works of art. Some of the finest monuments often regarded as the incarnation and efflorescence of Hellenic democracy were in fact erected over its dead body.

It all had to be paid for and how? The rich silver mines nearby at Laurion were one of the foundations of Athenian wealth, but as long as they were worked by free men their output could not be expanded fast enough to satisfy the demand for growth. So the free miners were phased out and replaced by slaves. More slaves were needed for the workshops of the growing industrial sector and to wait upon the citizens. Their lot was probably no harder than that of the theoretically free miners and skivvys and factory hands of Victorian England. But as in Victorian England, the horizontal stratification into social and economic classes became more pronounced and inequalities more extreme. Town planners like Hippodamus proposed reserving special areas of the city for the working classes, other areas for the 'armed defenders of the state', and so on.

For the army too had become professional, where originally it had materialised at need out of the voluntary and temporary mobilisation of free citizens taking time off from arguing, governing, acting, throwing the discus and tending their vine-yards. After all, there was great competition for resources such as slaves; there were other Greek cities besides Athens and some of them were slow to acknowledge the intrinsic Athenian right to supremacy which was so glaringly obvious to every native-born son of Athens. These inferior cities persisted in the supposition that the Athenian Empire was still, as in the early days, a league of free cities against Persia. And they complained loudly when the Athenians displayed metropolitan behaviour-patterns like dipping into the treasury to which all had contributed and using the money to adorn their own city, and finally moving these funds, lock, stock and barrel, from the offshore island of Delos into Athens itself.

The 'glory that was Greece' is sometimes adduced as evidence that some of the less acceptable attributes of urbanism are merely accidental blemishes that have crept in recently and can be eradicated. It seems equally possible to argue that fifth-century BC Athens provides a classic case of a folk-type community expanding under the impact of a sudden increase in wealth and power and inevitably acquiring, as it increased in size and density, all the universal hallmarks, good and bad, of *Homo gregarius* wherever he swarms.

Nowadays the men of power do not find much to worry them in the decline of the Athenian empire. It was superseded by superior and more efficient forces, and that can happen to anybody. It made mistakes which we have learned to avoid; for example, they never got around to replacing face-to-face town-meeting style democracy by the representative democracy of the ballot box. The ancient Greeks may have been very good at arts and sciences and philosophy and trade, but since they never quite got the hang of really efficient government, we don't feel that their passing bell truly tolls for us.

Rome was different. The fall of Rome – 'this almost incredible episode' – still has an insidious power to give us nightmares because Rome had strong government, military power, economic strength, administrative efficiency and experience, and established its authority over most of its known world as thoroughly as the late British Empire or any twentieth-century power bloc. And it was not defeated by an enemy even more efficient and civilised than itself. It fell because something went wrong, and reading about its decline and fall we find uncomfortably close echoes of the kind of malaise haunting more than one contemporary metropolis, and best summed up in W. B. Yeats's ominous line:

Things fall apart. The centre will not hold.

The power and wealth of Rome were founded from the beginning less on its merchants than on its armies, and as long as they continued to extend the bounds of its empire, metropolitan Rome flourished. It was the most exciting place in the world to live in. Its grave and eloquent senators debated and perfected the system of republican law and order which it then exported all over Europe and beyond. Wherever its soldiers marched, driving back the barbarians and establishing the Roman way of life, they built straight roads and established new towns all on a similar pattern, as recognisable as Woolworths stores, as square as their army camps, and all full of people eagerly learning to be industrious and to talk Latin and exploit the resources of their own immediate hinterland and climb on to the imperial gravy train. All the roads led back to Rome and loot, merchandise, profits and captives streamed along them unceasingly back to the centre.

Around AD 150 the limits of expansion had been reached and it was time to consolidate. But Romans by now were geared to the expectation of growth. They had come to regard the annual increment over the years from new provinces, brought one after another into their orbit, as if it was steady income destined always to appreciate. It was not at all convenient to them that it should dry up. It was inconvenient too that many client provinces, which had welcomed the products of Roman industry in exchange for local raw materials, had begun setting up similar industries on their own account – high class pottery, for example, and glass – which resulted in a loss of revenue for Rome. In order that the more affluent citizens might keep up their accustomed standard of living, including costly imports such as spices and silks from India, they began exporting gold.

In addition there were troubles on the home front. Some of them were minor irritations like the appalling traffic congestion. Julius Caesar nearly two hundred years earlier had been forced to ban wheeled traffic from the centre of Rome during the day, and things had got a lot worse since then. Juvenal was complaining: 'here in Rome many invalids die from being kept awake. . . . In the city sleep is a luxury that costs a fortune. This is the prime cause of illness there.'

The rent of a decent house in Rome had risen to four times that of other Italian towns, while the working people lived in flimsy, overcrowded, high-rise tenement buildings put up by dishonest building contractors. There was growing unemployment among them and growing discontent. Romans of all classes were increasingly manifesting the more undesirable of the qualities in Wirth's classical urban syndrome – anomie, boredom, violence, crime and corruption. In fear of anarchy republican Rome (like democratic Greece) turned back to the older urban system of the strong man as ruler, tyrant, dictator or emperor. The dissatisfied workers were pacified with doles – first corn, then flour ready milled for them, finally bread – and with shorter hours, more frequent holidays and gladiatorial shows of escalating violence and sadism. Sexual and porno-graphic elements were added to increase popular appeal, and by the end free shows were given on 175 days a year.

It all took a lot of organising. When victims for the spec-tacles of torture and killing were not forthcoming in large enough numbers from the jails, military expeditions were mounted to bring more in. There was a high consumption of human beings in the arena by now, as the sport element of the shows diminished and the amount of straight and disguised slaughter increased. It put intolerable pressure even on the system of refuse disposal. Sometimes as many as five thousand animals were slaughtered in one mighty spectacular, besides the human victims. They were all dumped in pits outside the city wall and periodically when plague victims from the typhus-ridden slums added to their number, the pits had to be left open day and night.

Other services which had been the pride of Roman efficiency began to creak also. The post might fail to arrive; the heating in the public baths fail to function. As time went on those who could afford it began to move out of the city. Some of them bought or retired to their own country estates and set about making them as self-sufficient as possible, because inflation had set in : Nero was covering his deficit by debasing the currency and putting up taxes yet again. Out in the provinces the new towns began to shrink, the public amenities fell into disuse or disrepair and nobody bothered or could afford to build them up again. For two hundred years the decline continued. By the time Alaric arrived with his barbarian horde, Rome was a push-over.

It is a narrative with too many uncomfortably familiar as-pects. Very few people can contemplate it without wanting to draw some sort of moral. In the last century it tended to be a simple, ethical one about the wages of sin, and pride going before a fall : those who wished to retain an empire should eschew orgies and exercise austerity and self-discipline. Later a Marxist version explained that the outward expansion into alien territory could have been, and ought to have been, replaced by an expansion of internal demand by paying the workers and slaves the full worth of their labour. Then everything would have been all right.

Non-Marxist economists will point out that no parallel can usefully be drawn with any crisis of our own; that effective demand can go on increasing as well under capitalism as under communism as long as it is properly manipulated; they will join with the Marxists in asserting that now we've got industrialisation and automation and computerisation the growth curves don't have to be limited by anything. We will never have to stop and consolidate. Unlike Rome we can go on expanding for ever – 'and', some of them seem to be adding under their breath, 'we better had, or else. . . .'

Because the trouble with expansion is that it becomes addictive. Poverty and underprivilege are highly relative concepts – the Wattstown rioters who stunned Los Angeles would have been regarded by millions of their fellow human beings as rich beyond the dreams of avarice. Moreover people think of themselves as poor not only by measuring themselves against their neighbours, but by measuring what they have against what they had been given reason to hope for. A man who has grown steadily better off for twenty years at the rate of five percent per annum can feel affronted and impoverished if this year he grows only two percent richer.

It is not easy to see how Imperial Rome could have solved its problems by paying its metropolitan proletariat the worth of their labour. Under such a system the worth of their labour to the community was frequently nil. How do you compute the social value of the personal servant of one of an emperor's overfed catamites, concubines and toadies? How do you provide space within the city's confines for productive labour at economic prices when urban land values are soaring and accommodation is being swamped with immigrants who come in penniless and hang around as beggars, or live off the crumbs that trickle down through various channels from the imperial table?

Draconian measures would have been needed – forcible eviction of thirty or forty percent of them and orders given to the rest that they must work or starve. But in the days before bombs and machine guns and CS gas it would have been madness to venture into those narrow alleys and try to implement such a policy. Far safer to hand out bread and circuses. The Greek word for the mob – *hoi polloi*, the many – is falling out of use; 'mob' itself comes straight from the Roman *mobile vulgus* – the fickle, the treacherous, common people. The dread of what might happen if ten thousand of these rose up in united fury was born with the first city. Such uprisings have only rarely come to pass but the fear of them has never quite died. So that if ever draconian measures have to be applied anywhere then the farther away from the capital city the axe falls, the less the danger to the wielder. The ones nearest at hand tend to get more than their share of both the circuses and the bread.

Thus the inequality between the city's rich and the city's poor was not the only factor unbalancing the economy. There was also the imbalance between what the city took and what she gave, an imbalance that has persisted down to our own days.

The imbalance is usually most evident in the case of capital cities, and Rome was a prime example. Arnold Toynbee in his historical recap *Cities on the move* ponders on the economic function of such places.

'The smallest and poorest market town produces wares to pay for the food that it buys. A capital city apparently reaps where it has not sown. . . .' But he ends up by giving them the benefit of the doubt:

Capital cities *do* make a return for the supplies they import though this is not a return in kind and is not an economic service either. Capitals justify the tolls they levy on the production of distant provinces by performing for the provinces political and military services that are valuable *though they may not in all cases be welcome.* (Those are my italics.)

D

He goes on to explain :

> A capital sends out civil servants and soldiers who conduct the administration, keep the peace within the frontiers and defend against attack from outside. . . . If the government installed in the capital city fails to provide the provinces with an efficient administration, an effective police, and a successful defence of the frontiers the revenues in kind or in money that have been flowing from the provinces into the capital will fall off and then both the prosperity and the number of the population of the capital will decrease. This was the fate of the city of Rome . . . and of the capitals of all other large states that have declined and fallen.

Some interesting points are raised there. The idea of demanding payment for rendering services which though 'valuable' have not been requested and are 'not in all cases welcome' is an ingenious one. Basically it is the same bright idea that inspired the South Africans to exact a hut tax from the blacks to defray the exenses of administering and 'protecting' them, and that inspires the urban protection-racketeer to collect a periodic sweetener in return for guarantees of immunity from violence and destruction – guarantees which are undeniably 'valuable though not in all cases welcome'.

Secondly, Toynbee's reference to a city failing to provide efficient policing and administration tends to suggest that apart from the occasional accident of such inefficiencies creeping in, the system is a viable one that might run indefinitely with the 'revenues in kind or in money flowing from the provinces into the capital' unceasingly and forever.

This I doubt. It seems rather like a subtler version of the relationship (which also lasted for thousands of years and was doubtless regarded by its practitioners as eternal) between the nomads and the settlers. That system finally broke down, in Dr Bronowski's succinct phrase, 'because theft is not a permanent state that can be sustained.'

Theft is obviously an overharsh word to supply to the *Pax Romana*. It suggests the actions of someone who knows he is taking something without the owner's consent and giving nothing in return, whereas Rome felt it was giving not only 'protection' (allow *us* to lean on you and we will guarantee to fight anyone else who tries to do it) but also the blessings of civilisation. There has never yet been a city or state which passed on this body of inherited knowledge to 'the barbarians' without feeling on the one hand the slightly smug sense of conferring a boon, and on the other hand a conviction that it had somehow acquired copyright in the ideas, and could expect to collect royalties in perpetuity from any of its pupils who began to make use of them.

This conviction was held regardless of the fact that the ideas themselves had originated in widely dispersed areas all over the known world. Some of the techniques which had the greatest economic impact had been discovered in the first place by obscure and illiterate people who certainly got no kick-back from their imitators. Thus it was probably to some unremembered Middle Eastern farmer that they owed the plough, to some villager in the south of Russia the wheeled cart, to the nomads of Central Asia the horse as steed, and to a barbarian tribe in the mountains of Armenia the economic smelting of iron.

What the swarming 'hot spots' of civilisation had done from the beginning was to provide a clearing house for all such discoveries that they encountered or got wind of; to corner by hook or crook enough wealth and raw materials and man-hours of servile labour to apply the techniques on a larger scale; and to hire, domesticate, enslave, corral or bribe the best brains within their orbit to come and contemplate the treasure house of loot and gadgets and dream up new ways of improving them, combining them and perfecting their uses. Once the system got under way the brains would barely need bribing; they would hunger for the pabulum of garnered facts and other men's ideas as a gourmet would hunger for the urban fleshpots, and gravitate to such places like moths to a candle. We may be thankful they did, for this led to such an explosive increase in the human potential that even for those who have not yet benefited from it – and they are many – it still constitutes their best hope for the future.

However, there was and is one built-in snag. Up to now it has always meant, and still means, the concentration of an overwhelming proportion of the world's best minds on the problems of the city and on more general problems as viewed *from* the city; and an unconscious predisposition to solve problems in ways that will mainly benefit the city, or by methods that only the city can employ, i.e. mass production methods requiring large capital outlay. By today, although this approach is running into unprecedented snags, the habit of looking ever more closely at the city for the cause and cure of its own malaise seems almost ineradicable.

But to return to the fall of Rome – the historian's view of it is like the Shakespearean Mark Anthony's view of the death of Caesar: 'Oh what a fall was there, my countrymen!' and the centuries that followed are known by common consensus as the Dark Ages. It might be worth trying to modify this rather spooky description as far as possible, if only because it prompts so many panicky forecasts that this or that dip in the economic graph must portend 'the end of civilisation as we know it'.

For one thing it was only on Europe that the 'darkness' fell. When Sir Kenneth Clark writes about civilisation 'coming through' by the skin of its teeth he remembers to qualify it (once at least) by the saving clause 'in so far as we are the heirs of Greece and Rome'. There were no simultaneous collapses in the civilisations of China and India; Byzantium, the Eastern outpost of the Roman Empire, contented itself with a non-expansionist policy and shrank away only very, very slowly over the centuries; and the forces of Islam which finally completed the demolition of Graeco-Roman culture certainly did not regard themselves as barbarians. By them, as by every successor civilisation, 'the science of the conquered nations was gathered with a kleptomaniac zest' and they quickly added notable advances of their own in mathematics (by adding the zero) and astronomy and chemistry.

But in Europe itself the process halted for hundreds of years. I cannot think of any history book that can be offered to a western child to read which treats of that as anything other than unalloyed tragedy – as if, to quote Mark Anthony again, 'then you and I and all of us fell down'.

Yet it can't be true that all of us fell down. Take a parallel : it would have been a set-back for civilisation in America if the Redskins had by some miracle recouped their forces and won, and sacked New York and Philadelphia and burned the books and the newspaper offices; but inasmuch as we are human beings and not just palefaces we must admit that there are extant inhabitants of the United States whom we should find it hard to convince that that would have been a black day for mankind. Geronimo, in resisting the advance guards of civilisation, felt with quite as much conviction as Churchill resisting Hitler : 'It is evil forces we are fighting against.'

When Rome fell the barbarians saw the Romans in much the same light as the Indians saw the cowboys, and with much the same justification. Yet while historians of the American conflict are now beginning to take a more sympathetic view of the Red Indians' doomed resistance, historians of the fall of Rome unconsciously but almost invariably identify themselves with the civilisers. This is partly because on that occasion the barbarians won, which naturally makes them much harder to forgive.

Fernand Braudel makes a very sound point when he says :

> When civilisations are defeated or seem to be defeated the conqueror is always a 'barbarian'. It is a figure of speech. A barbarian to a Greek was anyone who was not Greek, to a Chinaman anyone who was not Chinese.

The 'bar-bar' root of the word is only another version of the 'rhubarb' of actors in crowd scenes, an imitation of a lot of people making indecipherable noises.

As for the barbarians whose language fell so harshly on Roman ears, we have to remember that their deeds were written down only by their victims. It will be fairly safe to assume that in their own eyes the 'Dark Ages' would have been a meaningless phrase – to them the dark was light enough. Equally on the periphery of Rome's sphere of influence inhabited by the absolute losers, there must have been a period

when they began to cease cowering and lifted up their heads
and realised that the Roman army had not sent an expedition
now for many years and perhaps never would again. Even in
some of the near-autonomous colonial outposts during the long
sunset of Rome's power, when the post failed to arrive there
must have been some consolation in the fact that the tax collector didn't make it either.

I have no intention here of embarking on a panegyric about
barbarism (though perhaps the time is ripe for one – there
has already been a spirited whitewash job on Attila the Hun),
nor of reviving a Rousseau-style rumour that there was once a
Golden Age on the earth before civilisation came along and
spoiled it. Every strong and honest mind accepts that for its
beneficiaries, the blessings that civilisation has brought are infinitely precious. Sir Kenneth Clark puts it politely: 'People
sometimes tell me that they prefer barbarism to civilisation. I
doubt if they have given it a long enough trial.' Doctor John-
son put it more bluntly: 'Don't cant about savages.'

But the point about Roman civilisation, and our own too, is
that the world has never been made up exclusively of its beneficiaries. It is easy for Sir Kenneth to chill the blood of 'people'
(i.e. civilised people) by reminding them of the physical priva-
tions and boredoms and discomforts they would have to endure
if they went back to barbarism, but these things are highly relative and it would be nonsense to imagine that the barbarians
themselves found it blood-chilling. After all, most of us would
shrink from returning to the actual physical, medical, surgical,
and sanitational environment of Elizabethan England, even of
the Elizabethan court, yet to Shakespeare and his contempor-
aries they represented the last word in refinement.

And although the barbarians were so far inferior to the
Romans in knowledge and know-how, the accusations of moral
inferiority implicitly levelled against them are more dubious.
One such charge is that they were brutal and rapacious, and
that is certainly true. But they were not more brutal and rapacious than the Romans. No civilisation which treated mass
slaughter as a spectator sport was in a position to condemn its
adversaries for their cruelty. If they seemed more rapacious

to their victims it was because their raids were unpredictable and impossible to buy off, whereas the Roman Empire over the generations had institutionalised its rapacity in many of the provinces and colonies to the point where its annual exactions could be foreseen and allowed for, and the force behind them could remain latent.

Another charge is that the barbarians were senselessly destructive. This also is a somewhat one-sided judgement. If we are to regard Cato constantly plugging his slogan of *'Carthago delenda est'* (Carthage must be obliterated) as a civilised and far-sighted Roman statesman, we should not use different moral standards to judge a barbarian chief who decides that Rome must be obliterated – though in fact the vandalism of the vandals seems usually to have consisted less in knocking buildings down than in letting them fall down by neglecting them.

One way of looking at it is that their real crime was inefficiency. It would not have mattered so much if a new driver speaking a different language had slid into the driving seat of civilisation and taken over the controls as long as he knew how to drive it. But the barbarian ascendancy was more like a Rolls-Royce being taken over by someone who couldn't tell a car from a big tin box and would use it for keeping his chickens in – which makes it all the more mysterious that they managed to take over at all. It would seem on the face of it that they could no more have routed the Romans than the Red Indians could have routed the invading Europeans or the Bantu the invading Boers.

Perhaps the Romans exaggerated their backwardness. In this and all similar situations – the Mongol barbarians who defeated the Chinese or the Turkish barbarians who terrorised Islam – it must have taken more than blind fury and courage to win the day. Either their own native culture was more complex and integrated than their victims gave it credit for (a besetting weakness of the imperial mind), or else they had for some long time been penetrating this civilised society or been penetrated by it. Their sons perhaps had been conscripted or hired to fight for as long as they retained their youth and strength. Their daughters may have been enslaved and possibly later abandoned, their traders haggled with and cheated in the sublime conviction that these lesser breeds were too stupid to learn anything, or to take home what they had learned and profit by it. If Rome believed this she was wrong, as others have been before and since.

But the overriding factor was not the prowess of the barbarians, but the sickness at the heart of the Imperial city. Free citizens were moving out to escape the onerous taxes and the growing squalor. Men had to be compelled to serve in public offices which had once been eagerly competed for. Numbers of people, especially young people, revolted by the combination of luxury, incompetence, and creeping panic, looked on the whole scene as whatever was the Latin for 'dregsville, man': they became devotees of various mystical sects originating in the East and took to living frugally in small communities, sometimes even in caves, which they scrawled over with the signs of the zodiac. The urban unemployed, finding that the glory and the rich pickings had departed and that the Emperors were getting madder and greedier, began slipping away from the metropolis and taking refuge with the landlords of some of the great estates.

For when Rome fell, the people for whom it was most traumatic were those nearest the centre and those who had become most narrowly specialised in order to serve its needs.

Some people see a biological parallel here. Evolutionists are always telling us that the quality above all which contributed to man's survival and success was that he remained biologically *unspecialised*. Therefore when faced with climatic or environmental changes which would have spelt extinction for more highly adapted creatures, he was able to roll with the punch and survive. Biologically he remains unspecialised, but in his urban habitats as *Homo gregarius* his behaviour comes closer to that of the social insects. Individual members become specialised to fulfill certain allotted functions with supreme efficiency, at the cost of becoming totally unfitted to survive outside the hive.

In the insect case this has not proved maladaptive even over millions of years, because they have learned (as we have so far failed to do) to make their cities autonomous self-sufficient units. In our case, whenever from time to time the top-heavy civilisations have collapsed, the people most immune to the shock wave have been those who were least penetrated by the behaviour patterns of the urban-centred regime.

One of the commonest misconceptions about the period that followed the fall of Rome regards it as a change from a system of dynamic urbanism to a static condition where a serf was legally tethered all his life to the same status, the same land and the same lord. The impression is sometimes given that the old good life of mobility and individual freedom died with Rome, and feudalism was clamped on Europe by the sullen barbarian hicks who rushed in to fill the power vacuum.

That was not how it happened. An urban economy on the scale of Rome's doesn't stay inside the walls of the city. A lot of the countryside had become urbanised too – that is, it was geared to a money economy and to fit into the city's needs. The land was bestowed on or bought up by a breed of hard-faced men who had done well out of civilisation. As had happened in Egypt, the neolithic-type cultivator who worked a piece of land 'because it was there' had become extinct within the ambit of the city economy.

When the Roman economy began to show signs of cracking, the reaction of these landowners was to batten down their hatches and aim for greater self-sufficiency by building small-scale smithies, potteries, tile works and brick kilns on their own estates and discouraging their workers from leaving. Rome had no objection at all to this : it made it easier to collect the poll tax if you knew exactly where everyone was. So by easy stages the Roman villa began turning into the medieval manor. In AD 332 Emperor Constantine made the attachment of the share-farmer to the manor enforceable at law. In 371 Emperor Vespasian decreed : 'We do not deem that *coloni* are free to leave the land to which their condition and birth attach them. If they do let them be brought back, put in chains and punished.' In return for legalising the landowner's control over his workers, the emperor required him to raise and supply a contingent of soldiers when the need arose. You don't really need to get much more feudal than that. And it was not a system that came in from outside: it was Roman urbanism itself, stiffening in *rigor mortis*.

The centuries that followed remain 'dark' to the historian in the sense of largely unchronicled, and 'dark' to the archaeologist in the quality of the relics they left behind. To a highly cultured character like Sir Kenneth Clark this is the touchstone of the quality of life. 'I should believe,' he says, 'the buildings.' The scarcity of good architecture and high-class artefacts in the Dark Ages certainly establishes that nearly all Europeans – instead of as in earlier civilised periods only perhaps ninety-eight percent of them – lived in shoddy dwellings with shoddy clothes and tools. It might have been that the heart was still as loving and the moon was still as bright, but those things leave no traces for historians to decipher or for archaeologists to dig up.

The completeness of the collapse of the whole system that Rome had built up is usually taken as a shattering condemnation of the boorishness and ignorance of their successors, and a consequence of the flux of fear and uncertainty which hung for a long time over parts of Europe because of the Roman defeat and the barbarian raids. All that is true enough.

Yet it must stand as a condemnation of Rome too, of a system so monolithic that when the head was cut off the whole thing disintegrated. After the dust settled almost the entire cultural heritage of Rome appeared to be evaporating like fairy gold.

V. Gordon Childe pointed out:

Although the Roman Empire formed a unique reservoir for the pooling of human experience . . . not a single major invention was suggested by all the data accumulated. Despite the existence of a large leisured class of cultivated and even learned men, Imperial Rome made no significant contribution to pure science. In applied science too the advances made under the Empire are disappointing. Roman architects and engineers applied and amplified inherited techniques without any revolutionary innovations. . . .

For the Roman genius had been political and military, and perhaps there is not much incentive to lighten the burden of labour if you have enough political genius to arrange that other people carry most of that burden and to ensure that they will not or cannot put it down.

The colonial settlements, with cities on the Roman pattern, collapsed also. They had been encouraged to feel autonomous, and to believe that they were carrying the torch of enlightenment into the murkier corners of the globe (like the British Isles), but the ultimate motive power was always the drive to increase the wealth and power of the imperial city. Rome expended money and manpower on its provincial outposts for the same reason that a multinational company invests capital in the Third World, or a fly deposits its saliva on a sugar lump – to render the contents more easily ingestible.

Once the fear of military sanctions by the imperial army had been removed, the natives proved surprisingly ungrateful for having been incorporated into the system, as natives often do; and the physical destruction in a few of those cities was not wreaked by the barbarians at all, but by beleaguered enclaves of occupying Romans who pulled down their own beautiful temples to use the stone for fortifications they had never expected to need.

Amid so much that was disintegrating, literacy survived – somewhat against the odds. There were plenty of instances of urban collapse where it had been irretrievably wiped out. For scholars, like architects and sculptors and pyramid builders, were luxury products dependent on wealthy patrons supported by an urban surplus; if Europe regressed to a subsistence economy, who could afford to hire scholars and pay them to think? It is a phony question, and the answer shows why.

The conservationist element in this case was an improbable one. It evolved out of one of the proliferating underground mystical sects, an originally clandestine group who believed in the doctrines and the immortality of a deviationist Jewish preacher, Jesus of Nazareth.

It is not very unusual for religious groups to decry worldly possessions, as the Christians did, and assert that holiness can go hand in hand with poverty. A guru with a begging bowl can survive and meditate on very small handouts. But the groups of early Christians who lit out from cities of the Roman Empire to escape persecution and spiritual contamination were not moving, like the guru, through a continent full of believers. Fortunately they had an extra and sturdier tenet unshared by the Brahmin, which stated that not only were poverty and austerity OK but work was OK too, even hard or menial or dirty work. 'To labour,' they declared, 'is to pray.' They set up little communes group hermitages where they hoped nobody would bother them. They dug and built and ploughed and sewed with their own hands. When they found they weren't going to be left alone after all (after the Romans had become converts and stopped pestering them the barbarians often took over), they built high walls around their monasteries and wrote in books about the wickedness of their enemies, or else they sighed and pulled up stakes and moved again to places even more inaccessible and even less worth pillaging.

Because Christianity is a religion of the book, they kept literacy alive. They also preserved and passed on some of what had been achieved – Greek discoveries, for example, about medicine or Virgil's poetry. In fact they retained in encapsulated form many of the old urban qualities. Their dwelling places were built to last, their manuscripts were often beautiful above and beyond the needs of legibility, and they retained the concepts of hierarchy, discipline and obedience. If the Spore-theory of dissemination of civilisation is a true one, then what happened in the Dark Ages was analogous to what happens in organisms like yeast when the environment becomes adverse: they give rise to specialised individual thick-walled cells which can survive unchanged for long periods like dormant seeds until conditions improve.

At least they succeeded in establishing that if a man really wants to read or write or pray or think, he does not necessarily have to find someone else who will hire him to do it. For a time indeed they seemed to have found the knack of preserving a good many of the things that had been good about urban civilisation, without encountering too many of its drawbacks. At a time like the present, when not dissimilar groups with minority views about life are trying to insulate themselves from our own civilisation and learn lessons about survival, there is bound to be speculation about how they managed it.

For one thing in those early days they never aimed at conspicuous consumption or what Keynes calls 'pyramid building'. For another thing the leisure for prayer and contemplation was not provided for one set of people by another set of people's hard labour. The theory was that everyone should work with maximum energy and efficiency for part of his day to bestow on himself peace and quietness for the rest of it. Also these places attracted a higher than average proportion of what we should now call intellectuals, for in those days when everything you could contemplate was believed to be God's handiwork the distinction between thinking and worshipping was not so clear as it is today. And an intellectual is a special breed of man. He has been defined as someone who has found something more interesting than sex; one could perhaps go further and say that he's found something more interesting than money, and it's comparatively easy to work economic miracles when you're dealing with that kind of material.

Finally these establishments, whether for monks or nuns and however primitive, austere and self sufficient, were all receiving one valuable, invisible and often overlooked subsidy from the world outside before they ever began receiving tithes. It may be one reason why they proved economically viable while nowadays so many highly motivated communes fail to make the grade. In the convents and abbeys, every new recruit arrived fully grown and able to pull his weight. The burden of feeding, clothing and supporting him until he reached maturity had been borne by laymen. Go to any economic social unit in the world – town, city, state or federation – and offer to relieve it of the costs incurred in shepherding its citizens through their first sixteen years and it will throw its cap in the air and swear that all its problems are solved.

Of course, while the dormant seed may be very good at surviving, it can do nothing at all about evolving. The urban component which the monasteries signally lacked was flexibility – few people left them and the ones that came in were subjected to a rigorous process of assimilation. Yet this did not mean that economic change came to a dead halt with the fall of Rome. It was only the European city that had received a near-fatal setback. The European village was far less fragile. It simply continued from where it had left off before the Roman interlude, almost as though nothing had happened, on a path of progress very slow, but very solid. Its innovations were of the kind that no political cataclysms can throw back into limbo.

For example, by the end of the period known as the Dark Ages, they had introduced agricultural rotation in the three-field system; they had introduced oats into the rotation; they had learned to plough with horses instead of oxen. Wherever Rome had passed on to them a practical technology which could benefit small scattered communities as well as large centralised ones, they had no intention of letting such technologies die out – they extended and improved them. Water-wheels, for instance, continued to be constructed and their use continued to spread – by AD 700 they had reached England. And their own technology kept pace with the demands set up by their own improved practices: horse-shoes were introduced for the first time. An improved design of harness was invented which enabled the horses to pull the heavy plough. Men were now able to open up land formerly regarded as non-arable. Great areas of wilderness in Central Europe were brought under the plough; independent fishermen in Flanders got together with their shovels and created new land for themselves by building dykes.

These rural innovations are not celebrated in the school text books like the spinning jenny and the steam engine, partly because they were anonymous and their effects less dramatically swift. They receive less attention than the introduction of the crossbow and gunpowder, because people are more interested in war than in peace. Nevertheless, they were not fossilised bits of Roman imperialist know-how embalmed in the monasteries and reissued for the guidance of a grateful peasantry. They were genuine and striking advances, and resulted in an increase of real wealth.

The result was that over much of Europe, in spite of less favourable conditions of climate and natural fertility than had obtained in Egypt and Mesopotamia, there came into being that familiar indispensable pre-condition of urbanisation – the Potential Surplus. At first, no doubt, people simply lived a bit easier and ate a bit better, which showed a pretty sound sense of priorities, because more of their children survived, and the population began gradually to rise. Then, they began secreting cities.

When the cities came back, they came back at first with a difference. This time, the incentive for producing more than their needs was supplied more by the priests than the kings, and therefore was exerted by moral pressure rather than military force.

For the Church now left its ascetic phase behind it and decided, as other and earlier priesthoods had done, that its god could be properly worshipped only in temples of outstanding splendour and with a large retinue of full-time organisers and servants. By 1314, for example, the little town of Cirencester had 105 acolytes, 140 sub-deacons, 133 deacons, and eight-five priests. The king would have had nothing like that number of civil servants there. Besides, if we want to confirm which was the major wealth-centralising catalyst at the time, we could do worse than 'believe the buildings'. New cathedrals were going up in greater numbers than new castles and attracting far more excitement, architectural imagination and devoted voluntary labour. The results in stone were often breathtakingly beautiful. The result in demographic and economic terms was to draw off wealth from the countryside by means of tithes, the sale of pardons, etc, and spend it freely in the cities. Even today a standard English dictionary defines a city as : 'a large town, an incorporated town that has or has had a cathedral.'

A small number of these places began to grow quite rapidly.

In the north of Europe and its off-shore islands the concept of the nation-state was struggling to be born, renewing the need for capital cities to be crystallised around the royal courts. With the aggregation of wealth came a revival of international trade and a substantial new merchant class. At a few key points on the major trade routes they became the dominant element in powerful and autonomous city-states such as Venice.

They were places full of pride, ambition, callousness, corruption, fawning, hypocrisy, tyranny, self-indulgence, avarice, violence, intrigue and smells and dirt. They were also full of talk and laughter and colour and confidence and creativity and the highest class of art and craftsmanship. Because the prelates, princes and merchants had a taste for splendour, their courts and palaces provided the seedbed for a new flowering of art and scholarship and science. They were places where almost everyone of any spirit who heard about them would want to go and live.

Of course this could not be tolerated. That was the period when as Mumford puts it :

> The antagonism between town and country sharpened. For the city was an exclusive society based on voluntary associations for a common purpose. Every townsman in relation to the country folk born to the land was something of a snob with such snobbery as only the upstart and the *nouveau riche* achieve.

In the more prosperous cities like Venice there were two grades of citizenship. A newcomer needed fifteen years' residence to apply for the first grade and twenty-five for the second, and Marin Sanudo records that when too many peasants arrived there, hoping to work their passage to citizenship, the street people would attack them shouting : *"Poltroni, ande arar!* . . ."* (Oafs, go away and till the land). In other words, go back where you come from – a cry that has echoed sporadically down the centuries through city streets in every corner of the globe.

However, the handful of great trading cities was less typical of the period than the hundreds of little independent walled market towns and cities that sprang up in the middle ages at remarkably regular intervals right across the land surface of Europe in the interstices of the feudal system, sometimes near a monastery or castle, sometimes near a crossroads or the traditional site of a fair or market.

They didn't vary much in size, and the average population came fairly close to the theoretical optimum dreamed up by Plato and Leonardo and Howard. They didn't measure their own success in terms of expansion either of population or living standards, and were perfectly content for those indices to remain stable over the generations. They didn't succumb to galloping elephantiasis or wither away and die of discouragement, so that if they built a city wall they expected it still to be a good fit three hundred years later.

They were obviously not immune to a degree of urban snobbery, for all the European languages bear early traces of the fact that any adjective for a human being 'belonging to the countryside' tends to collect a whole raft of secondary meanings implying stupid, clumsy, oafish, crude, ignorant, and generally inferior.

But unlike earlier versions of the city, they neither laid claim to, nor charged for, the administration and defence of the surrounding countryside. They took responsibility for their own defence, but nobody else's. They minded their own business and conducted it in a fairly democratic and low-key style which kept the power widely dispersed, with burghers and deacons and guildsmen and merchants and abbots all confined to running their own separate bits of the show.

Their most imperishable works of art, the cathedrals, were largely communal efforts to which even the most naïve and anonymous stone-cutter might contribute a couple of idiosyncratic gargoyles without being censored, and without wrecking the whole concept. There were not many freeloaders. It has been calculated that four-fifths of the citizens were actively engaged in productive employment producing goods to be consumed within their own region, so that the balance of trade between town and countryside stayed on a fairly even keel.

They offered pretty good value and a bit of colour, excitement and entertainment to the country people when they came in to sell eggs and buy ribbons.

There was a period up to and after the First World War when some people wildly over-idealised those medieval cities, depicting them as idyllic places where the pious and god-fearing citizens were full of innocent gaiety and sportiveness, and implying that things have gone a long way downhill since then. That is not a tenable proposition. If we went back there we should find life nasty, brutish and short, the mental climate smug and inward-looking, the social distinctions stifling and the sanitation appalling. The over-romantic versions provoked equally extreme counter-attacks, like the blistering denunciation of Merrie England in Kingsley Amis's *Lucky Jim*.

But whatever was wrong with them one thing was right, and that was their stable and symbiotic relationship with their immediate hinterland. They were uppity and complacent, but neither parasitic nor menacing. The element of cream-off was low, and the element of mutual usefulness was high. It was almost the last period in Europe in which the countrymen, when they were laughed at, could laugh back with total conviction that the city people were an odd lot with comical manners and pompously inflated ideas about their own wisdom and importance, but condemned by the facts of life to remain a small harmlessly eccentric minority of the human race.

6 Industrial cities: Adam Smith and Karl Marx

Up to this point the argument has been on fairly straight-forward lines, whether you agree with it or not. It has been concerned to challenge the concept of cities – ancient, classical and medieval – as the chief generators of wealth and the showerers of riches and blessings and civilisation on all the world around, and to suggest that in those days the greater part of their wealth was appropriated rather than generated, and that while cities made life richer and more enjoyable for the people in their immediate vicinity they made it poorer and much less enjoyable for a great many others. At the times when they were least rapacious they did not grow so rich or so big, but encountered fewer problems and lasted longer.

When we move on to the period of the industrial revolution this proposition is not only harder to uphold, it is much harder even to *discuss*, because for people living at that time, and for historians describing that time, the functioning of cities for good or ill had ceased to be a topic thought worthy of exercising the best minds.

One major reason for this was the advent of the nation-state. Once people had begun to think of themselves as 'belonging' to large sovereign territorial, ethnic or linguistic blocs they learned to identify passionately with the interests of their own particular bloc. In times of need, all other conflicts of interest would be submerged in order to serve and save it.

The vast majority of human beings are still in the grip of that passion. For some in the newly emerging states it is an emotional allegiance as new-minted as it was to Europeans at the turn of the millenium, and no less powerful for that. No matter how often people have had it proved to them by post-war carve-ups and boundary changes that the nation-state is a political artefact (sometimes a cynically arbitrary one) they usually find themselves at any crisis responding to it with their blood.

Another important consequence is that when Adam Smith sat down to write the trail blazer of all economic textbooks, he entitled it inevitably *The Wealth of Nations*. It is perhaps unfortunate that Aristotle when he was busy blocking out parameters for Western thought on the topic of politics, philosophy, mathematics, physics and drama, never found time to expand his few pages on 'chrematistics' into a full-scale treatise on *The Wealth of Cities*. It might have shaped our thinking along different lines and would have been in many ways a more realistic approach even in Adam Smith's day. For within, and quite regardless of, the mesmerising framework of the national boundary, individual cities were making the running and triggering off the amassing of wealth precisely as they had always done, while the nation at that date was doing little more than holding a small kitty and preparing to swing the whole of its influence behind whichever vested interest could capture fifty-one percent of a parliamentary vote.

In opposition to Adam Smith there arrived an economist who refused to see the nation-state as the significant unit in any discussion of what was really happening in the economic life of the time. That was Karl Marx, and the units he chose to conceptualise were not England, Germany, France, etc, but Capital and Labour. His followers hoped that the horizontal loyalties of the class war were going to prove stronger than the vertical ones of patriotism, and slice across all state boundaries like a knife through butter. The hope appears to have been premature, but the dynamism of Marx's concepts and the passions they can mobilise exercised a mesmeric power of their own over all subsequent economic thinking.

The fact that there are these two basic viewpoints, conceived as being in opposition, strengthens the partisanship of their respective adherents, and strengthens also the assumption that no one need look any further for the truth : one or the other must be basically right. We can just about tolerate the idea that there are two ways of looking at any question, but it is pretty upsetting if someone comes along and says that perhaps there are three.

The risk of provoking that kind of annoyance is one that sometimes has to be taken.

What this chapter proposes to do then is to try to look at the economic events of the nineteenth century not primarily in terms of nation-states and not primarily in terms of class warfare, but as a further instalment in the continuing story of urban civilisation. To carry that narrative into and through the industrial revolution, and keep it on a straight course without being deflected by the giant minds that have set up their own signposts all over the map, will need a good deal of impetus: that is why we have taken such a long run-up. From time to time it will be necessary to halt and enquire more closely into what the giant minds were saying, and in what points their versions differ.

Most economic historians take the view that with the advent of capitalism and industrialism we are into an entirely new ball game and have to start from scratch. 'Continuity is broken,' says Carlo Cipolla, 'and a new story begins, a new story dramatically and completely alien to the previous ones.' But not everything about the story was new.

For one thing, this latest leap forward in population and urbanisation was preceded, as it had been on all previous occasions, by a quite dramatic increase in agricultural output. This is very rarely made plain in the accounts given in school textbooks and TV documentaries. In England, for example (their version usually runs) there was this great spurt of industrial invention – Hargreaves' spinning jenny, Arkwright's mule, the cotton gin, James Watt's steam engine, Stephenson's Rocket, the coal mines, the iron foundries, the railways, the mills, etc, etc – leading to immense new quantities of wealth being created, first in the industrial towns and then pouring out of them to enrich the countryside, resulting in a rapid rise in the population because of higher living standards and advances in public health and medicine.

The facts do not support this version. There was a considerable ground swell of population increase and of urbanisation for quite a while before any of those factors can be used to explain it. For instance between 1650 and 1750 the population of London increased by sixty-nine percent, yet at the end of this period, in 1750, James Watt was only fourteen years old and the steam engine wasn't even a gleam in his eye.

It is perfectly true that the rate of population increase in England as a whole speeded up considerably in the second half of the eighteenth century, when the industrial revolution might plausibly be given the credit for it. On the other hand there was in the same century an equally astounding expansion in the population of China. Braudel assessed it at an increase of 135 million, over eighty percent between 1740 and 1790, yet no dark satanic mills were going up over there. Then again the population of Russia *more than doubled* between 1722 and 1795, from fourteen millions to twenty-nine millions, although by 1795 the industrial revolution hadn't even laid a finger on it.

This suggests that the necessary fore-runner of the new step upward in civilisation was the same as the fore-runner of all previous steps, that is a marked increase in non-urban productivity. In England certainly this had been happening – there had been changes such as the phasing out of the strip system and improvements in animal husbandry and above all, for well over a century, a steady extension of arable land over heath and pasture. This was achieved by landowners simply pushing the hitherto self-subsistent peasant off the common land, enclosing it, and farming it themselves. At the other end of the world the Chinese were clearing forests, irrigating plains and introducing ground nuts, sweet potatoes and maize to areas where they had never been grown before. There was also a surge of pioneers to the Chinese west ousting the 'backward peoples' that inhabited the wide open spaces of inland China, and bringing great tracts of wilderness under cultivation, closely parallelling the Cowboys and Indians experience in many ways, though it hasn't given rise to the same worldwide folklore. At the same time the Cossacks were moving southward against Nogai and Tartar nomads, and Russian peasants came in their wake and began to farm the land.

In all those areas the demographic figures shot up at exactly the same time as in England. At the same time too European migrants such as the Conquistadors were manifesting a surge of energy which drove them to advance against the 'barbarian' cultures of central and south America with a greed and savagery which easily outclassed that of their victims, and made the Vikings look like a peace corps party.

Nobody likes to be thought simplistic; but historians who are not too intimidated by that charge have put up the proposition that perhaps there was in that century a perceptible improvement in the world's climate; that there was consequently a whole series of good harvests at least in the northern hemisphere (Africa's population did not increase in the same way). This would mean that men had more breathing space from hand-to-mouth toil to sit and think and try new methods. They had more sons surviving to maturity and wanting land of their own so that the younger ones *had* to go west (or south or overseas) to find it, and had been putting enough proteins under their belts in their growing-up years to give them the energy to do it.

Professor Rostow has convincingly argued that the industrial revolution could not and would not have taken place but for these changes in agricultural productivity. His beliefs now command such widespread support that 'an entire literature has evolved', according to Dr Frank J. Coppa, which regards such changes as 'no less than a pre-requisite' for all past and indeed all future improvements in human productivity. Unfortunately none of this has made much perceptible impact on governments or planners. They proceed almost unanimously on the assumption that cities have always been the mainsprings and creators of all wealth, that by taking thought and contemplating their own navels they can pull themselves up by their bootstraps, and that once they have solved their own internal problems the rest of the world (which they sincerely believe 'depends' on them more fundamentally than they depend on it) will automatically come right.

This attitude was strongly reinforced by events in Great Britain during the eighteenth and nineteenth centuries. Doubtless it benefited together with the rest of the world from a streak of climatic benevolence and the new lease of energy and optimism which it produced. But Britain was something else again. Using this agricultural upsurge as a springboard it took off with a leap into a new economic plane. This was the 'deep breach in the continuity of the historical process'. Many other cities all over the world have since then followed Manchester up the same springboard and into the same flying leap – some of them with a velocity which has left the British pioneers a long way behind – and launched themselves comparatively effortlessly into orbit.

That would be fine as long as they recognised that orbit is what they are in. Unfortunately the bigger and faster they grow, the more solid their apparent conviction that they have reached not orbital velocity but *escape* velocity, and can and will soar higher and higher inevitably an *ad infinitum* with no tug from the earth to bring them back again. That is a conviction as paranoid as any delusion of Ozymandias's or Nero's.

Another feature about the take-off was not new. The thing that originally made it feasible was, just as with the very first civilising impetus in the Middle East's 'fertile crescent' thousands of years earlier, a new relationship between man and plants. This time the plants were not grasses, they were lush wetlands flora such as calamites; they were not alive but a long time dead; and he used them not for eating but for moving things.

He had long since found ways of economising on his own energy by directly exploiting the energy stored up by the metabolism of the horse and the ox. As far as plants were concerned he had not been so lucky. He was, of course, even more dependent on the metabolism of plants than on that of his flocks and herds, but had found very few ways of utilising the energy they provided which did not involve swallowing them and so converting their calories into muscle-power. And this was not really saving him work. It was only enabling him to perform it.

One of the other ways he utilised their energies was by the burning of wood. By lighting a fire and cooking his food, for example, he saved his stomach some of the hard work involved in the initial processes of breaking down the tougher plant and animal fibres. However, the muscles involved in the process of digestion were, in any case, among those whose functioning he most enjoyed; it was his arm and leg and back muscles that he often got fed up with operating. The genius of James Watt lay in seizing on the idea (suggested to him by a cranky and long forgotten professor of physics) that if the energy of the fire could move the lid of your kettle it could, properly harnessed, move other things as well. If there was enough of it, it could work for you as hard as a horse.

Now that was a very interesting discovery. But if the steam had only been producible by throwing wood on to a fire it would not have taken mankind very long to realise that burning vegetable matter is not really an economic way of moving objects from point A to point B, because a tree grows slowly, much more slowly than a horse, and much more slowly than the grass which the horse eats. Besides, there are a great many other uses to which timber can be put, both utilitarian and aesthetic, whereas there are very few ways of economically disposing of grass other than by letting animals eat it.

However, when the British began exploiting steam power they were not burning dead oaks and elms and yews – they were burning dead tree ferns, since they had been lucky enough to unearth great caches of them buried underground and fossilised into coal, and the British after all are only human. They reacted as human beings always react to the sight of a very great deal of anything – just as the white Americans reacted to the sight of skies full of passenger pigeons and prairies black with buffalo by wiping out the pigeons entirely and coming within an ace of wiping out the buffalo. In much the same frame of mind the British waded into the coal, throwing it into their capacious fireplaces by the bucketful (which was rather like burning the yield of ten years' growth of an acre of timber to heat one small room between tea-time and supper), and into their blast furnaces and locomotive tenders and steamships by the thousand ton; and as soon as they exported the know-how other countries followed suit. Mankind had lifted the lid on a finite supply of stored-up vegetable energy and immediately proceeded to spend this inheritance 'like', as the Americans say, 'there was no tomorrow.'

Once he embarked on this binge there was not too long a time before he realised that the sea as well as the land had been laying down a cellar of corked-up energy for him. Not having a stomach like a whale he is still trying to figure out an economic way of using today's plankton, but *yesterday's* plankton has obligingly turned itself into petroleum. For the last few decades he has been racing around pulling the corks out of every store of the stuff he can lay his hands on and burning it up with the luxurious abandon of a film star taking a bath in vintage champagne with the plug out.

In theory it was now possible that cities would no longer have to grow rich by releasing the latent energy in (i.e., slave-driving) the less fortunate categories of human beings : they could release the energy from the rocks instead. This time the cities could pile up their wealth and achieve even higher standards of refinement and gracious living without anybody's lives anywhere being made more wretched or more arduous.

In the initial stages nobody could have fooled themselves that this was happening. Somebody had to dig out the coal; somebody had to dig the canals; somebody had to move mountains to make way for the railways. The means employed differed in no way from the methods of previous civilisations except perhaps in carrying those methods to unprecedented lengths. Hundreds of thousands of men, women, children and horses were spurred, beaten, starved, bribed, inspired or conned into prodigies of murderous physical toil in conditions of total misery, squalor and degradation. No anthill or termitary ever treated its inmates more ruthlessly as anonymous and expendable units. Employers illuminated their attitude of mind by naming their employees after the only piece of their anatomy they cared about − a dehumanising figure of speech more normally applied only in a sexual context − and referring to their workers simply as 'hands'.

Like previous spasms of economic expansion this one was based on slavery. Partly this consisted of the old-fashioned kind of chattel-slavery which produced cheap Virginian raw cotton to swell the profits of Lancashire's mills. For the most part however it was found more convenient to use hands rather than slaves, because when the hands became unserviceable due to the sickness or maiming or old age of the bodies they were attached to, the employer was under no constraint to put food into the associated stomachs, and he suffered no loss of capital if the bodies expired of hunger or cold or filth-borne infection; he simply had to replace the hands with another pair. There were plenty of them available because people were imploding into the growing cities at a tremendous rate.

For anyone living in the cities it must have appeared that the thronging crowds of people were being generated by the new economic order in much the same sense as the miles of yarn and the acres of cloth and the nuts and the bolts and the cheap tin trays. Consider, for example, this world-famous description of the achievements of the new order :

> Subjection of nature's forces to man, machinery, application of chemistry to industry and agriculture, steam navigation, railways, electric telegraphs, clearing of whole continents for cultivation, canalisation of rivers, *whole populations conjured out of the ground* – what earlier centuries had even a presentiment that such productive forces slumbered in the lap of social labour ?

The italics are mine but the sentiments are those of Marx and Engels in the *Communist Manifesto* of 1848. 'Conjured out of the ground' is, of course, only a metaphor, but it was the metaphor of a man who took the growing numbers of the urban proletariat as a datum. Capitalism was primarily an urban manifestation : the city was where it was all happening and the environment in which Marx and Engels were most at home; naturally it was to the urban centres that they turned their attention. Once the hands had arrived in London or Manchester, Marx concentrated the whole of his intellect, compassion, indignation and analytical powers on trying to understand the forces that contributed to their poverty and despair. He paid less detailed attention to where they had come from or what was happening in the places they left behind, or to the fact that far from conjuring populations out of the ground they were consumers of men – sucking them in from outside their borders and killing them off faster than they could replace themselves. He knew enough about the operations of the bourgeoisie (the term comes from a word meaning 'townsmen') to realise that they would be as ruthless in ensuing the constant supply of hands as in maintaining a smooth flow of raw material, and that this could only be done by making sure that the miseries of the rural poor outstripped the miseries of the urban poor by a decisive margin.

However, he did not seem to regard this aspect of the operation with any particular disapproval. Possibly he regarded the cityward drift as a necessary pre-revolutionary move and therefore an ultimately progressive one, rescuing the peasants from – in Marx's own words – the 'idiocy of rural life' and politically educating them by bringing them into contact with the urban proletariat. It was among this urban proletariat – and therefore in the most highly industrialised western countries – that he confidently expected revolutionary communism to score its first victory.

As it turned out he was wrong about this. Marxist theorists between the wars used to comment on the effects of the unforeseen – and in some way they felt unlucky – 'historical accident' which brought communism into power first of all in non-industrial Russia. They waited eagerly for the next Red victory which must surely this time take the classic form of a victorious urban uprising in the foetid industrial slums of some western capital. They were wrong again: it was China. And wrong next time: Cuba. The most spontaneous and popular Marxist victories have all occurred against a rural backdrop of landless peasants. No one can seriously believe that such a long string of historical accidents is really accidental. One reason may be that the spirit of Marx's teaching had more effect on people than the economics of it. If you preach with sufficient conviction against exploitation, your most fervent admirers will be found amongst the most exploited sections of the world's population, and they have never yet been located in cities.

If Marx saw the cityward drift as progressive, the new capitalist class was even more in favour of it. Earlier civilisers, when the need arose for extra supplies of labour to be brought in from the hinterland, had had very simple methods available: the emperor would dispatch an army and bring in slaves. By the nineteenth century the problem was more delicate and the means had to be more devious.

In Great Britain, where the energy explosion first manifested itself, an area in the northern half of the country was undergoing an attack of civilisation more feverish than any that had preceded it.

The eye of the hurricane had centred on a little place called Manchester which was growing by the hour and howling for more and more hands, and more and more money, and more and more raw materials. Its hour had come and nothing was going to stop it. It was momentarily hampered by the fact that it happened to be embedded in the body politic of an off-shore island where the balance of political power lay in the hands of a landowning aristocracy with a conservative philosophy and headed by a hereditary peerage. Within a very short time Manchester had burst out of this strait jacket, taken the British economy by the scruff of its neck, upset the balance of political power in its own favour and produced a whole new crop of political thinkers – the Manchester School – to discredit and demolish the conservative philosophy.

The question is, how did they manage to sharpen the urban/rural differential in living standards to the point where people flocked willingly by the thousand to live in the cellars and hovels of those appalling cities and work in those appalling factories and pits? And how, while doing it, did they convince themselves and a majority of the British population that this was a humanitarian undertaking?

The decisive battle centred around food. The growing industrial centres needed simultaneously a large intake of workers to man the machines, of raw materials and fuel to feed the machines, and of bread to feed the workers. These demands were so exorbitant that even the whole of Britain was not hinterland enough to enable the new factories to keep going and make a satisfying rate of profit.

The new manufacturers hated the Corn Laws which prohibited the import of cheap foreign grain in order to protect the home-grown product. They urgently wanted the price of bread kept down for all possible reasons. If corn was cheap, the mill owners could pay lower wages without having their workers die on them. If corn was cheap, people in general would have a little more money left after feeding themselves to spend on Manchester's manufactured goods. If corn was cheap, there would be less profit in British arable farming. More land-owners would turn to sheep-farming and bring down the price of the raw wool for the woollen mills. Also turning to sheep-farming meant driving labourers off the land and into the manufacturing towns where, by competing for jobs, they again helped to keep wages low and increase profits.

So in the 1830s there followed a political battle between the lords of the countryside and the masters of the towns conducted for the most part in terms of the Higher Hypocrisy. In 1838 the Anti-Corn Law League was founded to conduct a propaganda campaign, and since working men had now been given the vote they could hardly mount it on the slogan 'Repeal the Corn Laws and keep wages low'.

Instead the League spent all its energies issuing propaganda, organising meetings and paying writers and orators to expatiate on the terrible sufferings of the poor who were kept hungry because the price of bread was too high. These sufferings were only too real. Its speakers thundered against the selfishness of England's traditional gentry, their unearned wealth, their snobbery, their game laws, the callousness of the rich landlord in his castle towards the poor man at his gate, and these charges were only too true. They pointed out that in Ireland where the potato crop had failed people were dying of hunger because they were too poor to buy bread, and that was true too. Working people all over the country rubbed their eyes in wonder to see how the tale of their sufferings moved the rich to indignation and loosened their purse strings. In one single meeting of the League held in Manchester in 1845 local businessmen subscribed £60,000 in an hour and a half to help the League to fight the good fight.

They did not however, in all their denunciations of the past sins of the rural aristocracy – the Enclosures and the evictions – go so far as to suggest that those wrongs ought to be undone and the land given back to the people who had formerly worked it. The last thing they wanted was to see their hands trickling back to the countryside and the price of wool going up. All they wanted was a very simple and human thing – to maximise their own profits.

They could strive for that now with the clearest of consciences, because they had on their side the teachings of Adam Smith, who had said in his book on *The Wealth of Nations* that free trade was not for the exclusive benefit of either town or country, buyer or seller, producer or consumer, master or man. It was for the benefit of everybody. As long as no one interfered in any way with the desire of every individual to buy goods at the lowest possible price and sell at the highest, everyone in the end would be better off in the best of all possible worlds.

In well under ten years the battle was fought and won and the Corn Laws were repealed. It was a swift and brilliant campaign and seemed to notch up a victory for the humanitarian principles of the Manchester School as against the reactionary views of the old guard. It is possible to take a less starry-eyed view. One of the most famous of the radical free-traders, Joseph Hume, was a staunch defender of the Opium War and the Punjab War (waged to enforce the boon of trade with Britain on lesser breeds who didn't appreciate it), and had retired from service with the forces of the East India Company with a personal fortune of £40,000. And he was far from untypical.

Another thing that besmirched the democratic image of the free-traders was another political tussle, in the year following their victory, when a committee of trade unionists tried to promote a Bill limiting the working hours of young persons to

ten hours a day, since children of thirteen were currently working a seventy-two-hour week in the mills. The businessmen,
with one or two honourable exceptions, protested that there
was nothing they would like better than improving conditions
in this way if they only dared to do it, but they had to resist
on principle, because such a provision would constitute a law
in restraint of trade, and Adam Smith had shown that any such
law must inevitably end in disaster.

The demographic effect of all this in Britain was rapid urbanisation. The effect of it further afield was the same that
had always accompanied rapid urbanisation. After an initial
period of coercion, shock, and upheaval all areas in the vicinity
of the urbanisers gradually began to benefit from the overflow
of the concentration of wealth, while the absolute losers remained far out of sight and out of mind. The method of achieving this was the time-honoured one : expansion against the
barbarian was intensified.

Conveniently (since the supply of barbarians in Europe had
virtually run out) the world had been opening up and there
were plenty of indigenous peoples in India, Africa, North and
South America and Australia ripe to be evicted, or exploited,
or both, while further east the Chinese and the Europeans were
glaring at each other with mutual incomprehension, each side
deeply convinced that it was a civilised race confronting a
barbarian one.

Manchester did not view the economic expansion into overseas markets as exploitive. Its attitude was never one of swash-
buckling and conquest : on foreign strands it wanted to see not
corpses but customers. The only time the Manchester Chamber
of Commerce brought pressure on Parliament to use strong-
arm methods against foreigners was when they came up against
stiff-necked people like the Chinese, who refused to open their
economy to trade with the West until the British battered the
doors down.

Manchester didn't want slavery either. It only wanted the
best raw cotton at the cheapest price. If the price was such as
to stir the greed of American planters, line the pockets of a
generation of slave-traders and necessitate unspeakable brut-

alities against African tribes who had never heard of England, let alone Arkwright and Watt and Stephenson – well that was to be deplored. At least nobody was importing them for the arena.

Manchester didn't need any laws to protect it against foreign competition. It was the first in the field with a new technology and its strength was as the strength of ten because it was using for energy the new miracle ingredient, fossil fuel. It advocated free trade because free trade favours the strong, but it had enough of the nonconformist conscience to wish to persuade itself and everybody else that free trade and laissez-faire favoured the whole human race. This was not immediately apparent to the overworked hands in its cholera-ridden slums, to the children falling asleep under its looms and being beaten awake by their own parents, to the starving country people dispossessed and pauperised, to the half-naked men and women harnessed like animals and hauling trucks in the depths of the coal mines, or the casualties in the foundries splashed with molten iron, any more than it would have been apparent to the Africans. The theory was, however, that the system should not be interfered with since these were merely temporary disadvantages on the way to the new Jerusalem and the system was being cruel only to be kind.

To most readers those examples will have a familiar ring. They feature frequently and justifiably in denunciations not of urbanism but of capitalism. At the time when Karl Marx was writing the two processes were forging ahead simultaneously and hand in hand, so tightly enmeshed in a complex chain-reaction of cause and effect that it was very difficult to consider the two concepts separately.

Since then we have had well over a century of human experience to add to the available data on capitalism and on urbanisation, operating sometimes together and sometimes apart for they are by no means Siamese twins. In the light of all this additional evidence it is time to look again at some of the things that Marx was saying, and why.

E

The thing that spurred him on to the immense task of writing *Das Kapital* was his reaction to a situation where tens of thousands of men and women were working extremely hard in conditions of poverty, hunger and dirt, while a few people were growing very rich on the proceeds of their labour; yet the rich sincerely regarded themselves as benefactors because their thrift and initiative and financial risk-taking had 'provided employment' for the poor who would otherwise have starved. Many of the poor accepted this view of the transaction and almost all of them regarded the relationship as a fact of life, eternal and unchangeable. Marx's aim was to convince them that this state of affairs was not permanent but one stage in the development of a dynamically changing society : that in the wealth-creating process it was labour and not private capital which was the absolutely indispensable partner; and that the then existing balance of power between Capital and Labour, so far from being eternal, could not possibly continue. He was right on these three counts.

One of the ways in which he tried to convince working people of their rightful claim to a bigger share in the wealth they were helping to produce was by formulating the Labour Theory of Value. He postulated that the value of an object was governed by the amount of socially necessary labour which had gone into the production of it. Thus a coat was worth more than the cloth that went into it, the cloth was worth more than the yarn it was woven from, the yarn worth more than the equivalent amount of raw wool and so on, only because more man hours of necessary labour had been put into them. On this reckoning the labourer was the creator of the real value of all commodities. On this reckoning he should be receiving back not a pittance sufficient to enable him to stay alive and replace himself, but the full equivalent of the amount of value his work had added to the material he was working on.

The alternative, the classical or non-Marxist version, argues that value is only a function of relative scarcity : it is a matter of the 'relationship between ends and scarce means which have alternative uses'. So the price of flowers goes up on

Mother's Day because more people want to buy them and a doctor costs more than a dustman not (as Marx would argue) because more essential man hours of education have gone into producing him, but because a man who can take out your appendix is in shorter supply than a man who can empty your dustbin.

Either of these explanations can be used with some plausibility to explain the magnetising of wealth and population into the industrial cities. According to the Marxist version it would be because a greater amount of necessary social labour was being expended there. The articles turned out there compared with the unprocessed raw materials coming in from outside were highly wrought products absolutely stuffed full of labour-generated value.

According to the classical version the reason would be in broad terms that the raw materials the towns were bringing in were in plentiful supply whereas the products they turned out were relatively scarce in relation to the demand for them. Yet neither of these explanations is totally satisfactory. Let us consider them in turn.

I can understand and sympathise with the passion behind Marxist's formulation of the Labour Theory of Value, but I could never quite swallow the logic. For example, it seems to me if an African boy was paddling in a river and felt something hard between his toes in the silt and picked it up and found it was a large diamond, the diamond would at that moment have considerable value even though he had contributed to it only a second's worth of labour. On going back on the actual text of *Das Kapital*, I discovered that Marx himself had worried a bit about that diamond. 'Diamonds', he wrote, 'are a very rare occurrence on the earth's surface and hence their discovery costs on an average a great deal of labour time. Consequently much labour is represented in a small compass.'

Up to a point, yes, but they're not such a terribly rare occurrence in diamond mines, the only place where labour is regularly expended on looking for them. The bit about 'on the earth's surface' and 'on an average' almost seems to imply that their value is derived from the amount of labour time per jewel that would be expended if we all went out and hunted for them in our back yards and over the prairies and under the snow and in the rice paddies and under the date palms, and that is a lot of highly hypothetical labour.

Because he so badly wanted the theory to be true Marx could in the last resort get himself out of all such tight corners in one neat manoeuvre by separately defining 'value' and 'use-value' and 'exchange-value'. For example, he will grant that the air I breathe or the blackberry on the bramble bush do in a sense have value even though no human labour went into producing them, but that he claims is 'use-value' and not the same as value in his sense. He will grant that even though a commodity may be the product of many hours of labour and be useful in itself, if the demand for it is missing then the price goes down to nothing. But what has gone down, he explains, is the 'exchange-value' and not the value in his sense. 'An object may have a price without having value.'

Very well, you can score debating points in that way but if you're saying that an object has a value which has nothing to do with anything I might use it for and nothing to do with what I might sell it for, then I suspect that that value is as hypothetical as the diamond-hunting Eskimo; and when you tell me as Marx does in so many words that 'uncultivated land is without value' (even though it may be both extremely useful and highly expensive) then you are arguing in circles. You are saying in effect 'human labour is the only thing that can create value because value in my definition is that which has been created by human labour'. And I would submit that that particular tenet is a dead duck for any purposes of practical analysis. This doesn't greatly affect the validity of many of his conclusions (it will become clearer later in the book why I am making rather a fuss about it), and the Labour Theory, inasmuch as it helped to put heart and hope and self-respect into generations of exploited workers, certainly possessed 'use-value' in the very highest degree. But in case you think that Marx was not sufficiently human to obfuscate an argument a little bit in order to win it, you might read a letter he wrote to Engels about his (Marx's) article for *The Tribune* on the probable outcome of the Indian Mutiny. He remarked that in the event that his prophecies were not precisely fulfilled, 'with a little dialetic one will still get away with it. I have actually given to my considerations such a form that in being wrong I shall still be right.'

The alternative theory, the supply and demand one, was more cynical, according to Oscar Wilde's definition of a cynic as a man who knows the price of everything and the value of nothing. It was not at all concerned with the value of goods in Marx's almost mystical sense, but a good deal concerned about their exchange value, i.e. prices.

It was based, reasonably enough, on the civilised assumption that what everybody wants is more. (If any sizeable section of the population were to revert to the ancient belief that all a man wants is enough, orthodox economists would find that attitude very difficult even to think about.) It is also based, much less reasonably, on a type of hypothetical norm which assumes that in a right-thinking world everybody would be allowed to buy goods and labour as cheaply as possible and sell them as dearly as possible, in open and equal competition with everybody else and without interference from any source.

If everybody would only conform to that norm, they would come moderately close to converting their proposition into a kind of science. They could use it to predict, say, what would be the effect of a rise in the price of commodity A on the price of various other commodities provided everything else remained the same. Their predictions are very elegant but seldom fulfilled, because all other things never do remain the same. And one reason why economists so seldom agree as to what should be done is that they are all making different guesses as to what other things are going to be different, and why.

The other limitation on the usefulness of their discipline is that as soon as monopolies, tariffs, trade unions, selective taxation, social security, public enterprise, price fixing, minimum wage legislation, or any such source of frictional interference creeps in, then any attempt at practical application of classic economic theory encounters an escalating and finally prohibitive degree of 'mush'. And when confronted with a totally planned economy it becomes quite simply irrelevant as a tool of understanding, even though a great many of the phenomena it was designed to 'explain' continue to operate.

Consequently, by this time, as anyone can tell who has heard them floundering around disagreeing with one another in the last year or two, non-Marxist economics is likewise a dead duck for most practical purposes of diagnosis, prognosis or therapy.

Like Marxism, it was often used – and is still sometimes used – not solely as an analytical tool but as a kind of moral tenet or ideal. Adam Smith was implying not merely that men *do* conduct themselves so as to sell their goods or their labour at the highest possible price and buy at the cheapest, but that it was ethically desirable for them to keep on doing so and mistaken for anybody to try to impede them in this endeavour, because in the long run everybody would benefit from it. It did not work out like that. Free competition, like a free fight, does not conduce to the advantage of everybody – it conduces to the advantage of the strongest. That is why it has always been most popular among the nations, and the groups within those nations, which are economically in the healthiest state at any given time.

I can find no support from either of these schools of thought for my proposition that among all the things that were happening in the industrial revolution the most deep-rooted, the most significant and, in the long run, the most menacing, was the steep upturn in the graph of urbanisation, and that the apparatus of capitalism was chiefly a piece of up-to-date machinery for operating this five-thousand-year-old rake-off.

Both Adam Smith and Marx regarded urbanisation unequivocally as a good thing. Smith's reasons were obvious enough – he was the apologist of the manufacturers; he was very keen on opportunity and growth and not much exercised about equality; he believed in the almost magical qualities of free competition, and the manufacturing cities were the places featuring the fiercest competition and the most glittering prizes for the winners.

Marx's reasons were more complex. There was the ordinary

human fact that he himself was urban to the fingertips and could never have had much rapport with anyone who didn't at least appreciate that that was the best way for anybody to be. Then there was the ideological reason, that he hoped for the overthrow of a system that had brought in its train so much misery and injustice, and he believed the only force capable of stopping it was an urban proletariat, politically educated by first-hand experience of capitalist methods and made conscious of their own power by being brought together in large numbers.

It was already beginning to be obvious that, as a result of capitalism, wealth was not only being concentrated in an up-ward direction from the workers to the employers – it was also moving sideways and becoming geographically concentrated in some areas at the expense of others. Marx was aware of this, and said so, but to him it was an unimportant side-issue : from his point of view it would have been politically cretinous to lay any stress on it. All his strategy was concentrated on emphasising and strengthening the horizontal loyalties : to point out that the interests of different groups among the working classes were sometimes divergent or in conflict would have been to give aid and comfort to the bosses with their policy of 'divide and rule'. So he paid no further attention to it.

For his successors, however – notably Lenin – it gradually became obvious that the *geographical* concentration of wealth had gathered such impetus and strength that it was the most explosive political issue of his day; and he had to write a book to explain what was happening in terms of Marxist ideology. He called it *Imperialism: the highest form of capitalism.*

It was by then becoming clear that if the breakdown of cap-italism was indeed becoming imminent in any Western country, it was not going to take place as a result of the rich becoming ever fewer and richer and the poorer becoming ever more numerous and more wretched as Marx had predicted (or was believed to have predicted). For the British working classes, by the end of the century the worst appeared to be over; their working conditions and living standards were slowly but un-deniably improving, as living standards throughout the whole of Latium had improved with the rise of Rome.

Just to put the record straight, although Marx had forecast the polarisation of wealth he had also hedged the prophecy by cautioning :

> It is possible, with an increasing productiveness of labour, for the price of labour power to keep on falling and yet the fall to be accompanied by a constant growth in the mass of the labourer's means of subsistence. But even in such a case the abyss between the labourer's position and that of the capitalist would keep widening.

That is a rather more tenable position. Even so, if Engels had revisited Lancashire in Lenin's day he would have found the living standards of the workers in the back-to-back houses, inadequate as they still were, considerably improved. It would not have been easy to demonstrate that the living standards of the boss in the big house on the hill had gone up by a sufficiently *greater percentage* to justify the description of 'widening abyss'. Many people felt that the abyss, if anything, was narrowing.

However, as Lenin saw it, this did not invalidate Marx's thesis. It only meant that to take a total view of the operation of British capitalism it was no longer sufficient to examine its working inside the British Isles. He claimed that it had so extended its sphere of operations that the proletariat it was now exploiting included all the workers in all the overseas countries which Britain had taken over.

In his book he pointed out that in the period between the publication of *Das Kapital* and the end of the nineteenth century Britain had more than doubled the extent of its colonial possessions, adding between six and seven million square miles and over 150 million new subjects to its empire; that in roughly the same period the national income of Great Britain had approximately doubled while the income 'coming from abroad' had 'increased *nine times*' (Lenin's italics). He maintained that such imperialism was creating a new form of the economic parasitism which had weakened 'former empires' (like Rome's, presumably), vastly enriching the ruling class and enabling it to hand over to the lower classes living nearest to the power centre enough of the loot 'to keep them quiet'.

In this way Marx's forecasts could be vindicated. It was obvious in Lenin's day that if the proletariat was considered in this global light, then the abyss between their standards and the standards of the capitalist overlords was indeed widening. It is equally clear that in our own day it is widening still.

Implicit in Lenin's analysis are two inferences which are worth examining more closely. The first is the implication that the situation he was describing was specifically characteristic of capitalism. He himself makes the comparison with earlier empires and the end result – the convergence of wealth and power towards the central location, the disbursement of parts of it to the adjacent population 'enough to keep them quiet', and the absolute losers at the periphery – all this displays a very close correlation with historical events which took place before capitalism was ever thought of. It would seem possible that at least some of the forces at work had been in operation for many centuries.

The importance of this distinction is hard to overestimate. If the forces had operated before the introduction of capitalism, the possibility exists that they might continue to operate *after the demise* of capitalism in those countries where it has been abolished. Anyone in pursuit of equality may ultimately have to face the fact that socialism and communism in themselves are not enough; that power and privilege still inexorably drain towards the centre; that the communist world may have eliminated some of the inherent contradictions of capitalism and succeeded in ironing out booms and slumps, but has left intact a slow burning fuse of imbalances and injustices which is much older and harder to extinguish, is common to both the Eastern and the Western World and the Third World also, and may prove in the end a more urgent problem than any of the issues which divide them.

The second implication contained in Lenin's analysis is that twentieth century imperialism chiefly concerns the relationship between nation states and their colonial dependencies. This was one reason why the concept was dynamite. Lenin like

Marx did not indulge in theoretical exposition as a mere intellectual exercise. He was using his pen as a lever to move men to political action, and the most effective way of doing this is to weld together large numbers of people by creating in them a passionate sense of common purpose. The springs of political action in the world as we know it are such that this can best be achieved by pointing out to them a common enemy.

In Marx's original version the group he was trying to weld was the International Working Class Movement and the common enemy was capitalism. In the Leninist extension the group in any colonial dependency consisted of the native population, and the enemy, while still theoretically capitalism, was vividly symbolised by the occupying power. It is not at all surprising that the fight against colonialism met with swifter and more complete success than the fight against capitalism. For one thing the colonial freedom fighters were geographically more compact than the 'workers of the world'; for another thing there was usually a convenient visual aid in identifying the enemy: he was a different colour. More important still, the original Marxist campaign was attempting to cut across nationalist feelings whereas the anti-imperialist campaign could enlist them on its side. Anyone who can do that is halfway home.

Thus the followers of Marx and Lenin had no hesitation whatever about what attitude they should adopt to the centripetal drift of wealth away from overseas dependencies and towards the metropolitan imperial states – Britain, France, etc. The tactic was to urge the native population of the colonies to detach themselves at the earliest opportunity and reclaim their independence as a first step to breaking the economic chain that kept them poor, dependent and underdeveloped. The white soldier policing their country might be himself in his private capacity a wage slave of capitalism, driven to enlist by chronic unemployment in his home town. But this was not to inhibit them from exhorting him to 'go home'.

However, the almost total success of this policy is now beginning to throw into higher relief another aspect of the matter which the Marxists seem no more concerned than the capitalists themselves to draw specific attention to, since it is very hard to see how either of them can derive any political advantage out of it. That is the fact that the identical process is continuing all the time *inside* national boundaries – within the boundaries of ex-imperialist states, within the boundaries of non-imperialist states, and now within the boundaries of the ex-colonial states themselves.

Take, for instance, the archetypal example of twentieth-century imperialism, the British Empire. It must have seemed to millions of inhabitants of the far-flung territories as they fetched and carried for Sahib, Effendi, Tuan or Baas that the British Isles, the heartland of the Empire, was one monolithic bastion of wealth and privilege and that everyone there – all white and free and equal and enfranchised as they were – must be well fed and contented and literate and rich. Yet at the same time in Ireland people were starving to death. Very well, that was obviously imperialism too, for Ireland was a conquered overseas territory. In the north of the mainland over large areas of Scotland the natives were being turned off their land without hope of redress, as cavalierly as if they were Red Indians or black Africans. That also may be imperialism, for after all Edinburgh was once the capital city of a bona fide nation-state. In the west, Wales was being exploited like many other parts of the Empire as a rich source of raw materials. Her rural areas were becoming depopulated and the industrial ones were the first and hardest hit victims of every recession. We can still, if you like, use the word imperialism since the Welsh had a different ethnic origin and preserved their own separate language.

But now come to Newcastle-on-Tyne. Nothing happened to Welsh Rhondda or Scottish Clyde that didn't happen to Tyneside. There too whole generations of men spent their lives fuelling the new civilisation with labours as arduous and in conditions as gruelling as any overseas colonists. Tyneside is a longish way from London and by some strange inevitable economic alchemy the wealth it helped to produce somehow failed to stick. It wasn't simply that, according to the Mark 1 Marxist model, the gap between the Tyneside workers and the Tyne-side capitalists widened. What happened was that the wealth trickled away from that place altogether and in the course of a couple of generations a widening gap appeared between the living standards of the workers on Tyneside and the workers in the South East of England who enjoyed, on average, higher wages and better health and longer life and better education and lower infant mortality and taller and heavier children and more doctors and better housing and more amenities and lower rates of unemployment. It was in fact a classic happening on the Leninist model in every respect but one: that the Tyne-siders were English. So the process is never referred to as imperialism. It is a process that has never been properly christened at all.

Move down a hemisphere and consider, say, South America. If you had been a poor peasant in that continent when your country groaned under the European yoke and its riches were flowing back to Spain or Portugal while you were growing poorer, then you were a victim of imperialism. If you are a poor peasant there now, and your district is growing poorer because its riches are trickling away and ending up in Rio or Santiago or Buenos Aires that can hardly be imperialism be-cause it is not being done to you by foreigners. But it must be very hard for those on the losing side to tell the difference. Marx himself saw no difference. In the passage concerning the terms of trade from which much of Marxist thinking on im-perialism is derived, he specifically assumed that the imbalance could occur between different communities in 'the same or different' countries.

There are many reason why no major international political movement has found it expedient to call attention to and de-nounce this centralising process as a major plank in its plat-form. For one thing the object of most political parties is to gain control of the machinery of central government. They have no wish to undermine the concept of the unity of the nation-state or the belief that it is possible to administer it from the centre in a way that will be in the interests of all its citizens. Thus there has never been the same general support for the detachment and independence of underdeveloped peripheral regions as there was for the detachment and independence of underdeveloped colonies.

Most political parties have their headquarters in the capital city. They share the unspoken conviction of the central headquarters of every other national organisation that they have a better understanding of what is going on in the world than any provincial branch could possibly have, and that any plan or proposals which might risk antagonising the most influential and densely populated area of the country would be counterproductive and political suicide.

In the international arena, Communist countries are eager to point out and to wax indignant over any anomalies and shortcomings which are exclusive to capitalist countries – and, of course, vice versa. But in this particular respect there is a tacit gentleman's agreement to keep silence and let sleeping dogs lie. There is no great power which would care to go to town on this issue.

There is no small power which would care to either. The Third-World bloc at the United Nations contains many countries which are freer than most to make moral denunciations of other governments, since they have not been in power long enough to make as many mistakes or commit as many sins as older established administrations, and many of their people's misfortunes can still be blamed on problems they inherited after decades of colonial misrule. But in 1975, watching New York in the throes of its fiscal agonies and noting the willingness of large areas of the US hinterland to watch it go under for the third time, they showed no desire to make public speeches about the arrogance of metropolitan areas. Such speeches might in some cases have aroused unfortunate echoes back home, not only because the gap in living standards there between metropolis and hinterland continues to widen, but because independence has usually done nothing to close the gap or slow down the pace at which it is widening.

If New York's problems ever become really insoluble there will be a great many cities in every part of the world knowing only too well for whom the bell tolls.

PART III

The Rise of Megalopolis

7 The anaemia at the extremities

The archetypal image of the industrial cities was a powerful one. Once money became more plentiful there, they were often places high in morale. The first of the self-made employers were able to remain sturdily independent and free of sycophancy because for the first time in the history of the world some people were able to become rich by producing *for the poor*, and had no need to court the patronage of the aristocracy and kowtow to their vanity. The workers frequently took pride in their new cities, the workshops of the world. They knew they were visibly enriching their own countries, paying their way, taking in raw materials and sending out manufactured products which all the world needed and wanted.

This version of the economic functions that bring wealth to a modern city was a stereotype which maintained its hold on people's minds long after the reality had changed out of all recognition, and after many of the large industrial cities had passed from a phase of apparently irresistible dynamism into decline and stagnation. Several forces were at work to bring this about.

For one thing it was becoming clear that the process described as urbanisation does not consist simply of people moving from agriculture into urban centres and occupations. It proceeds undiminished in highly industrialised countries even after the numbers engaged in agriculture have sunk to a barely reducible minimum (in Britain around three percent). The movement is most characteristically a step-by-step affair of people moving from farm to village, village to town, town to city, city to megalopolis, until the smallest settlements are no longer able to survive.

All over Europe small-towns studies repeatedly confirm that the smallest units are being wiped out. Rural hamlets and mountain villages which have been inhabited uninterruptedly for centuries prove no longer viable. Sometimes, when the last couple of dozen inhabitants of an off-shore island give up the struggle and climb into a single boat and leave the place un-inhabited for the first time since the Vikings, a television camera will record the move and ask them why and play poignant music on the sound track, but more often such places are deserted quietly and piecemeal and simply weather into the ground.

In the United States seventy-five percent of the population already lives crowded into three percent of the land. It might be imagined from all the talk of American cities drowning in the morass of their economic problems that this concentra-tion had just about reached saturation point by the end of the second World War, and that there would be no pressure for the emptier ninety-seven percent of the land area to become emptier still. On the contrary, half of all the counties in the United States suffered an actual decline of population in the 1950s.

What is being done about it? The White House, as quoted in US *News and World Report* (6 July 1970), after calling a conference of urban planners and demographers, reached pre-cisely the same conclusion as the rulers of any banana republic – that the process was indeed inexorable. They decided that 'No amount of money or other federal help could stop the de-cline of small towns in rural America and that the government should concentrate rather on improving the planning and development of metropolitan areas'.

If the drift is visible at one extreme in the disappearance of the smaller units, it is equally visible at the other extreme in the largest ones. The conurbations around New York, London and the 'Golden' Triangle of north-eastern Europe are continu-ally and rapidly expanding, swallowing up what were once small independent towns and converting them into suburbs and boroughs, integral parts of the urban machine.

And the last thing we are accustomed to contemplating is that the cities themselves are not immune to the pull. A pro-vincial city such as Glasgow or Newcastle is a very solid entity. An immense amount of material and human capital has been sunk into it. Within its own area it is accustomed to exerting a quasi-metropolitan degree of influence and magnetism. It must have acquired a great deal of hardheaded urban experience and know-how, just as it has created its own lifestyles and inspired its own loyalties.

But with every advance in technology, communication, and speed and facility of transport, the magnetic pull of London and the south-east is exerted more powerfully and over longer distances of the British Isles. The demographic and economic tides in Great Britain flow primarily inwards towards an urban bloc described sometimes as a 'coffin', sometimes as an 'hour glass', polarised diagonally from the Merseyside conurbation through the Midlands to London; and within that block itself the tide runs strongly south.

Among the cities remaining outside, the fortunes of course vary widely. Some may have been hit extra hard by the collapse or weakening of a staple industry. Others may have received a shot in the arm from tourism. But generally speaking all efforts they put into growth or rehabilitation are tapped and sapped and drained by the same invisible forces that are sapping the villages. And the further away they are from the economic centre of gravity in the South East, the more heavily the dice is loaded against them. Over the last ten years 50,000 people per annum have been moving out of these 'development' areas. At a time when the Home Counties around London were enjoying tolerably full employment, a school-leaver in the north-east could apply for a poorly paid job as a van boy and find thirty-five others ahead of him in the queue.

Urban theorists sometimes used to read little homilies contrasting the exuberant economic health of Birmingham, that humming hive of small businesses and live-wire entrepreneurs, with the 'stagnant' conditions of cities further north where people were apparently too tired or too stupid to try out the same tricks and make the same fortunes. This kind of talk is the sheerest romanticism. In present conditions it lies not in ourselves, Horatio, but in our geography that we are underlings.

The process is world-wide, and in most countries it has long been obvious to everybody in which direction the tide is flowing – in Europe, inwards towards the prosperous Golden Triangle; in the United States, towards the eastern and western seaboards and the 'sunbelt'; in Scandinavia for the most part southwards; westward in the USSR; eastward in China; and in most of South America towards the coast.

The effect of this on urban population patterns is not always the same. In the older developed countries, it produces what is known as a 'rank-size order' in urban distribution – a gentle steady graph descending from the small number of very large conurbations down to the large number of villages, with correlative numbers of all intermediate sizes in between. But in Third-World countries such as many in Africa, South East Asia and South America, the Western-style step-by-step urbanisation cannot take place because the provincial cathedral cities, market towns, and industrial centres of previous centuries do not exist. Anyone there wanting to leave the land has to choose, as the Australians put it, between 'Sydney or the bush'.

This results in the rise of the so-called 'primate city' – a single very large, magnetic capital city, with a rapid uncontrollable growth rate and a rash of slums around the outskirts sometimes stretching for miles.

The oedematous growth of the primate cities causes great anxiety to their governments. There is always danger that a rich capital city with a poverty-stricken hinterland will crystallise out not into one nation but two. If the gap in the living standards and lifestyle widens, the city will appear and function less and less like a symbol of national pride and more and more like an occupying power. Envy and discontent in the interior might conspire and harden into rebellious separatism, or it might build up into an avalanche of immigration into the primate city which would overload its amenities to breaking point.

Brazil, India, Chile, the Ivory Coast, Morocco, Kenya, Nigeria, Turkey, Thailand and Korea are among the many lands attempting to redress the urban balance by methods varying from tax incentives, or residence permits, or providing amenities for new settlements in rural area, to Brazil's method of constructing a brand new capital in the interior, scores of new towns in the south and development programmes in the north-east.

In only one case was the drive to end primacy promptly successful, and that was in Israel – an example not easy to follow, because the motive was as much military as sociological, and any nation which believes itself to be fighting for its life can always pull off the odd miracle.

In most cases the efforts are fruitless. Growth continues to concentrate in a single centre which acts as the seat of government, the residence of the Westernised élite, the showplace for visitors, the recipient and distribution centre for foreign-invested capital, the central headquarters of communications media and banks and institutes of Higher Education, and foreign embassies, the site of the airport, and the radial centre of the transport system. The primate city hurls itself into the twentieth century at impressive speed, leaving an ever-widening gap between its standards and amenities and those of the rest of the country, like a locomotive which has become uncoupled from the rest of the train.

In Western countries the problem does not register itself so dramatically, but it is present nevertheless. In Europe, for instance, it makes itself felt in the central areas by problems of congestion, overcrowding, soaring prices, traffic jams and housing shortages, and elsewhere by a kind of creeping economic blight that paralyses the peripheral regions. The national capitals keep shovelling government financial aid out to these places; they keep christening them in more and more optimistic terms, from 'Depressed Areas' to 'Special Areas' to 'Development Areas', but inevitably the aid appears to soak away into the sand and the stagnant towns and cities repeatedly and soggily fail to achieve a take-off into unaided prosperity and growth. The twin symptoms of this malaise have been aptly described as 'apoplexy at the centre and anaemia at the extremities'. No one has yet found a cure for it.

Some will see this perhaps as just another manifestation of the failure of capitalism to resolve its own contradictions. It cannot be quite that simple.

The *Communist Manifesto* of 1848 advocated 'the gradual abolition of the distinction between town and country by a more equitable distribution of population over the countryside.' What has actually happened in the Soviet Union is described by Isaac Deutscher in *The Unfinished Revolution*: 'Soviet urbanisation in tempo and scale is without parallel in history.' After fifty years the USSR is almost as urban as the United States, and more than forty million people have left the countryside for the city since the second World War.

In the early days of the revolution some of this urbanisation was deliberately planned, but it has long since become obvious that the Russians are riding the same tiger as the rest of us. To take the classic example of Moscow, it was firmly decided in 1935 that its growth was to be strictly limited. No more industrial expansion, an absolute ban on net immigration enforced by a system of work permits and a ruling that even the natural increase, that is the excess of births over deaths, must never be allowed to push the population above five million. It passed six million as long ago as 1960. In 1967, for example, natural growth added 11,000 to the city's inhabitants but the population increased by more than 60,000.

When this matter was the subject of public debate in 1972, some economists, such as V. V. Perevedentsev, took the line that big is beautiful and the attempt to control urban growth was essentially misguided. It is significant that one of his strongest arguments was the proven fact that, planning or no planning, controls or no controls, such attempts *do not work*. 'Many large cities' he pointed out, 'have long had rigidly limited registration; they grow and grow just the same.'

In China, if anywhere, the anti-urban bias behind official thinking is well documented and world-renowned. Mao like Marx hoped to abolish 'the three great differentials' – between brain and hand, worker and peasant, and city and countryside. There, if anywhere, the aim is 'industrialisation without urbanisation'; there, if anywhere, the hammer and sickle emblem of communism might figure in the public mind in the reverse order of esteem: sickle and hammer. There the most determined and constructive efforts have been made to implement the realisation that you cannot keep people out of cities by forbidding them to come, only by improving the conditions of life outside the cities.

That the Chinese repeatedly proclaim their determination to pursue this goal is admirable and among the Great Powers unique. Yet in spite of it all the most that can be said is that without those efforts things might have been ten times worse. In 1957 the Communist Central Committee was complaining of 'a blind emigration of peasants from the rural areas' – 800,000 of working age moved in during the first Five-Year Plan. Between 1960 and 1975 the population in the cities almost doubled, bringing the urban numbers up to 246.5 million, over a third of them living in cities numbering over a million.

We must conclude that if there are any inherent contradictions in our urban-based civilisation which may cause it one day to grind to a halt or collapse, there is no Great Power or economic bloc which can look forward with any complacency to watching the rest of the world go under. It will be too busy swimming for its own life.

If this process continues to operate everywhere against the clearly expressed wishes of the powers that be, even in places where those powers keep a pretty comprehensive grip on all facts of economic life, there has to be some explanation. It could be that their expressed wishes are not really as fervent as they sound; they themselves dwell *ex officio* at the centre of things and the gripes and discontents of the metropolitan sector are bound to reverberate more menacingly in their ears than any thin cries blowing in from the periphery. Or it could be quite simply that they don't fully understand why the thing is happening. Some of the mechanisms at work are not readily apparent to the naked eye.

It was in the 1960s that it became clear that the concept of the modern city outlined at the beginning of the chapter, as a place growing rich by the import of raw materials and the manufacture and export of processed goods, was obsolescent.

In 1961 Jean Gottman wrote a book called *Megalopolis* containing a detailed analysis of the urbanised north-eastern seaboard of the United States. He discovered, apparently somewhat to his surprise, that at a period when this area was increasing rapidly in population, it was producing a decreasing percentage of the nation's industrial output.

'Modern urban growth,' Gottmann wrote,

> thus appears to be less rooted in manufacturing activities than is usually believed and than used to be the case. . . . The labour force in megalopolis is no longer basically concerned with manufacturing employment. The fundamental change has been the steady growth of the white-collar army.

Gottmann documented three main characteristics of urban white-collar employment, and since that time all the trends he observed have been reinforced and have manifested themselves in all parts of the world.

'The most spectacular and most unique characteristic of the megalopolitan economy and growth today,' he wrote (it has become even more spectacular but has ceased to be unique), 'is the expansion of the white collar labour force of which the towering skyline is the rising symbol.' Already by 1950 white collar workers accounted for forty-five to fifty percent of the total employment in the New York, north-east Jersey, Boston, and Hertford areas, and over fifty percent in Washington DC. Those figures look low today, but as Gottmann pointed out : 'The most impressive feature of this rise appears to be its continuity.' There has been no break in the continuity since. He could have used the word 'inexorability' with no less truth.

A second characteristic was that 'this type of work demonstrates almost everywhere *more stability* (his italics) than the less regular income from manufacturing'. Similarly, in the United Kingdom the lowest rates of unemployment are to be found, together with the highest concentration of white-collar work, in the south-east around London. Whenever there is a hiccup in the economy the employment figures in that area acknowledge only with a gentle dip the kind of recession that further afield in areas of manufacturing and heavy industry is throwing thousands of people on the dole.

The third feature is the tenacity with which this type of work clings to the central location. 'White-collar employment appears to be the most difficult type to decentralise and scatter over the countryside.' Capital cities are spending money and effort on organisations like London's 'Location of Offices Bureau' with the aim of persuading offices to move out of the city centre to areas far removed where the air is fresher, the commuting shorter, and the cost of office floorspace very much lower. But even when financial inducements are added to reason and exhortation, such programmes are never able to push existing offices out of the centre as fast as new ones spring up or older ones expand. All over the world high-rise office blocks rear up thick and fast like a population of sub-terranean Krakens heaving themselves up out of the asphalt.

The inexorability of the growth of the white-collar sector is peculiar in that it seems not to be subject to normal economic laws. The bureaucratic sector of a corporation, or a Department of State, appears to continue steadily growing regardless of whether the output of the Corporation or the responsibilities of the Department are expanding, contracting, or stationary. This was pointed out a long time ago by C. North-cote Parkinson, and if he had expressed it more pompously and less readably he might have been listened to with more attention. So let us hear the same thing said again by a few less light-hearted observers.

Take one clear example: the business of labour-saving machinery. This is being constantly improved and refined – automation added to mechanisation and cybernetics to engineering – and the result is that fewer human beings are required per unit of output. Anyone investing capital in up-to-date plant expects this benefit to accrue and would complain bitterly if it didn't.

In those cases where the wage-earners resent and resist the

rise in productivity because it creates redundancies (instances often quoted are the dockers' opposition to containerisation, and the railwaymen's stipulation that a 'fireman' still continue to ride with the driver on a diesel-powered locomotive), these workers are denounced as Luddites, standing selfishly with arms outspread in the path of progress or throwing spanners in the works.

But here is a surprising thing: there are no Luddites in the bureaucratic sector. You can add computerisation to computation as freely as you like and no one will strike, or march up and down with banners protesting about the consequent redundancies.

This is not because office workers are any more amenable than dock workers to being made redundant. It is because no redundancies occur.

In other words this is one kind of labour saving machinery that does not save labour.

On this point too Gottmann seemed mildly surprised at the conclusion his researches had driven him to, namely that the various machines installed 'have not saved much in the way of payrolls'. He failed to come up with a reason for this, and a bulletin issued by the United States Department of Labour Statistics concerning the same mysterious phenomenon didn't get much further than restating the problem. It explained that the use of electronic computers, for instance, 'has created a number of new office occupations and has changed the functions performed by others. Some of the new jobs especially in programming require considerable related experience or education of the college level. Some of the other jobs related to operation of computing systems also require other types of clerical work. . . . The machines also require regular servicing by maintenance and repair crews consisting often of workers even more highly specialised than the people who merely operate them.' The inevitable conclusion is that the machines don't do much to reduce the total office labour force, but do tend to make the units which remain considerably more costly.

It is not easy to establish whether or not the people who

invest in the machines expect them to reduce the numbers of their office staff, but they accept the failure to do so with apparent equanimity. They sometimes point out that the staff are 'happier and more fulfilled' working with the gadgets than they were with pen and paper. Presumably when the competition for really first-class secretaries is so fierce, it pays to keep them happy and fulfilled.

Probably the real reasons for the curious statistics of this sector of employment are outside the normal scope of economics whether classical, Keynesian, Marxist, or what have you, for once you leave the factory floor and approach nearer to head office, economy counts for less and less and prestige counts for more. An executive in a large office with six people working under him feels more impressive than an executive in a small office with one fifty-year-old typist. He would be a fool to cut down on these items. They are tax deductible; they make him feel good; office expenses are anyway only a tiny percentage of the overall outlay of a large concern. If he suddenly announced he could manage just as efficiently with a quarter of the space and staff he would create alarm and despondency in his shareholders and suspicion in his rivals that either the firm was going downhill or he himself was going bonkers. If one of his assistants complains of overwork and demands a secretary of his own (to increase his own prestige) the executive has no very strong motive to resist the demand. Saying yes will make his assistant grateful, cost the executive nothing, create a stir of interest, add the presence in his near environment of a possibly delightful dolly bird and convince people that the work of the department is flourishing and expanding; he now has seven people working under him. Saying no means a week or two of coolness and disaffection and a built-in implicit answer from the assistant to any future charges of tardiness or inefficiency, or alternatively means all the hassle of firing him and breaking in somebody else.

If he learns that other executives of his grade are installing computers he is unwilling to tell any of them that his own work is not sufficiently complex and arduous to necessitate this. If someone privately hints to him that in practice the machine might not actually do anything to reduce his staff, this will be no deterrent. He doesn't in the bottom of his heart want his office staff reduced.

He will point out a few months later that the expense has been justified because although staff has not been reduced, output has been increased. By this he means not the output of the material product the firm produces but the output of the head office computer. It is indeed spewing out a great deal of information which has to be communicated to other offices and other interested bodies (what else can you do with it?) and read and initialled, thus creating more work at the receiving end in the way of opening, circulating, initialling, filing, and after a decent interval feeding into the shredder or other avenue to oblivion. Such time-fillers are sometimes welcome. When a secretary wrote a letter to the *Guardian* asking advice from other secretaries as to how they filled in the hours after they had done their nails, read their magazines and got fed up with their knitting and written to all their friends, a flood of correspondence poured in from girls who were faced with the same problem but had never liked to admit it. The victims of chronic if adequately paid underemployment seemed to outnumber by about eight to one the small minority whose bosses worked them off their feet.

The economic rationale of sustaining such a large pool of females in attendance for long hours of idleness interspersed with short bursts of activity cannot be explained in terms of normal market forces. We are in the world of courtiers and ladies in waiting and conspicuous consumption, for at the top levels of economic life the relationships between the protagonists become less mercantile and more monarchical. In this connection J. K. Galbraith has pointed out one often-overlooked reason why many firms continue to grow and grow by mergers and amalgamations and take-overs long after they have passed the 'technically optimum size – the size which most economically sustains the requisite specialists, the counterpart organisation and the associated capital investment'. They go on growing, he suggests, because in large and complex enterprises the power to make decisions passes out of the hands of the owners (i.e., the stockholders) and into the hands of the organisation men who use that power – not surprisingly, says Galbraith – to serve their own personal ends, which are by no means always identical with those of the owners. 'These ends – job security, pay, promotion, prestige, company plane and private washroom, the charm of collectively exercised power – are all strongly served by the growth of the enterprise.'

The other major growth point, Gottmann discovered, was in the service industries. The numbers employed in this sector were growing throughout the nation as life grew more complex and living standards improved; but they increased most of all in the cities. This was natural. Most service jobs are by definition serving people, and have to be carried out where people are. This doesn't merely mean that two million people need twice as much servicing as one million. The graph is steeper than that because in fact people in cities need a lot more servicing *per head* than people outside them, simply because of the vastly increased complexity of their relationships and interactions.

There has always been a knock-on factor in this service sector, even in former and far simpler days. By the time one well-to-do household had decided it needed a staff of nine servants to wait on its needs and look after its possessions, it would find it necessary to employ a tenth because of the extra work involved in organising, feeding, accommodating and cleaning up after the other nine. This factor applies with equal force when the private servants turn into public ones and the chauffeur has become a taxi-driver, the parlour-maid a waitress, and the lady's maid a hairdresser. And it applies more forcibly with every increase in population density and every increase in general living standards.

Every such increase brings us fractionally nearer to the theoretical and impossible time when every thousand people moving into a metropolis will create a demand for another five hundred to move in to lubricate their lives (and that five hundred for another two hundred and fifty, etc etc) and when every hundred workers made redundant in a declining industrial city will spell death to the jobs of another fifty and that fifty to another twenty-five and so on.

That time is theoretical, like the concept of an object moving at the speed of light. Before we could get anywhere near it the system would have seized up. The functioning even of long established services would deteriorate and become increasingly subject to breakdown; the problems of transport, communication, financing, and the maintenance of law and order would get out of hand. Anyone who hasn't noticed the signs of the system creaking under the strains it is already subjected to has not been living in a metropolis or reading the newspapers.

These two activities – those of the white-collar and service sectors – have now become the characteristic metropolitan activities. Among other things, this has transformed the impression the city makes on a visitor up from the country. In the nineteenth century he might have been struck by the wealth and extravagance of the place, but it would also have been easy to see how the city earned the money – there were the mills and the factories pouring out products which he among others might require to buy.

Today in any large metropolis he might have to look quite a long way for signs of any of that kind of thing going on. The factories for the most part have had to move out of the central location – the rates are too high for them. Gottmann had already noted this in 1960. 'Despite,' he wrote,

all the power of inertia and the expense involved in moving plant and despite the endeavour of municipal authorities to retain manufacturing plants in their territory or even to attract new ones, the migration of such plants out of the central cities especially out of the larger ones has been steadily going on and on.

Downtown Boston, for example, had already at that date lost nine thousand manufacturing jobs in a space of ten years. Of the kind of thing that still *does* go on in a place like

New York, Jane Jacobs' book, written even earlier than Gottmann's, gives a very vivid illustration. When she is *theorising* about the city she writes of the firms manufacturing brassieres and Scotch tape, but when she is describing at first hand those sectors which she commends as being in good heart and full of growth and vitality, it so happens that her eye never actually alights on anybody engaged in making these or any other exportable items.

She refers to a great many stores and restaurants and offices and theatres and cinemas and such splendidly varied enterprises as a health club with its gym, a dental laboratory, a studio for water-colour lessons, a man who rents out tuxedos, a Hawaiian dance troupe, a garage, a beauty parlour, an art gallery, a camera exchange, a laundry, a barber's shop, delicatessen, tailor's, meat market, a locksmith, a drug store, a dispensary, coffee house, candy store, florist, a store that rents diving equipment, a concert hall, a hamburger house, a lodging house, a fruit vendor and many other busy and contented citizens, all usefully and gainfully employed in adding immensely to the pleasures and conveniences of urban life, but producing absolutely nothing that anyone outside the city is liable to consume, all contributing to the task of shovelling around and redistributing the wealth already *inside the city*, all of them engaged in the process which used to be known as taking in one another's washing.

This then is one component of urbanisation: that recent technological changes lead to growth in white-collar and servicing jobs, and these are activities that inevitably aggregate together and multiply.

It is one of the invisible subsidies from the regions and provinces to the cities, that whereas everyone in the country pays taxes on equal terms for the privilege of being administered, the lucrative end of the process of administration – the buildings to house it, the salaries paid out for it, the subsidiary services – are concentrated disproportionately in the cities.

There is another such subsidy more considerable, and even more invisible. I would like to approach it by a detour through another problem which has been considered mysterious for a long time, but to which some economists now believe they have found the answer.

The problem was how the inhabitants of the newly settled United States of America managed to create so much capital in such a short space of time. To be sure, they were not starting from scratch in quite the way Europe had started from scratch. They could benefit from Europe's experience and Europe's know-how : they didn't have to re-invent the harness and the plough and the textile machinery. But then this common stock of human knowledge is equally available in all parts of the world and its availability certainly doesn't always lead to affluence.

The miracle cannot be attributed to national character, because many of the immigrants came from some of the poorest countries in Europe, and their ethnic virtues had not been able to enrich their homelands. True, the prairies were rich and empty, but the steppes were rich and empty too, and they had not secreted an equivalent of Chicago. Nobody would suggest that the settlers comprised the representatives of their respective races 'most likely to succeed'. A high proportion of them came from the bottom of their respective heaps : it was failure that drove them out. In colonies like Virginia some of the first settlers had been considered so worthless and undesirable that their country could not wait for them to leave but forcibly evicted them, and whoever coined the phrase 'there has never been a British refugee' forgot the *Mayflower* and its hundreds of successors.

One popular explanation has been that in America the huddled masses threw off the yokes of oppressive old-fashioned regimes and learned to breathe free, and it was this that released all that latent energy. There may be something in that, and there are many Third-World countries who hoped that with independence they would be able to repeat the trick. But it hasn't turned out so easy. They need capital to get their economies off the ground and without relying on some outside aid or investment it has proved very hard to accumulate. Russia and China both managed to move into a phase of rapid growth but not without coercion, tight control of the whole economy, constant exhortation and Herculean feats of labour in countries which already had urbanised sectors of long standing and some capital accumulation to build on.

But the people of God's own country, building from the grass roots, receiving no foreign aid and contracting no foreign debts, offering little guidance to the constant stream of newcomers beyond the general principles of the Gettysburg address and Samuel Smiles's *Self-help* appeared to an astonished world to levitate themselves into affluence as if there was nothing to it.

They attributed their success to the virtues of their political systems, their God-fearing philosophy, their pep and industry and republicanism, their freshness and ingenuity and democracy and get-up-and-go. When they visited the homes of their ancestors they lectured them on their deplorable imperial habits and their hide-bound hierarchies and they freely proffered advice to the world as to what it must do to be saved. They acquired the reputation of being brash and smug and full of themselves, though it would have transcended human nature for any nation to have lived through their experience and reacted any differently.

It was a long time before economists managed to perceive that the Old World had been heavily subsidising the American dream throughout its youth and adolescence. The reason it took so long is that until recently economists were all males. They constructed in all sincerity mental models of the workings of the economic system which have come to be regarded as standard. According to these models the work done by men contributed to the wealth of nations. The work done by their wives, if work it could be called, did not so contribute. Wives were dependants, they were paid nothing because they produced nothing. The results of all their labours registered zero when the gross national product came to be totted up.

This model is still widely adhered to. Now that women have moved into the field of paid employment, the work they do

F

in office or factory becomes visible to the economist and is accounted productive. But anything they do at home sinks below the horizon of his perception and as far as he is concerned she is on holiday. Occasionally an economist looks up from his labours and perceives before his very eyes a solid ten-stone housewife moving about and exerting herself for all the world as if she were usefully employed, and is struck by a sudden misgiving because in his mental model her activity has no way of registering.

They sometimes make little economists' jokes about the intellectual dilemmas this lands them in. A. C. Pigou once pointed out that in most countries the national income could be doubled overnight if all men agreed to swap their wives. If A hired out his wife as paid housekeeper to neighbour B and vice versa the national income would be transformed because the women's work would then become economically visible. It would immediately be seen as an immensely lucrative contribution to the gross national product, and the country would shoot upwards in the statistical league of the world's wealthy nations. This is clearly a nonsense, yet they go on employing the GNP yardstick and refuse to admit that there must be something radically wrong or missing either in the mathematical tool they are employing or in the information they are feeding into it. It looks like a case of what the computer men call GIGO – garbage in, garbage out.

J. K. Galbraith, one of the most brilliant and least hide-bound of his breed, is another who has noted the existence of these 'non-working' women and in a recent book he devoted more than a chapter to his discovery that Eureka! their activities do after all have an impact on the economic life of the nation. He describes their role as that of 'crypto-servant'. I should make it clear that he wishes to be on their side and considers them undervalued. He describes their economic function as 'to facilitate consumption – to select, transport, prepare, repair, maintain, clean, service, store, protect and otherwise perform the tasks that are associated with the consumption of goods. . . . This role is critical for the expansion of consumption in the modern economy. . . . As matters now stand (and for as long as they so stand) it is *their supreme contribution to the modern economy.*' (My own, stunned, italics.)

This is a by no means extreme example of the effect of economic models on the thinking if not the actual eyesight of an otherwise intelligent man. He would never dream of implying that the hen's supreme contribution to the economy of the farm is to facilitate the consumption of corn. But he is clearly capable of following a woman around a house, barking his shins on the pushchair, dodging round the diapers, stepping over the teddy bear and the toy lorry while protesting earnestly that all that stuff about consumption was meant to enhance her importance because she can't really pretend she ever *produces* anything. Can she?

Now back to America. The subsidy it received from Europe remained for centuries economically invisible for the same reason – because it was the end product of the life's work of uncounted thousands of Europe's women rather than Europe's men. It was the same subsidy that the medieval monasteries received from the laity which led them to think how easy it is to be self-sufficient and still have leisure for prayer and contemplation when God is on your side. The subsidy was people.

Belatedly an attempt has been made at costing the value of this subsidy. Corrado Gini has worked out that even the enormous capital stock built up in the United States in those years did not in fact exceed the cost of the burden which America was enabled to shift on to the European mother countries of its immigrants – the burden of producing, feeding, rearing, and educating them throughout childhood and adolescence – by reason of the fact that the great majority of them arrived full grown, ready and eager to go to work on building up the country. This particular form of foreign aid to that particular undeveloped country, since happily it did not take the form of loans or capital investment, did not saddle its infant economy with a load of debt or even the paying out of interest or dividends. It was a free gift.

This analysis is not aimed at belittling the American achievement or implying that the debt is still outstanding. America's growth rate has long been self-sustaining and she has long since squared the account through Marshal Aid and a dozen other channels. Nor is it intended to imply that New York today should thank heaven fasting for its influx of Puerto Ricans; we are into a capital-intensive world now and a whole new ball game.

But it should be borne in mind by any American who feels sore because US Foreign Aid seems to sink away into the sand, and looks back at America's own unaided lift-off and wonders why the Third-World goons can't show the same kind of gumption. They are not in the same position. Bangladesh, for example, is a country with a good many geographical and ecological crosses to bear. But if she could find a way of shifting the cost of feeding and rearing just a quarter of her children for just one generation, she would be a million miles nearer to achieving a little miracle of her own.

H. W. Singer goes a step further and suggests that it was in the final analysis the Third World, as we now call it, which really paid for the building of America. Liberals have always been aware that Africa paid in blood through the slave trade for the building of the South, but the Northern States have felt their hands were clean of exploitation. In any conscious or direct sense so they were. But it was the imperialistic adventures and depredations of European empire-builders which sucked into that one little continent enough excess wealth to enable it to equip and despatch its surplus sons and daughters to fill up the countries of the New World and the old Commonwealth.

'Perhaps in the final analysis,' says Singer,

it may be said that the ultimate benefits of the traditional investment-cum-trade system were not with the investing countries of Europe but with the new industrial countries of North America. . . . The industrialisation of North America was made possible by the combination of migration and the opening up of underdeveloped overseas countries through European investment and trade. To that extent Point Four and technical assistance on the part of the United States would be a gesture of historical justice.

If it seems that the argument has wandered rather far away from the question of urbanisation and centrism that is not really the case, because precisely the same economic blind spot is one of the factors that invalidates most of the pronouncements about provincial stagnation. In Europe for example we are frequently assured that the central governments of the United Kingdom, France and Italy pour out far more millions in financial aid to their stagnant and depressed peripheral areas than they ever receive back from them in taxes, and there are figures to prove it. But there are no figures to establish what percentage of the high-earning, high tax-paying metropolitan manpower was fed and nurtured through its childhood and subsidised through its education by the ratepayers of some decaying backwater.

When English scientists and doctors are lured to America by better pay and conditions in the States this 'brain drain' is sharply complained of, and seen clearly as a haemorrhage of actual money as well as talent. But the constant inflow of doctors, nurses, teachers and professional talent of all kinds from Scotland, Wales, Ireland and the North is never joyfully hailed as a blood transfusion and a concealed financial subsidy from the fringes to the centre.

And when explanations are sought for the impressive economic post-war record of West Germany, attention is rarely drawn to her employment, especially in the kind of jobs which are still labour-intensive, of 'guest workers' who spend not only their childhood but also their declining years and any period of slight recession, when they are not needed, in some far away place like Turkey. It is as though young America, having received her immigrants full grown from England, Sweden, Hungary, Poland, etc., had thriftily sent them back home again when they grew too old to work or there was temporarily no work available. That way her stock of capital would have grown even faster than it did. But statistics along those lines are almost impossible to get hold of. To most economists of East or West capital is capital, and people of working age are labour. Until then the gross national product knows them not, for babies are neither capital nor labour.

They are items to which Value is undoubtedly Added, but in amounts which there seems no point in quantifying, rather like home-knitted cardigans – items in fact which idle women make in their spare and unpaid time.

A pointer to a third hidden subsidy has recently had our attention drawn to it by Carol Greenwald, the Banking Commissioner for Massachussetts. Like Gini and Singer, she was not directly concerned about the economic relations between centre and periphery – she was in fact concentrating with vigour on the difficulties of the inner city itself. The problem that concerned her was why the aids and reliefs handed out to certain underprivileged areas of the city hardly ever resulted in those areas rehabilitating themselves and becoming once again prosperous and desirable places in which to live. She was not prepared to write off the failure as a sign that the people in those districts were intrinsically inferior to the people in more thriving suburbs and not worth trying to help.

She received the impression that somehow the money pushed out to those areas in welfare benefits was failing to stick, as though it were being clawed back through some subterranean channel. What she did was to go out to talk to community groups and ask the savings banks to disclose where they were getting their funds and where they were lending them out again. She revealed that they were to a large extent taking savings from lower-middle-class areas only to lend them out again in the wealthier suburbs. She maintained that there were underprivileged areas which the banks were mentally drawing a red line around, and she called the process 'redlining.'

It is a simple and obvious truth, and all I would wish to add is that the capacity of these more prosperous areas to suck in and make good use of the savings of less privileged sectors has a range that extends far beyond the cities' limits. There are whole areas of the country – of any and every country – which are tacitly 'red-lined' in the minds of the powers that be. Anyone living and working there is not only likely to find that all the effort and money expended on rearing his children over the years (recently calculated at well over £10,000 a head in Britain) means money earned and expended in the declining areas on talents later utilised and taxed in the prosperous ones. He is also likely to find that any-thing else he manages to save and put into banks or building societies or almost anything other than an old sock under his mattress will be deployed in a similar way.

It is not due to anyone's malignancy or spite: the financial institutions are merely trying to get the best return on their money in the interests of their customers. But in practice, a central decision that a certain precinct or town or region has 'no future' is a self-fulfilling prophecy. The decision does not have to be conscious or official. There may be no actual red lines on any document for any future Greenwald to put the finger on. But the word gets around, and the word is the kiss of death.

The psychological effect of this invisible and mysterious load-ing of the dice is as insidious as hook-worm. Projects embarked upon with high hope are twice as hard to get off the ground and twice as likely to founder. Not merely does the conviction spread that the place is regarded as a dump, but there is the be-ginning of a gut feeling that perhaps it *is* a dump. Perhaps we are in some depressing way inferior to the places where bankers smile and projects succeed. There is a haemorrhage of hope and confidence very hard to staunch.

It is very seldom that sociologists can get any kind of statis-tical glimpse of the economic value of such a nebulous factor as the people's morale. But somebody kept a finger on the pulse of Sunderland's productivity in 1973 when their team won the FA Cup Final. Shortly afterwards the magazine *Industrial Man-agement* devoted four pages to the effect of this success on pro-ductivity in the area. Factory after factory reported that production was up, industrial relations had improved, and even that vandalism in the town had decreased.

One final but vital point should be made in this connection. It is that this process we have just described is scarcely at all inhibited by the existence of frontiers. It is international.

London itself, though it has barely begun to realise it, is in the first stage of becoming provincialised. It will remain of great importance as a city, a capital and a gateway to Europe.

It will continue to recruit newcomers from the British provinces and from overseas, at least as fast as it sees its own brightest and best of talents and investment capital being creamed off into Europe. London will be to Brussels what Edinburgh and Cardiff are to London – or for that matter, what Dublin is to London, because the independence of Eire has not turned back the tide, and a British 'NO' to the Common Market would not have turned it back either.

It had, in fact, begun to flow that way long before Britain joined the EEC. Professor Peter Hall's book *The Containment of Urban England* prints two diagrams which reduce the net demographic migrations in the UK to their simplest terms and illustrate them by way of contour lines superimposed on a map of Britain like the lines of barometric pressure on a weather map. The chart for 1951 to 1961 showed the circle of highest magnetism centred firmly over Greater London. In a similar map based on the figures for 1961-66 the ring had moved south-eastward, its contours cutting the coastline, for all the world like an anticyclone heading firmly towards Europe's Golden Triangle.

If there is any validity in the analysis offered above as an explanation of peripheral decline, there should be no cause for surprise in the fact that the process can extend itself to London.

Bureaucracy, for instance, can seep across frontiers as easily as money can. It is the easiest and most natural thing in the world for a London-based firm to open a branch office in Brussels or Amsterdam because the European end of the business is expanding so rapidly; for the European branch office to augment its staff to cope with the fact that increasing numbers of the firm's top brass are having to spend an increasing percentage of their time there; and in the space of a few years for it to be transformed into the *de facto* head office, the one that generates a spin-off of white-collar and service jobs.

As already noted it is not in the nature of bureaucracy for the London office staff to contract as fast as the European end expands : they will merely have less work to do, less power to wield, and less thought and cash will be expended on keeping the premises impressive and the typists on their toes because that will no longer be the prestige address. The first signs of 'stagnation' will have set in and the first confirmation of it will be when an English-born executive on being given a transfer from Amsterdam to London experiences the sinking heart of a man being sent into provincial exile and wonders where he went wrong.

There are clear signs that the peripheral gangrene affecting the remoter fringes of the British Isles is creeping further south and has already laid a chilly finger on parts of the Midlands. Indeed to some testy Europeans it already appears that the whole of Britain is one large development area. It must arouse some chagrin in a London-based administration to read such comments as this from the *Bild* in Hamburg: 'The European Community pumps over three billion marks as subsidies into Britain annually. Every single German taxpayer has so far paid three hundred marks (£57) for Britain'. And the fact that Londoners have often adopted the same pained long suffering tone vis-à-vis their own regions makes it no easier to bear.

The question that remains in the balance as the outlines of the new magnetic centre of European urban growth begin to define themselves, is whether London itself will remain just inside or just outside of the invisible psycho-financial 'red-line' dividing the winners from the losers. If the answer should be 'outside' it would put Britain into a class of her own as the first (but certainly not the last) member of a Fifth World – the world of what has been christened in anticipation 'post-industrial' states, faced with problems in some respects parallel to the Third World's problems and possibly in search of the same solutions.

It would be an unenviable, unprecedented and rather lonely predicament. Not the kind of situation in which Britain or any other country would wish to find herself. On the other hand it is perhaps not too jingoistic to suggest that it is the kind of situation in which in the past she has been known to shine.

8   The apoplexy at the centre

If the only charge to be brought against unchecked urbanisation were its debilitating effect on outlying areas, the
remedy for the people in the sticks would be laughably simple,
namely : 'If you can't lick 'em, join 'em.'

It is everywhere obvious – in some places painfully obvious –
that they have been following this advice in large numbers.
Apart from the people who feel that this is deplorable but
nothing can be done about it, there are quite a number of
experts who have declared that the trend is basically sound
and ought to be applauded.

They range from Jane Jacobs in America, champion of free
enterprise and defender of the small entrepreneur, to Perevedentsev in the USSR, proponent and practitioner of the fully
planned economy, and their message is that any attempt to
limit the size or discourage the growth of large cities would
be 'profoundly reactionary.' The phrase is Jane's, but the sentiment is one they both share.

There are few people who would not share it, if the great
cities of the world were demonstrating that side by side with
their continuing accumulation of material goods they were
maintaining the lead they once held in respect of less tangible
blessings – if they were still top in tolerance, equality, freedom, efficiency, security, urbanity, graciousness, confidence,
optimism, and the quality of life, as some of them in their best
days undoubtedly were. Unfortunately, as the size of a conurbation increases, too many of these indices appear to move
into reverse.

For quite a long time after the grit began to get into the
works, the problems that arose were regarded as serious but
incidental and soluble – always soluble. Traffic problems were
a nuisance, but given wider streets, a ring road, a flyover, these
frustrations could be eliminated and everything once again

whizz along freely in a smooth and orderly fashion. There were pockets of deprivation and delinquency, but with a little effort and determination the slums could be cleared, the people would be given nice clean new housing, adequate schools, parks and playing fields, green belts, bathrooms, pedestrian precincts, and their children would grow up contented and useful citizens. There were juxtapositions of wealth and poverty which sometimes gave rise to envy and resentment, but the cities were growing richer and as time went by the standards of welfare and benefits to the needy could be improved; they would show their gratitude by greater loyalty and diligence and the inequalities would diminish.

These millennial prophecies never quite came to pass because the problems always kept one jump ahead of the solutions.

The two stock examples are traffic and the slums. Los Angeles has the most comprehensive, ingenious and ambitious network of roads and freeways of any city in the world. At the same time it is the city that gave birth to the wisecrack that anyone leaving his office in Los Angeles when it closes on Friday evening will be lucky to get to the coast before his licence runs out.

England has striven as actively and persistently as any country to eradicate the problem of urban slums for good and all. Yet in 1976 the Architectural Association reported on the results of ten years of multimillion-pound housing developments in Britain's big cities that these schemes 'have not merely done little to solve our housing crisis – they have in fact made it worse.'

No people are less inclined than New Yorkers to throw in the sponge and call any problem insoluble, and no one would accuse the *Wall Street Journal* of anti-urban bias, but a few years ago it stated:

One need only live in or near a major city like New York for a period of time to realise that the institution (taking the word in its wider meaning) of the sprawling metropolis is quite literally beyond human control, unable to provide a safe, let alone pleasant, environment for its helpless inhabitants.

Many people still doggedly maintain that the snarl-ups are temporary, that with patience and intelligence and above all with more wealth and more growth there is no reason why the thing cannot be made to run smoothly even if the urban area grows to five or ten times its present size. They urgently need to believe that, because all their forward planning is based on the assumption that such growth is acceptable, indeed desirable, and will continue. Their justification for believing it is that at previous stages problems have arisen and have always somehow been solved without restricting growth : therefore they always will be solved.

The argument is a weak one. Any architect could tell them that it was possible to solve successively the problems involved in a structure five storeys high, ten storeys high, thirty storeys high and fifty storeys high; but that does not mean that it will ever be possible to build a Hilton four hundred storeys high and make it habitable. It is impossible not necessarily because of any insuperable problems of materials, stresses or structural techniques, but because at that height the ration of space needed to provide access and services for an extra floor would have risen to more than the equivalent of the living space the extra floor would provide.

In some quarters the suspicion has been growing that the unfairnesses and disappointments and repeated strokes of bad luck which hamper the efforts of underprivileged city areas to rehabilitate themselves cannot any longer be regarded as fortuitous, or blamed on the design of the buildings or the racial mix of the immigrants or any such simplistic scapegoat.

Professor David Harvey is one who believes that the real cause is not minor or accidental or eliminable : the cause is the city itself. Perfect justice and perfect equality nobody anywhere achieves because life itself is unfair. But there are built-in mechanisms in the complexities of metropolitan life which exert a multiplier effect on inequality, ensuring that to him that hath shall be given, and for anyone who loses his foothold and starts on a downward slope the city will grease the slide.

Professor Harvey has written a book, *Social Justice and the*

City, entirely devoted to illustrating this thesis. He concludes:
'It appears that the "hidden mechanisms" of income distribution in a complex city system usually increase inequalities
rather than reduce them', and that these effects 'become disproportionately important as the size of an urban system increases.'

If he is right, that statement packs as much unexploded
dynamite as Louis Wirth's. Wirth was saying, *inter alia*, that
crime is an integral element of urbanism: David Harvey is
saying that poverty and inequity are integral elements of urbanism and grow worse as the city grows bigger. He has
worked out a closely reasoned case to back his claim and it
runs in part as follows.

Some of the universal characteristics of large cities are high
densities, rapid change and complex interdependence. As I.
Lowrie expresses it: 'In the city everything affects everything
else'. Anything that happens from the construction of a new
airport, or the decline of the cinema, or a craze for Carnaby
Street fashions, or a West Indian family moving into a street,
doesn't only affect the lives of the people immediately concerned but starts a whole chain reaction of economic side
effects. It can affect at several removes everything from
property values and traffic flow to the local going rate for a
daily help or the sales of fish and chips.

That is so obvious it's a platitude, as also that every such
change will leave some people better off and some people worse
off. Harvey's argument is that nine times out of ten the question of who is left better off and who is left worse off will be
settled according to who can adjust most speedily and flexibly
to these constant and accelerating crosscurrents of change, and
the most successful adjusters will be the ones with the most
information and education and political pull, but above all the
ones with the most money.

Take one concrete example, the invention of the motor car.
There are many small places on the earth's surface and even
in England, where the fact that one or two people are able to
buy cars gives pleasure to the owners of the cars, proves fatal

to the odd hedgehog and unsettling to the nerves of a few sheep, but has no downgrading affect on the lives of the rest of the population. If anything it slightly upgrades them, for if you've got a perforated appendix or a wife in labour there's always the chance that you can tap your affluent neighbour for a lift to the hospital where formerly there would have been no way.

In the cities a great and as yet by no means exhausted chain of effects flowed from the fact that there was a time-lag of decades between the time when the middle classes had the automobile and the time when it became available lower down the scale.

It had a striking effect on relocation, because the first car owners were able to move away from the city centre and take advantage of land and house prices in pleasant areas away from bus and train routes while those prices were still low. Lower-income families were unable to shop around in this way. They remained trapped in the centre where the jobs then were, but where the housing supply was inelastic and housing demands were competing for land with commercial users which drove rent constantly higher.

It had an effect on rates. It affected the collection of them because many of the motorists were now able to live just outside the city limits, paying low rural rates but enjoying an urban level of earnings and amenities; the losses from these defectors had to be made up by bearing down harder on those remaining inside. However often the city extends its boundaries to try to catch up with this drift it is usually several steps behind. It also affected the spending of the rates because more of the public money had to be spent on roads and car parks and traffic regulation, leaving less for other purposes. As more people took to the automobile, public transport services lost income. Their standards of efficiency and comfort and even cleanliness began to decline and their fares to go up.

By the time car ownership had begun to be accessible lower down the scale – so that theoretically the benefits of lower suburban land prices could have afforded cheap housing for low-income commuters – it was too late. The middle classes were there first and had dug themselves in and property prices had rocketed. Inner London Boroughs asking outer London Boroughs for facilities to rehouse people displaced by slum clearance received chilly and non-cooperative answers. When they opted for high-rise housing it was not wholly an architectural fad; it was partly an economic squeeze. Socialistic local authorities who managed to force through a few rehousing schemes in high-toned suburbs, where really nice people had invested their hard-earned savings, were showered with vitriolic abuse. In America such a move would rarely even be attempted owing to what economists delicately call 'strong social contiguity restraint', which means we don't want your sort in our neck of the woods. American real estate agents apparently have a rule against selling property to such undesired newcomers and they call it an 'ethic' as though it were the Hippocratic oath.

The latest ironic turn of the screw came when older firms started to move out to the suburbs. A factory, after all, is usually a low-rise structure covering a lot of ground and high rateable values were driving them out of the centre. Factories were often admitted even to quite nice areas in the outer ring (sometimes in America they were admitted on condition that they were not accompanied by housing for their workers). The one thing that had trapped the poor of the urban slums and ghettos into living where they could least afford to live was the necessity to stay where the jobs were. In the end the jobs moved away from them and left them with the worst of all possible worlds. They were living in the expensive and stagnant centre where there were large numbers of white-collar jobs, but few for unskilled labour. There were high rates of unemployment and those who did find jobs in the suburbs had to pay to commute out.

In London, a further stage of this process is now under way. Some of the more comfortably-off sections of the community are returning to carefully selected central city locations, repairing and refurbishing the dwelling accommodation and curing the blight. Environmental legislation has lifted the curse of the smog-laden air and polluted water from the inner areas.

Long-distance commuting grows more time-consuming and nerve-racking now that the roads are so crowded and the distances so long. People have discovered that some of the older houses in the centre are far more solidly built than the modern stuff on the outer rings – it is only, they remark, that the low-income people who've been crowded into them simply don't appreciate the possibilities or look after them properly; anybody who can outbid or displace three or four of these families and spend a few thousand on improvements has a really sound investment. Of course, in the first instance they are the young and trendy and carefree who can laugh off the current unfashionableness of the area and tell gay stories about their salt-of-the-earth working-class neighbours. But you only need to get a few congenial friends to follow your example and before long you have a nice little community going and the place is worth six times what you gave for it and most of the amusing salt-of-the-earth characters seem somehow or other to have disappeared. But the pressure on low-income accommodation in contiguous areas has increased yet again, and the charitable organisation known as 'Shelter' reports annually on the alarming growth in the numbers who are now literally and totally homeless. . . .

This is not a description of the behaviour of wicked or heartless people. It was entirely reasonable when the urban sprawl began for a man to spend some of his money on a house where his children could see the trees and listen to the birds. He had probably worked hard to earn it and could certainly have given you a list of other desirable things he had gone without to get it. Nobody could possibly have demonstrated to him that any other individual would be better off if he refrained from laying out his money in that way, where it would give him the best value and the most satisfaction. The same comment can be made at every stage of the process. Yet the final effect is that, as David Harvey concludes; 'It is the economically and politically weak who suffer most unless institutional controls exist to rectify a naturally arising but ethically unacceptable situation.'

The above example illustrates how private economic activity in the urban situation tends to increase inequality. More often than not *public* activity tends in the same direction. It is partly, as Harvey suggests, because in such a complex situation where every policy decision will inevitably benefit some people and disadvantage others, such decisions are bound to be influenced by group pressure. He quotes several American and other researches in urban sociology which reveal that:

> The smaller groups – the privileged and intermediate groups – can often defeat the large groups – the latent groups – which are normally supposed to prevail in democracy . . . because the former are generally organised and active while the latter are normally unorganised and inactive.

The reasons why the poor are unorganised and inactive are many. They may have inadequate access to advance information – it often happens that whole streets only learn of a decision to demolish their area after the plan has already been passed by the relevant committee. Once they do become aware of what is happening they may be unfamiliar with the most effective channels for applying pressure. In the old folk phrase 'it's not what you know, it's who you know'. Because they are more numerous than the rich, conflicts of interest and arguments are more likely to spring up inside their own ranks and divert their energies. They may on occasions mount a surprisingly strong (even if ineffective) protest against something they *don't* want to happen, as for example a new flyover or the loss of a play space. But in an open-ended situation they will be far less coherent and decisive than the affluent about what they *do* want to happen, because their more limited experience makes them less able to imagine alternatives. For one thing they are less accustomed to exercising choice. A man and wife paying to have a house built for them will have ideas and plans submitted by an architect and make their own decisions. But a man and wife being rehoused by the city council – or fifty or three hundred men and their wives – will be treated as if they could not be expected to know either what they wanted or what was good for them, or else as if what they wanted was irrelevant.

Quite apart from such political influences the very dynamic of change imposes a built-in tendency to favour the 'haves'. The great majority of innovations are expensive when first introduced. No great city can reasonably decide not to expend scarce resources on an airport just because, in the first instance, only the well-to-do will be able to fly. Such a policy would mean the end of progress. So they build the airport at great cost in preference to modernising, say, the underground railway which was a miracle of twentieth-century engineering in its day: it's getting rather tatty and inadequate to its task but it's still good enough for most of the people who still use it and after all the world has got to move on.

As I. D. Sherrerd wrote of New York in 1968,

> The slum is the catch-all for the losers, and in the competitive struggle for the city's goods the slum areas are also the losers in terms of schools, jobs, garbage collection, street lighting, libraries, social services and whatever else is communally available but always in short supply.

You may demur that all this is merely a bleat of protest about the unfairness of life in general, since after all somebody has got to end up on the bottom of the heap. But it is more than that. The tendency towards a vicious cycle of deprivation and a tendency for well meant public action to widen the gap of existing inequalities always increases with the size of the community. If we go to the other extreme and think of a village there will be unfortunate and deprived people there too. But there is simply no mechanism by which public money spent on improving the village school or lighting the village street or building a public convenience could benefit their 'betters' without also benefiting them and their children. In any city such mechanisms do operate. In a megalopolis they operate to the nth degree.

You may also object that in the case of some of these services it would hardly make economic sense to provide them in the poorer districts – libraries, for example, or museums –

since there is so little demand and anyway such amenities are usually centrally placed so as to be equally accessible to everyone who really wants them. But they are not equally accessible and it is not only distance that makes them less accessible. Cultural differences can have the same effects. 'Two individuals can command exactly the same resource but if they value it differently they have different real incomes'. Public money spent on cultural activities is always administered by a small influential subculture promoting activities which it enjoys and/or feels to be 'good for' people. Thus money may be paid out to keep theatres and opera houses running but not cinemas. It may be used to subsidise the provision of good books but not the provision of good television.

Harvey concludes his survey of the mechanisms governing the redistribution of income in the urban system by suggesting that 'they seem to be moving towards a state of greater inequality and greater injustice'. Ask any social worker in any great Western city and you are unlikely to hear that conclusion challenged. The problem is of such scale and complexity that no one has any clear solution to offer. Some people advocate some form of small-scale neighbourhood government within the city structure to improve the administration of underprivileged districts. But if such local government is locally financed it will simply 'result in the poor controlling their own poverty while the rich grow more affluent from the fruits of their own riches'. If it is not locally financed the tune will still be called from somewhere over its head – and in any case many of the decisions that wreak the greatest havoc may concern developments taking place many miles away. Others advocate ever larger and more all-embracing administrative units. But innumerable studies have established that the larger the unit the greater the alienation and apathy, the lower the voting turn-out, the weaker the 'participation potential'.

That these things take place is well known to everybody. Jane Jacobs was quite as aware of them as David Harvey. 'People who got marked with the planners' hex signs,' she wrote, are pushed about, expropriated and uprooted much as if they were the subjects of a conquering power. . . . Whole communities are torn apart and sown to the winds with a reaping of cynicism, resentment and despair that must be heard and seen to be believed.

What she wrote about the iniquities and stupidities going on in the cities was as full of eloquence and passion as Rachel Carson's *Silent Spring* and, other things being equal, might have exerted as steady a cumulative influence on the way people actually behave.

But other things are not equal. The new dimension that Harvey has imported into the argument is the contention that this kind of behaviour is *endemic* to urbanism. No chairman of a company, even if he has read Jane's book and been impressed by it, is going to report to his shareholders that the firm has decided to erect an office block on the third most profitable of the available sites because two others which might have brought higher dividends were occupied by some people who were repainting their tatty old houses and singing in the streets. 'Nobody,' as Jane herself sadly admitted, 'pays any attention. The protests are discounted as the howls of people standing in the way of progress.'

Almost equally sad is another one-time urban bonus that seems to be turning into a deficit – the former certainty that by moving from the boring, monotonous old countryside to the exciting metropolis anyone could be certain of broadening his sympathy and understanding by mixing freely with a wide variety of people of every class, colour and creed.

Now they are all splitting up into ghettos with invisible boundaries growing more rigid as time goes by. They hive off into groups according to colour, race, religion and ethnic origin. Also the bigger the city, the more minutely it grades off areas suitable for precisely defined income groups. Part of the jumpiness of the lifestyle of a city dweller rapidly climbing the ladder of promotion, particularly in America, lies in the necessity of moving house with every rise in income if he is not to feel out of step with his neighbours. Some people are developing the habit of leaving the furniture of each house *in situ* for the next occupant during this game of musical chairs, since it is hardly worth the bother of transporting it every time.

E. W. G. Timms wrote a book about all this called *The Urban Mosaic*. He described and documented the sifting-out process and deplored some of the effects such as the creation of racial ghettos, but on the whole he took an optimistic view. He seemed to see no reason why, in future, the sifting-out tendency should not take a happy turn and result in the creation of cultural suburbs full of stamp collectors or health food buffs or balletomanes. Optimistically he wrote : 'The importance of social rank, ethnicity and preferred lifestyle in the organisation of the western cities may be but a passing phase.'

However, it shows no sign of passing and every sign of tightening its grip, and even acquiring a further dimension by subdividing also along generation lines and creating special reservations for that chronologically underprivileged group, the Senior Citizens.

The trouble with money, rank and race as mosaic makers is that they are liable to lead to mutual misunderstanding and mutual mistrust, and in times of social stress even to mutual fear and hatred. Jonathan Raban – the same who uttered some of the glad pro-urban cries quoted in an earlier chapter – was somewhat sobered by being told so often in America that it wasn't really wise to go too far in that direction, or that one, or that one, because in those places the city had been 'taken over' by the Irish, or the coloured, or the hippies, or the Jews. 'I like cities on principle' he reaffirmed in 1974, 'but in America my liking was rapidly turning sour; my enthusiasm was beginning to seem to me glib and blinkered.' In one city he drove out to a black suburb to prove to himself that it could be nothing but the fevered imagination of prejudiced WASP acquaintances which seemed to drop an iron curtain between them and whole sections of their own native city. Nothing worse happened to him than having a couple of kids yell after him an astonished 'Hey, Honky!' Nevertheless, he drove straight back again without getting out of his car and wrote:

> If I had believed in a city freedom which permits every-
> one to roam into other social worlds, here was proof of the
> reality of those boundaries about which I'd been so sceptical.
> I was in the wrong place and anxious to get out.

Such disenchantment about cities is a not uncommon emotion even among those who love them best. It is getting harder to find any place in a modern metropolis where a poet could stand and feel with Wordsworth:

Earth hath not anything to show more fair.

Undoubtedly there are millions who would like to 'get out'. They get sick of the dirt and the noise, the anonymity without privacy, the frustrations and hostilities and the carbon mon-oxide. Commuting out to areas of relative emptiness gets less rewarding and more expensive and in some places will soon become impossible, as executives retreating southwards out of one city find themselves backing into their counteparts exur-banising northwards out of another and all the intervening spaces gradually get filled up and built over, as is beginning to happen on the eastern seaboard in America. Some of them work themselves into ulcers and coronaries with the sole aim of earning enough money to be able to quit the place altogether and retire to somewhere green and quiet before they are too old to enjoy it.

Yet still coming in are the millions who have left the quiet green places because these places are full of despair. In the shanty towns of the new world – the *favelas* and *bidonvilles* and *geçekundus* and *barrios* and *bustees* and *kampongs* – the inhabitants of most of these stinking suburbs are full of hope that the urban magic is going to work its miracle yet again and qualify their children if not themselves to take their place among the urbane, the privileged fifty percent, the lords of humanity, the city dwellers.

These are the places that some urban sociologists designate 'the slums of hope'. But even hope, the most ubiquitous of all the urban virtues and the last to weaken, has deserted the rotting centres of some of the large and affluent cities of the West. Throughout the nineteenth and most of the twentieth century, whatever discomforts and indignities were suffered by incoming immigrants, they were borne up by the conviction that things would certainly be better for their children and better still for their grand-children.

That conviction is no longer there, and there is no place where the absence of it can be quite so bleak. At most times and in most places when a boy growing up has decided that the place he is in feels like a cul de sac, there has always been a road out in his mind if only he has the strength to take it. From the decaying villages to the towns, from the stagnant towns to the cities, boondocks to bright lights, emptying islands to the mainland, West Indies, Pakistan and Puerto Rico to London and New York where everything will be different and better. But now that frontier is gone. If you happen to be born or bred in one of those magnetic centres that beckon to outsiders like some Shangri-la and if it *still* feels like a cul de sac, it is very hard to find anywhere to channel your energy and frustration except into anger and violence.

These are the slums of despair – not only the despair of those condemned to live in them, but the despair of everyone who tries to combat or eliminate them. Trying to eradicate urban blight is like trying to exorcise metastatic cancer – you cut it out in one spot and it springs up more virulently in another. Wherever anyone has stopped and calculated the net effect of their best endeavours on the totality of the problem it has added up to a negative : they have lost ground.

In a dozen different ways the problems of these areas echo the problems of the worst hit areas of the periphery. In precisely the same way the population grows older, the young cannot wait to get out, there is not enough money to maintain the buildings : confidence and wealth and incentive are drained out of the communities in ways they cannot understand. In both cases they look for a reason for these things and grasp at explanations that are never precisely the right ones.

In American cities coloured or ethnic minorities may fasten

on racial or religious prejudice as the core of the trouble, and fight back with Black Power or Mafia-type tactics – yet the problem manifests itself in the same economic terms in cities outside America where there is no racial or ethnic mix. In European fringe areas militancy coheres in a precisely similar fashion around submerged or semi-submerged national groupings – Scots, Welsh, Bretons, Basques, Corsicans – although their economic troubles are precisely the same as those of other fringe areas who share the metropolitan language and blood group. Colour in the ghetto and nationalisms on the fringe offer an aid to morale and a focal point for militancy. They help to defeat the sense of *cul-de-sac* and to attract attention to the sources of their malaise. But they do not necessarily illuminate the nature of the basic problem, and they often create divisions among people who in economic terms are fellow victims and ought to be allies.

Saddest of all is that the victims of the apoplexy at the centre and the anaemia at the extremities tend to regard one another with mutual suspicion and resentment. Londoners get impatient with the Regional Aid constantly and fruitlessly being shovelled out to development areas which never quite get themselves developed to a point where they cease to need aid (What can be happening to all that money? Are they spending it all on beer and whippets? Has it stuck to the pockets of corrupt councillors and building contractors? Are they all loafing around on Social Security up there?). Provincials look askance at the London Weighting Allowances paid as standard bonus to a wide range of London wage and salary earners and public employees (Who is paying for all that?) and at the soaring sums in 'Rent – Plus' Social Security handed out to the metropolitan unemployed (If they claim London is overcrowded why are they bribing people to come and live there?).

The same reactions obtain elsewhere. New York stands high among developed nations for the complexity of its economic problems and the degree of alienation this has aroused in the rest of the country. Home bodies in the Middle West read about the level of its welfare payments and its escalating debts.

They are shocked to their thrifty puritan souls and fear that if they offer to bail out this one particular rich relation a score of other prodigal cities will line up behind it with palms extended and there will be no end to it.

And the rest of the world looks on with horrified fascination because the seeds of New York's trouble are beginning to sprout all around the globe. A spokesman on London's perplexity said recently that if something drastic (but unspecified) is not done over the next three years London will inevitably become 'a city of the very rich, the very old and the very poor.'

It is that particular combination of riches and poverty which chiefly differentiates central blight from the peripheral kind. Out on the extremities living conditions are harder in a hundred ways that most city dwellers have forgotten how to imagine, but there is not the close constant obscene galling juxtaposition of the extremes of poverty and wealth. It is easy to advise a city administration that it should say to claimants 'We cannot help you because there is no more money. We cannot raise taxes any further because people cannot afford to pay them.' It may well be true that additional impositions would be self-defeating and only shrink the tax base further. But it will not carry the ring of truth to people who are struggling to live half a mile from the mink and limousine belt when you tell them 'there is no more money'. Clearly there is God's plenty of the stuff around. And if there is no work to be found, if money is the chief way of commanding respect as well as commodities, if there is no legitimate way of getting it spread around a little more evenly, the temptation to use more direct methods of getting hold of it is bound to escalate, and the city becomes a place of fear.

In the circumstances it is very hard to understand the thought processes of those who still claim that the answer to all our problems is more growth, bigger conurbations, and full speed ahead to the World City.

Before long it will not only be pusillanimous to say 'We are riding a tiger we dare not dismount.' It will also be futile.

For the signs are multiplying every day that the tiger is getting ready to unseat us.

9   The urbanisation of agriculture

Meanwhile, as they used to say in the old movies, back at the ranch....

Every time we cover another thousand acres of land with houses, shops, banks, parking lots, snack bars, strip clubs, boutiques, and flyovers, every time another thousand land-workers knock the mud of subsistence agriculture off their boots and stick their feet under the urban table waiting to be served, somebody somewhere has to grow more food to make up for it.

In every city it is regarded as a categorical imperative that food must not only be available; it must be cheap. People may feel they would like the price of a TV set or a deepfreeze or a motorcycle to be lower than it is, but they do not express this opinion in the voice throbbing with moral indignation which they use to demand cheap food and cheap fuel. They can tolerate the prospect of night clubs increasing their cover charges, poodle clippers and health farms upping their fees, corporation lawyers and pet-food copywriters making a bomb, but if the farmers or miners demand higher remuneration, that is seen as not only greedy but wicked, because 'these are things that people must have'. The attitude is entirely understandable. But it results in the very curious situation that the more un-necessary the service you provide, the more ethically OK it is for you to charge the earth for it.

Over the millennia, as we have seen, urban populations have applied much ingenuity to thinking up ways of ensuring a reliable food supply on terms advantageous to themselves, and as long as the cities grew fairly slowly this could often be done amicably and without provoking resentment.

But in the last few centuries the pace has been hotting up. The speed at which they walk the pavements is only one small symptom of the fact that urbanites operate on a different time-scale from hinterlanders, and it has never yet entered their heads that this difference is one that might be bridged by a spot of compromise: you try to walk a little faster and I will slow down a bit so that we may keep in step. Their attitude is that anyone who won't or can't voluntarily keep up with the pace of change they desire must, in the vivid metropolitan phrase, be 'dragged kicking and screaming' into whichever century or decade they are currently hellbent on entering.

In Britain, as it led the way into the industrial revolution, the screaming was often loud and the kicking vigorous, and not all the trauma was due to the private landlordism and industrial capitalism on which it is most commonly blamed. Most of the phenomena accompanying urbanisation transcend the differences between free enterprise and managed economies.

To take a comparable example from further east, what happened in Russia after 1917 has been well described by E. H. Carr as 'an industrial revolution carried out by Communists.' Michael Barrett Brown comments:

The process has never yet been accomplished except by dictatorship and repression. The excesses of Stalin have to be related to the Combination Acts, Tolpuddle and Peterloo in Britain, and slavery in the British colonies.

You can relate them to what you like; the fact remains that quite apart from the savagery of the treatment meted out to the Russian peasants, the attitude of the central government proved conclusively that quoting the Communist Manifesto and socialising the economy is no guarantee of an even-handed approach to the hammer and sickle respectively.

One mistake they made was to believe that productivity could be improved by so-called economies of scale while still leaving agriculture at the tail end of the queue of investment priorities. This policy came to be known as the 'nationalisation of wooden ploughs', and its results were disastrous. The harsh measures used to enforce it were so counter-productive that the numbers of livestock, for example, did not regain their pre-1929 level in the USSR until after the second World War.

Britain was able to maintain the speed of her industrialisation without any such head-on clashes with her own food producers by having other nations to do the job for her. Once you accepted it as part of God's plan that food producers were and ought to be lower paid than the producers of most other things, the best way to increase the Wealth of your Nation was to ensure that it included as few of those unfortunate creatures as possible. Britain at the height of her power was content for her own land to produce enough to feed her people on Saturdays and Sundays – the rest was brought in from overseas. She pushed the job outside her own borders in much the same frame of mind as the Japanese are now transferring the more pollutant industrial processes away from their own island and paying for them to be performed elsewhere, such as on the Asian mainland – or even, in the case of processing nuclear waste, at the ultra-safe distance of halfway around the world in England.

The British did not of course view their free trade policy in that light. It was meant to be in the best interests of everybody. Foreigners, they said, are the best people to grow food because they have a better climate and lower expectations concerning living standards. We, on the other hand, are the best people to make, for example, textiles because we are cleverer. Occasionally the thought arose that lesser breeds might treacherously develop a streak of cleverness of their own, and the British sometimes took perfunctory precautions against this, but on the whole in the early days their belief in their own innate superiority was perfectly honest and sincere.

But fairly soon the stage was reached when the demands of large-scale mechanised industries and the people who manned them could only be adequately met by large-scale mechanised agriculture. Things passed beyond the stage when a farmer might take it into his head to hop into his buggy on a fine Saturday morning and drive into town to offer Chicago five sacks of grain, three dozen eggs and two little pigs. Chicago didn't want to know about two little pigs. A mass market for food means mass marketing and that gives rise to standardised mass packaging and mechanised mass processing, and so the pressure built up for mechanised mass food production. A similar back-tracking process had taken place when Lancashire invented the power loom for weaving cotton yarn, which necessitated a power-assisted process for spinning the yarn, and that necessitated introducing the cotton gin in the States because it was intolerable for all that expensive machinery to be slowed down by the old-fashioned operations of a lot of cotton-picking slaves.

There was one striking difference between mechanised manufacturing and mechanised agriculture. As more and more machinery was introduced into the towns and cities, they attracted more and more people; on the other hand, as the countryside became more mechanised it grew emptier and emptier. Individual farmers could now grow rich, acquire expensive machinery, drive large cars, hire skilled labour, and some of that skilled labour could command high wages. The price they paid was that they became thinner on the ground, the one farmer growing rich on an area of land that would once have supported 150 farmers, the one employee spending all his solitary working day driving an agricultural machine across an empty horizon.

In the cities the labour released by mechanisation levitates into decision-making or diversifies into services; but on the land there are fewer amenity jobs because there are fewer amenities, and there is a very much lower ratio of white-collar workers to the other kind. A farmer working his way up may still deal with his own paperwork (or very probably get his wife to do so), long after the enterprise has reached a size and complexity where an urban businessman would have a secretarial staff of three girls and an office boy; and he will deal with it on the dining room table when his city counterpart feels duty bound to install a larger office desk, a deeper carpet, and a more nubile receptionist.

It is not that large-scale food production generates less bureaucracy than large-scale anything else – it is merely that it is generated elsewhere than on the land, for agri-business on the largest scale is no longer a rural occupation. Most of the labour is employed (and most of the profit retained) in the factories that make the tractors and the combine harvesters, the banks that advance the loans for their purchase, the enterprises that package and transport and retail the inputs and the produce, the fertiliser plant, the chemical combine that makes the insecticide and the aviation firm that makes the helicopter for spraying it, etc etc. Somebody has to be there on the spot the way somebody has to be out on the oil rigs in the North Sea, but in both cases they are only one link in a long chain. Jane Jacobs somewhere loftily remarks that 'rural people by themselves can't even solve their own food problems,' and I have to admit that nowadays this is largely true. (I would only add that the prospect of urban people by themselves trying to solve *their* own food problems is an even more harrowing one.)

The results of the agricultural revolution were impressive. Apart from the new machines, there were new scientific methods of soil analysis, advances in plant breeding, resulting in new improved strains, artificial insemination of cattle, new fertilisers, new insecticides, and hundreds of other innovations; and agricultural productivity steadily increased.

Naturally, the new methods were first applied in the most urbanised nations and they were the first to benefit. In developed economies such as the USA and Japan the output of cereals per acre has tripled since the second World War. In such regions productivity rose so high and agricultural labour requirements sank so low that it seemed the last conceivable brake on the emergence of a Doxiadis-type World City had been removed. The problem of undernourishment was replaced by the problem of obesity; the spectre of starvation receded and people began to worry instead about their intake of cholesterol, agene, cyclamates, excesses of sugar, alcohol and nicotine, and inadvertent doses of lead, insecticides, nitrates, hormones, carbon monoxide, strontium-90, mercury, and other unpleasant things which were leaking into the air, the water, and the food chain. To the hungry half of the world these preoccupations must have appeared neurotic : they would gladly have embraced all those anxieties in return for a guarantee of two square meals a day, or in some areas only one.

The hope was of course that in the end everyone would benefit. For thousands of years the archetype of a genuine benefactor of mankind has been the man who could make two blades of grass or two ears of corn grow where only one grew before, and this was undoubtedly being done. Looking at the problem globally, measuring the rate of increase of food production against the rate of increase of world population there was no lack of optimists to point out that as a species we now had the available technology to close the hunger gap.

If we take the crucial example of food grains, the output from North America alone was rapidly transforming the world picture. There the urban know-how and freely available capital were combined with favourable geographical factors – soil, climate, contours and plenty of space – and in the space of a single generation this area leaped forward to an unprecedented position of dominance in the world's grain trade.

Going back to the 1930s, most of the major regions of the world were self-sufficient in grain (the exception was Europe, a net importer to the tune of twenty-four million metric tonnes). Many of them had a surplus, and among these was North America which exported five million metric tonnes.

By 1966 the North American exports had shot up from five million to nearly sixty million tonnes, and almost all the rest of the world had moved into deficit. Only Australia and Latin America were still, on a comparatively small scale, exporters. Since then Latin America has gone into deficit too.

Now, there is more than one way of looking at that transformation. It is possible to reflect : since almost all the rest of the world appears to have become practically overnight too feckless, overpopulated, ineffective or bone idle even to be able to feed itself any longer, what a very lucky thing it was that at least North America remained industrious, inventive and efficient enough to make up for their shortcomings.

Alternatively, it is possible to point out a great variety of specific reasons why some of the other areas were falling short of self-sufficiency. Some had climate problems; in Europe living standards were improving and people were eating more and better; some of the Communist countries were concentrating on catching up with the West industrially; there were all kinds of incidental reasons which could be advanced as to why during those thirty-odd years so many regions of the world happened to fall short of their own requirements, in which case it *was* providential that the USA was able to step in and supply their needs.

It seems more likely that the reason was single and simple – that in agriculture as in other economic fields a great pile-up of economic wealth in one place is not possible without somebody else losing out, not merely comparatively but absolutely; not merely standing still but sliding backwards. Just as the spectacular success of Manchester in textiles had killed off formerly thriving units of textile production in other parts of the world, so the heating up of North American grain production incidentally imposed a touch of permafrost on the lives and endeavours of other agriculturists in distant places all around the globe.

Take the case of India, and consider one fairly representative statistic which emerged from a conference held in Oxford in 1974 under the general title of *The Exploding Cities*. I quote: 'Even the impoverished gutters of Calcutta and Bombay support a standard of living forty-five percent above that of the surrounding countryside.'

That is not India's fault specifically. You could parallel it in a thousand other places all around the globe. It is so familiar that we sometimes forget to be outraged and astonished by it, to wonder how this situation arises and why it has been tolerated so long, by what maniacal brand of economic alchemy an urban immigrant engaged in sub-subdividing the profits on re-retailing some wretched piece of merchandise in a city slum – which is how many of the newcomers in the Third-World cities get their first toe-hold on the urban economic ladder – is immediately worth so much more than he was a week before he arrived. In the impoverished Indian countryside he was probably producing little enough in Heaven's name – now he is producing nothing. But he is better off producing nothing in the streets than producing something on the land.

No one can doubt that if any one of these swollen Third-World cities together with a large tract of its hinterland were islanded and cut off from all commerce with the outside world, this process would move sharply and agonisingly into reverse. Every available ounce of energy, every cent of capital, every gallon of water, every serviceable piece of equipment, every scrap of organic refuse, every pair of hands and every active mind would be diverted out of the city to save the people. The market forces that now exert such a powerful centripetal effect would then operate as powerfully in the opposite direction. Nobody could wish such a disaster on them, because the process has already gone so far that the suffering would be unimaginable. But to the extent that this proposition is self-evident, it must also be self-evident that it is some force operating over a distance that is presently sucking them *into* the cities, and militating against any efforts made by their governments to stem the tide.

Unfortunately, solving the problem of how to grow enough grain to feed the world did nothing to solve the problem of how to get it to the people most in need of it. Even the most efficient of farmers cannot stay in business by growing food to give away, and the people with the emptiest bellies were also the ones with the emptiest pockets.

Idealists might argue that governments or charitable organisations should buy the food from the haves and distribute it to the have-nots. Sometimes when the hunger has deepened into famine this has been done, and has had to be done; but the secondary effect has always been to intensify the problem. If cheap food from abroad damages the economic viability of native agriculture, *free* food from abroad can only damage it further. You cannot solve the problems of car workers in Detroit or Coventry by a consolatory issue of free foreign automobiles.

It was clear to everybody what the next step in the urbanisation of agriculture would have to be. The new methods would have to be introduced in the developing countries them-

G

selves. Research was intensified into the staple energy foods of Third-World countries, into producing heavier-yielding and more disease-resistant strains, into how far the new mechanised methods could be adapted for different climatic conditions, and the firms producing tractors, combines, fertilisers, etc, got ready to step up their exports.

This time the euphoria was more marked and success followed swiftly. By this time the graph of per-acre productivity in the USA was near levelling off: not much could be gained there by increasing inputs still further. But experiments on test farms in such places as India, Mexico, the Phillipines, indicated that yields in the developing countries could be multiplied more spectacularly than they had ever been in the States, and occasionally even by a factor of ten.

By 1970 the miracle had happened. India declared herself able to support all of her burgeoning population, and a year later managed to feed ten million Bengali refugees in addition. The Phillipines stopped importing rice; Pakistan produced a small surplus of wheat. Stockpiling in the world's granaries was at a reassuringly high level. In places like the Food and Agricultural Organisation the professional worriers began to breathe more easily.

Then almost immediately it began to go wrong.

When food prices began to go through the ceiling, beleaguered and bewildered ministers in various democratic assemblies stood up and attributed it to an unlucky combination of adverse weather conditions in different parts of the globe. Towards the end of 1972 they blamed it largely on Russia, for sneakily buying up thirty million tonnes of American grain in such a way as to conceal the size of their purchase until the deal had gone through.

As for the reason why Russia should need to behave in this way, some blamed bad weather again, this time the Russian weather. There had been a couple of short, cool summers which had done some damage and caused the Soviet grain yield to fall short of expectation. Others cited the situation as evidence of the inefficiency of the Soviet system. The Russians were no more likely than their detractors to put forward the idea that a Russian deficit was simply one more spin-off of a couple of decades of American surplus. They preferred to think their system was too well insulated against Western economic vagaries to respond with a knee-jerk to the tap of an American hammer.

But the world had shrunk rapidly during the high-energy years, and the laws by which development in one place creates underdevelopment in another cannot be blocked off by closing a frontier or nationalising an economy. It would require total autarkie. Any reasonable Russian planner observing the fertility of North America and the rising harvests of the Green Revolution elsewhere would have felt safe in assuming that the terms of trade which had favoured the industrial sectors of the world ever since there had been industrial sectors would continue to do so, that world grain stocks averaging well over a hundred million tonnes would not quickly evaporate; and that when it came to planning the allocation of resources it could do no harm to take a calculated risk on the agricultural side because other things could always be exported to buy food.

The consciousness of purchasable stocks existing elsewhere must have played a crucial if inexplicit part in many of the day-to-day decisions which led up to this sudden debut as a major importer.

At roughly the same time, the Green Revolution in many of the developing countries slowed down. The system was not quite as foolproof as it once looked. The new hybrid strains are indeed capable of yielding much more grain per acre, but they don't do so for free. They demand a lot of water and a lot of fertiliser; as the years pass they demand increasing doses of fertiliser not to produce more than last year, but to produce the same amount.

Mass methods and mechanisation require a mass market, preferably not too far away (that means not merely people but people who can pay), good roads and up-to-date transport, an available supply of skilled labour to operate the agricultural machinery and mend it when it breaks down, etc, etc. So for all these reasons it seemed best to introduce the Green Revolution first in places not too far from the cities.

This proximity made it clear that the urban/rural relation-ship had radically altered. Throughout the ages, although (like male and female) they were not necessarily treated with parity of esteem or remuneration, town and country had always (also like male and female) retained a roughly complementary and non-competitive economic relationship. This was no longer true. With the growing sprawl of the cities and the growing urbanisation of agriculture they were coming into direct com-petition for at least three indispensable but finite resources – land, water, and oil. The realisation of this was slowly dawning all over the world: it merely dawned more harshly and ab-ruptly in some of the developing countries because the com-peted-for commodities were often in shorter supply to begin with.

Generally speaking, if a food grower is bidding for land against a developer, there is no contest: he is on a hiding to nothing, and has to retreat. No city, in any kind of economy, has yet stopped growing because the sprawl of speculative building or the extension of public housing development or the festering rash of favelas or bidonvilles or shantytowns has come up against a patch of arable land in good heart. Often it is the best land which is soonest engulfed by the concrete, because towns and cities tend to be established for preference where the land is level to build on and the water supply is secure and transport easy – the banks of lakes and rivers and fertile plains are favoured places now just as in the beginning.

But now they do not remain neatly inside a surrounding wall. A roof to shelter them is, to be sure, one of the things that 'people must have,' and there are some cities (like the Yoruba cities in Africa) where that is what they settle for. But as affluence grows, the cars become far more greedy for space than the people or even the bureaucrats, and the space occu-pied by the offices people work in and the houses they live in all rolled into one is dwarfed into insignificance by the amount of space it takes to enable them to get from the one to the other. This process has gone further than anywhere else in Los Angeles: it is part of the syndrome Americans refer to when they speak of Californication.

Even in Britain, which is not nearly so badly californicated, where unusually strenuous legislative efforts were made to confine the urban sprawl within some kind of limits, where every time anybody calculates the percentage of the population still engaged in agriculture they acclaim it as an irreducible minimum (which is thereafter further reduced), still every decade an area the size of Nottinghamshire is eaten up by urban extensions and transport requirements. And in any country, to calculate the amount of land actually falling out of production, the acreage actually engulfed by the cities gives far too low a figure; because it forces the remaining agricultural acres into becoming even more capital-intensive and agribusinesslike or else they would go under, and the competition administers the final *coup de grace* to owner-occupiers on hill farms and marginal lands who simply give up the struggle and move out and let the farmhouses fall down and the fields go back to bracken.

Professor Georg Borgstrom of Michigan University has done a few calculations on what our best efforts have done to the available area of cultivable land in the world. We have done a good deal, for example, to bring into use more of the world's marginal lands (which are often the semi-arid regions) by extending irrigation. Over the past century we have scored notable successes in this direction, multiplying the amount of irrigated land by four or five times; the hope is of doubling it again by the end of the year 2000.

It sounds like progress, doesn't it? But Professor Borgstrom has worked out that the amount of land man has had to vacate – for example has turned into desert by overgrazing and overpressure – is about five times greater than the amount we have irrigated. In India one quarter of the entire acreage has been so heavily eroded that the topsoil will be gone before the end of the century: there have been demonstrations there by women wrapping their arms around the trees and refusing to be moved, to prevent any more being felled. Drought areas are spreading in the Caatinga zone of north-east Brazil; and in the Sahelian areas of Africa the Sahara desert is moving southwards at the rate of nine kilometres a year. In the Andes fifty million people are trying to live on soil that is vanishing from under them; but nobody is going to spend capital on staving off that disaster when the GNP is so much higher in the cities on the coast. The authorities would rather wait thirty or forty years till the greater part of that fifty million streams down from the mountains and settles in cardboard shacks on the urban fringes and hopes to be fed.

Irrigation of course is one of the white hopes, but for water as well as for land the competition between city and hinterland is naked and direct. In Zambia, at a time when the need for increasing food production was so urgent that the country was forced to buy grain from Rhodesia at four times the local price, the city of Lusaka had increased its water consumption in ten years from four-and-a-half million gallons a day to twenty-seven million gallons a day. Mexican farmers near the banks of what had once been the lower reaches of the River Colorado went bankrupt, because the demands of California had escalated to the point where the river gave up the ghost and sank away into the sand before it ever reached them or its one-time outlet to the sea.

For most of the developed world the idea when it was first mooted that anything they really wanted to do could ever be limited by the shortage of anything as plentiful as water struck them as coming from the lunatic fringe of the Doom Brigade. (At least it so struck the city dwellers among them. The rural section – however privileged, mechanised and capital-ised – does have an instinctive realisation of some of the basic facts of life, such as that to keep a dairy herd requires rainfall to the tune of 1100 gallons *per quart* of milk. That figure is from Borgstrom, too.)

But the impression persisted that we had moved into an exponential growth curve which nothing could arrest. Futurologists like Herman Kahn painted pictures of a time approaching at a rate of knots where his own lush suburban-American style of gracious living would be available to, and surpassed by, every single human being on the wide earth. One nice touch he added was the prospect that every family could expect to have its own dandy little submarine – in addition presumably to two or three cars and a small yacht and a helicopter on the roof.

As for water, that was held to be no problem. The greater part of the earth's surface is covered with water. We need only apply a little technology – pipe Canada's water to Mexico, Finland's down to the Sahara, melt the polar ice caps, desalinate the sea, discipline the clouds, and presto! you're home and dry and everything you want to be wet is wet. The projects may look ambitious but, said the scenario, we have or can acquire the know-how. We have machines that can give a man not the strength of ten but the strength of ten thousand. We have unlimited power . . . and anyone who demurred that the sources of the power weren't unlimited was a nit-picker.

That was before 1974.

Before OPEC.

For the Green Revolution that was the bitterest blow of all. It was not too easy trying to compete with the cities for land and water, but that at least was a local struggle. When it came to oil the underdeveloped countries were bidding against nations which were simultaneously the world's wealthiest and its most oil-dependent, as hooked on the stuff as a junkie on heroin, and equally ready to play rough rather than endure withdrawal symptoms. Nor was it only a question of oil for the tractors: the agriculturalists were now brought hard up against the fact that in effect the miracle crops were also being *fed* on oil, since it takes five tons of oil to produce one ton of fertiliser.

In the poorest countries the green miracle ignominiously petered out. Energy-intensive agriculture with oil at a dollar a barrel had seemed a good idea – with oil at eleven dollars a barrel it was a farce. In a year when local output was crucial to the people, because world food stocks had shrunk dramatically and American food aid was cut by two-thirds – the beautiful growth curve came to a halt. Even if the farmers had somehow managed to pay the going rate for oil, fertiliser was for a time simply unobtainable: food prices were worrying even the rich countries, and what they had they held on to. Somebody rather bitterly calculated that the Americans were scattering enough fertiliser on their lawns and golf courses alone to have made up the whole of India's deficit, but that's the way the cookie crumbles.

Since that time statisticians and experts have been making a new and more critical reappraisal of the benefits of urbanised agriculture, and have employed quite new mathematical approaches to it.

Under the old methods of calculation – ie measuring output per acre and output per man-hour – the picture was still bright, and North America methods remained outstandingly efficient. But even by these yardsticks a team of specialists conducting an investigation in Washington under the auspices of the National Academy of Science detected some 'tapering trends', indicating that in some departments the graph was now levelling out. It appears, for instance, that no additional amount of selective breeding, environment control or high quality inputs will induce a hen to average more than 230 eggs per annum. They discovered too that you cannot measure agriculture's loss to urban expansion only by the acreage actually taken out of production, because the cities cast a longer shadow than had been realised. For example, Connecticut potato crops, although the potato is hardly a hypersensitive plant, were found to prosper only in inverse proportion to the amount of airborne pollution from the adjacent metropolis.

Possibly more serious than any of this, the team produced two new measuring rods by which American agriculture was shown to be actually in a state of decline. There was a decline in the number of Americans being supported by each farm worker, and being fed or otherwise supported by each acre of agricultural land; in other words, a decline in the degree of agricultural self-sufficiency.

This is a tricky situation and not one that can be dealt with by the agricultural sector alone, for the variant here depends not solely on the producers of food, but as much or more on the consumers of it, and American consumers were eating more, drinking more, wasting more, giving more food to their pets, and above all demanding that a higher percentage of their diet should consist of the least economic forms of food.

An acre of soya beans will feed a man for 2224 days; an acre of wheat will feed him for 877 days; but an acre of beef pasture will feed him only for seventy-seven. And Americans like steak.

There is a conventional belief among economists that the demand for food is non-elastic, since we each have only one stomach and there is a limit to the amount of food we can put into it. It does not follow that a man's pressure on food resources cannot increase dramatically as he grows richer. If he was brought up rough in the sticks on pork and beans and moves to the city where the GNP index registers that as a hirer out of tuxedos he rates eight or ten times the remuneration, he will promptly change his diet to one requiring ten or twenty times the acreage to keep him satisfied.

This is not exclusively an American development: it is a universal one. In the pivotal year of the notorious Russian grain-drain, among all the feverish statistics that were tossed around at the time and all the speculations about what could have caused the 'failure' of the Russian harvest, there was one figure which made very little impact – the fact that that particular harvest was a very good one, which had only been surpassed four times in the whole history of the country. The only 'decline' was like the USA decline – a decline in the numbers of Russians an acre of Russian land will support.

However, that measure of decline was a bagatelle when compared with the results that emerged when an assorted bunch, including the ecological lobby and the Chinese, came up with yet another yardstick, which immediately established that North American agriculture was just about the least efficient in the world.

This was arrived at by measuring its output not in terms of output per man per acre, nor in terms of the number of compatriots it supported, but by comparing the number of calories it put into the ground with the number of calories it took out again. In this respect it was and had been for a very long time deficit farming.

It takes the amount of energy you get from burning five tons of coal to make one ton of nitrogen fertiliser. Add in the energy used in transporting and spreading it, manufacturing, transporting and applying insecticides, manufacturing and fuelling the farm machinery, top it up with the calories used to feed the farm workers, and you end up deep in the red.

Top of this new-style post-OPEC roll of honour came the operators of the oriental wet-rice agriculture practised in parts of China. The calorie input there, it was claimed, consisted almost exclusively of the farmer's food, and a family of four could live on half an acre of good bottom land because they used organic fertiliser and no fossil fuel. For every calorie they put in they got forty out.

By this time, too, some of the horny-handed oldtimers who had looked askance at the new methods and from time to time crumbled the soil between their fingers and shaken their heads, could be heard in various parts of the world uttering little grunts which roughly signified 'I told you so'.

In clay soil areas of Britain around Warwick and North-amptonshire, after fifteen years of intensive mechanised one-crop agriculture, the soil was found to have deteriorated to the point where two wet seasons made it impracticable to continue with arable farming. In East Anglia the destruction of hedges and the diminishing organic content of the earth (in some areas down to three percent) has been causing the farm topsoil to be blown away. Draining and irrigation, no doubt, are not what they used to be there. The trouble with having a ten-thousand-pound combine harvester is that while it does wonders for one week in a year and doesn't eat any-thing for the other fifty-one, it will not fill in its spare time with a spot of hedging and ditching. However, in an urban-dominated economy a farmer must cut back on labour costs if he is to survive at all. (In some peripheral areas where these labour-saving methods of husbandry were reluctantly being applied, jobs in industry were being 'created' by the Regional Development Boards at the cost of around £6000 per head.)

There is an old Latin tag to the effect that if you drive Nature out of the door with a pitchfork it will climb back in through the window. Certainly it was endlessly inventive in the varieties of backlash with which it combated agribusinessmen's onslaughts of chemicals and poisons. The answer was always more chemicals and more poisons. If by cutting down all the hedges and destroying the habitat of small birds you are plagued with small insects on which they used to feed, apply massive doses of insecticide. If after eliminating the insects your orchards are ravaged by the red spider mite on which the insects used to feed, back to the drawing board and ask for a new chemical which can be massively applied to destroy the mites. It's all good for business, because the best brains are all hired by the big firms and they only deal in large quantities. Their rule is that to break even on the land you can and must always go on applying more and more of everything – everything, that is, except people; and they are applied so sparingly you would imagine they were a commodity in short supply.

For a brief period when the first shock of the initial OPEC price rises were sending tremors through every section of the world economy, there was a ripple of doubt as to whether this policy could continue indefinitely, some questioning of whether if there was not enough power to go round the agricultural sector would be sold short in favour of the cities, and some anxious senatorial lobbying of the Federal Power Commission to ensure that nitrogen fertiliser plants would be assured of emergency supplies of fuel if the emergency deepened.

But the moment passed, and the flicker of doubt about the wisdom of applying urban methods to rural problems subsided. After all, people pointed out, although we all now realise that the supplies of fuel oil really are finite, the 1974 squeeze didn't mean we were nearing the end of them. It was merely a ploy by the Arabs which threw a bit of a scare into people. It didn't take the developed world very long to adjust to the higher price of petrol, no longer than it takes a committed smoker to adjust to a rise in the tax on tobacco.

The main way of adjusting has been to intensify the search for hitherto untapped deposits of oil, and these have been found without too much difficulty, even though they are not quite as accessible as could be wished. The result is two-fold;

that the yield of oil per dollar of expenditure continually goes down (North Sea oil extraction costs ten times Saudi Arabia's) and the day when we really will get to the end of it approaches more quickly. Meanwhile we continue to make hay with it, and corn too, and in 1975, mindful of Earl Butz's dictum that 'food is a weapon', American production reached record heights. The crisis was apparently over and we were back to square one.

With one difference; everybody now knows that sooner or later it will be back. They only disagree about when.

OPEC may not have been a sign that the end of the world's oil supply was immediately imminent. But it was a clear sign that something else was coming to an end, something which has vitally contributed throughout history to the creation and continuance of centralised urbanistic and imperialistic economies.

It is a process that might best be described as the wampum factor. Wampum was the cheap and trumpery merchandise, consisting of glass beads and whatnot, that Europeans used to take with them to trade with primitive natives in newly opened countries in return for commodities like mink and ivory.

This kind of trading has been a prime contributor to urban wealth, and it is based on the assumption that the peripheral partners to such deals are more scattered than the central ones so that they are less likely to compare notes or form monopolies, and that they have lower living standards and expectations, so that it doesn't take much to please them. But above all it is based on the assumption of their ignorance.

An Indian chief might accept wampum because he liked the look of it and because he already had a perfectly viable lifestyle where his real needs were few; but he would certainly not have been so satisfied with the deal if he had known that back home in the big city the trader would sell his purchases for the worth of a whole truck load of glass beads rather than a handful. The key to being on the winning end of these transactions is knowing more than the people you are dealing with. It depends on having the most comprehensive and up-to-date information concerning all the factors which affect the commodity being traded. It depends, in fact, on what the city (in the commercial sense) calls Intelligence. It was this commercial necessity to be the first with the answer to the eternal query of 'What news on the Rialto?' that originally created fact-gathering organisations like Reuters, placed them and anchored them in the very heart of the city, and provided the spur for the development of ever faster methods of communication. The press itself is partly a spin-off of this process and clings equally tightly to the central location where the lines of communication converge.

It was the wampum factor that enabled the West for so long to buy oil from the Middle East at prices so abysmally below what the market would bear that the Governments of purchasing countries were able to skim off a sizeable chunk of the surplus into their own treasuries and still allow the stuff to be sold at a profit. They did this quite sincerely, with no consciousness of exploitation but rather with an age-old centralist conviction that they were doing their suppliers a favour by providing the know-how for extracting and utilising the formerly valueless black mess that lay below the sand. Their attitude was precisely that of Daniel Defoe when he wrote: 'The whole country is dependent on London for the consumption of its produce', sublimely ignoring the fact that the dependence was mutual. The Middle East in the same way was felt to be dependent on the West for the consumption of its oil.

But the power of the wampum factor has been gradually and quietly eroded in the course of the twentieth century, largely by the very techniques that had once added to its power, namely, the improvements in communications. It is much harder to swindle a Red Indian Chief once he is able to look up the price of glass beads in a Sears Roebuck catalogue and discover from the financial press, or by a phone call to an agent, the precise figure that mink pelts are currently fetching on the New York market. You may still, if you are very agile, beat him to the draw and pay him five percent under the fair price, but never again five hundred percent or a thousand percent. 'Intelligence' in the information sense is now widely disseminated through all the media, and intelligence in the know-how sense is hirable anywhere.

The scatter element has also diminished in importance. In Britain, for example, after the coming of the railways and the penny post, it was not possible to go on for much longer employing South Wales miners for less pay and under more arduous conditions than miners in other areas, on the assumption that they were too isolated and under-educated to do anything about it. The miners in the various coalfields not only became aware of what was happening in other areas, but since there was a clear identity of interest they were able to co-ordinate their activities almost as effectively as if they had all been geographically concentrated in one place.

By the time the members of OPEC were ready to act, communications had progressed from steam engine and letter post to the jet plane and the international telephone; distance as a brake on united action had been eliminated, and the wampum factor in this particular instance was immediately shown to be stone dead. The only thing that had prevented it from lying down earlier was a delay in perceiving the extent of the identity of interest. Possibly too there was a psychological factor, the hangover of a hundred years at the wrong end of imperialist economics, but it was nothing that could not be eliminated overnight in one blaze of anger.

The third ingredient of wampum trading is the assumption that the peripheral partner, besides being ignorant and isolated, will be content to make less out of the deal because his living standards are lower. He has never had so much, therefore he doesn't 'need' so much, and it would be outrageous for him to expect so much.

This assumption has sunk so deep into all our economic thinking – since it has held true since the beginning of time – that most people are unconscious that they are making it. It is a nettle that Karl Marx never quite got round to grasping. When he talked of the cost of labour and stipulated that this must include the cost of the labourer replacing himself – ie, being paid enough to bring up a family – he came up against the fact that this cost varied from one area to another; that it cost less to replace a Chinese coolie than a British factory hand. It was a fact of life; he nodded at it and moved on. He had too much else on his plate at the time to go into all the implications.

In terms of ethics, let alone economics, it is a ticklish problem. It is a simple human fact that those who have never been accustomed to amenities do not suffer from their absence as acutely as those who have long enjoyed them, so that a superannuated distressed gentlewoman would undergo acute misery in conditions in which a superannuated charwoman would find comfortable and jolly: should we therefore say that since the charwoman has always had less it is a reason why she should have less now?

There is a whole range of clichés to support the proposition that she should: 'It's all according to what you've been used to. . . .' 'What you've never had you don't miss. . . .' 'No point in them having good things, they wouldn't appreciate them, they don't know how to look after them. . . .' 'They haven't got the same expenses, they don't need to keep up appearances. . . .' and there is a grain of truth in all of them. During the 1973 strike of the British miners when it finally dawned on their rulers that there was no way of doing without the coal, and no way of extracting it without their willing co-operation, among all the outbursts of fury and frustration there was a repeated note of genuine bewilderment: 'But what do they want all that money *for*? What can they do with it? They live in those poky little houses, they don't have the school fees to pay. . . .' as if the fact that they had so long been relatively deprived was in itself a good reason for the relative deprivation to continue.

This attitude isn't exclusive to the bourgeoisie, either. Trade unionists are displaying the same assumption when they proclaim the sturdy working-class concept of 'differentials', which means nothing more or less than if you have always been at the bottom of the wage scale the ones higher up are going to do their damnedest – on 'principle', no less – to see that you stay there. If a farm labourer stands up to speak at one of their national congresses they give him a big hand, as they do to any representative of the chronically underprivileged; they would gladly help him to screw more money out of the man who employs him (as long as it didn't involve them in anything wicked, like asking people to spend a higher percentage of their income on food and a lower percentage on consumer durables); but they are used to seeing him at the bottom of the scale, and if asked to justify it they would offer some variant on the theme of 'What does he want the money *for*? No point in buying posh clothes, stuck out there on the farm . . . no entertainments to waste his money on . . . very few public amenities to force up the rates. . . .'

But OPEC drove a coach and horses through that idea, too. The people who couldn't understand what a man living in a terraced house could possibly find to do with £70 never wasted a second on wondering what an Arab living in a tent could do with a million: they were too busy rolling out the red carpet. They didn't enquire whether he was truly capable of appreciating the good things in life or would know how to look after the precious ones; they were too busy selling them to him.

Finally, there used to be in classic wampum trading an unspoken assumption that not only was one side more ignorant, less united, and grateful for small mercies, but in the last resort the other side had bigger guns. Hopefully they would never need to be used, but they were there. Frequently of late this has been shown to be irrelevant. The Government could have called out the troops to discipline the miners, but it would have been counterproductive: you can't dig out coal with bayonets, nor with dead miners. The Americans could have descended with massive force on the Middle East and commandeered the oilfields, but it would have been fatal: it would take only a handful of Arab terrorists to blow up the installations and the pipelines and keep on doing it until the Americans got out.

What has been challenged is a long accepted tradition that people near the end of a production chain have always tended to receive higher remuneration than people nearer the beginning of it. Marx implied it was because the man-hours of labour that Lancashire weavers were adding to the value of the final product were more skilled man-hours, and therefore more expensive to replace, than the man-hours put in by the cotton pickers in America. According to market economics the reason is, in its simplest form, that manufactured goods are scarcer and more in demand than the raw materials from which they are manufactured. Thus, in a television discussion at the time of OPEC's first bombshell, an 'expert' cried out in anguish when someone suggested selling the Arabs some refineries to pay for the oil: 'We mustn't do that! That is the profitable part – you don't make money by producing oil, you make money by refining it.'

He ought to have realised, by his own tenets, that that is not necessarily an eternal truth. It is perfectly possible to envisage situations where an unprocessed product is more in demand, and can command a higher price, than a processed one. After a severe famine, corn might be worth more than the bread you could make from it, because the corn could be planted. There is absolutely no intrinsic reason why the oil refiner must always get a larger cut than the oil producer, or the weaver a higher wage than the cotton picker, since each is indispensable to the other. It is only that one side has been slower to appreciate this fact and act upon it.

Even regarding the matter purely as one of relative scarcities, if you continually accelerate the speed at which you use up finite resources and spew out manufactured commodities something is bound to happen. It is unlikely to be apocalypse. What it will be is that the terms of trade will begin to move against those at the end of the production chain and in favour of those at the beginning of it. Of this OPEC was a first portent. It will not be the last.

It is not at all surprising that conventional economists are currently at a loss to agree either on diagnosing or prescribing for the present turbulences. Too many longstanding 'certainties' have been cast into the melting pot. We are crashing through a whole series of economic watersheds, like the first test pilot crashing through the sound barrier and finding that the instructions he had been confidently given were suddenly and unexpectedly producing the wrong results.

We are passing the mark which indicates that more than fifty percent of the world is now urban; we are passing the mark which indicates that in the urbanised sectors less than fifty percent are engaged in producing anything; urbanised agriculture has passed the mark which indicates that we now put more energy into the land than we get out of it; and we are passing the highwater mark of the oil bonanza so that the costs of energy and transport, which had been constituting a steadily decreasing percentage of production costs, will henceforth absorb a steadily increasing percentage.

It is a formidable combination of circumstances which makes any forecast of future developments a very hazardous business. At the same time the necessity of attempting such a forecast is more urgent than ever before, if only so that we can make some effort to steer into the skid.

PART IV

The Tide Turns

10   The economics of exodus

Predictions of social events in the old days, when they were not made by examining the entrails of a dead hen or watching the flight of magpies, frequently took a Utopian form. Men would say: let us imagine an ideal society and work towards it.

It was sometimes set in the future like Plato's Commonwealth, sometimes in the past like Rousseau's society of the noble savage, sometimes in a faraway place like Utopia itself, or Butler's Erewhon.

By now human history is so littered with Utopias that have proved abortive or stillborn that this genre would appear recently to be falling out of fashion. Modern prophets do not say: this is how I imagine things could be in a better world than ours, and we must all fight to achieve that world. They say: I have perceived these trends which are inherent in human society and I conclude this is how things will *inevitably* be. (Karl Marx was taking no chances and in effect said both things at the same time.)

Prediction in some form or other is more necessary today than ever it was. The scale of modern organisation and technology means that planners need a vision of the future stretching a long way ahead: you can't decide to draw up a blueprint for Concorde today and launch it next Christmas. At the same time the pace of change means that the distance we can peer into the future with any confidence grows shorter and shorter. This is a highly inconvenient combination of circumstances, and one effect of it in the field of planning is a tendency for some of the prophecies to be *self-fulfilling*.

Urbanisation is a star example. One of the most widespread assumptions in the minds of all planners and predictors is that urbanisation, having spread and accelerated to our own day and to the point when the world is fifty-percent urbanised, will continue to spread – will probably continue to accelerate – until only some irreducible minimum of the order of perhaps two or three percent will be left outside, and the mutant genus *Homo sapiens gregarius* will have inherited the earth. It is widespread alike among those who welcome the prospect and believe with the Hudson Institute that it means continuing economic growth and unparallelled affluence for all, and by those who dread it and believe it is heading into some apocalyptic disaster, and react with a cry of *'sauve qui peut'* and head out like the early Christian hermits to the wilderness.

The belief has plenty of facts to support it. The current figures on global urbanisation are devastating. In 1960 two-thirds of the world's people made their living on the land. At the present rate of implosion, by the end of this century the ratio will be reversed and two-thirds of the world's people will be living or trying to live in cities. Most of them will be in the Third World. Their city dwellers will outnumber those of the developed world by a factor of two-and-a-half to one. They are arriving so fast that many of these cities are surrounded by illegal squatters numbering hundreds of thousands (1,2000,000, for example, in Seoul alone), families living in tents of tin or cardboard shacks or waterless, drainless hovels. A recent official count in Ankara showed that these newcomers constituted two out of three of the total population.

Practically every decision involving forward planning, public or private, is based on the assumption that these trends are universal and can be extrapolated into the future. Now, if you accept as axiomatic that in X years' time your city will be ten percent bigger, then you plan housing schemes, educational provision, parking space, office accommodation, hotels, roads, air terminals, water supply, etc, etc, to accommodate the extra ten percent, and avoid the charge of having failed to foresee their needs. The process of carrying out these ambitious plans calls for perhaps an extra four percent; perhaps another three percent will be attracted by the very existence of the amenities; another three percent will find occupation in pro-viding services for the seven percent. You will realise that your plans are only barely sufficient to keep pace with the growth, and over the next period of X years you plan for twelve percent expansion to be on the safe side.

Conversely, in a village where population has shown signs of declining there will be a tendency to cut back on existing amenities rather than take the risk of introducing new ones. Schools will close or amalgamate, frequency of bus services will be reduced, mortgages will be harder to raise, the sub-post office will be closed and with it the village shop which it alone made viable – and every one of these developments features as the last straw to a few more inhabitants who are otherwise reluctant to leave.

As long as the underlying trends remain constant, all this will be acclaimed as intelligent anticipation. If and when the trends change, things are not so simple. In the case of the village, because it is small, a reversal of economic fortunes can be quickly responded to: decline could give place to expansion at fairly short notice. In the case of megapolis a change of the underlying predisposing economic conditions from growth even to standstill, let alone decline, might take anything up to forty years to be reflected appropriately in the conduct of affairs.

It would take fifteen or twenty years to overcome the sheer incredulity that such a development could be other than a temporary hiccup which it would be pusillanimous not to ignore. Then there might be a half-built airport or a ring road with some of its sections constructed at an astronomical cost in terms of compulsory purchase and demolition and years of local political in-fighting and horse-trading, which will remain a monstrous white elephant forever unless the other sections are completed at even more astronomical cost.

Projects like these develop their own dinosaurian momentum and lumber on remorselessly while even their onetime champions feel their blood run cold at the escalating estimates and the unpredictable side-effects of their unstoppable forward march.

Let us go further, and come clean, and take that proposition out of the subjunctive: there are already clear signs in the most highly developed countries that the underlying trends *are* beginning to go into reverse, even though in the Third World they may still be accelerating.

In the first stages it was easy to misread the signs. For example, it was long ago pointed out by someone who had consulted the electoral register that the City of London, the very heart of the metropolis, had turned into a demographic desert inhabited by absolutely nobody except a couple of janitors and the Dean of St Paul's – which on the face of it suggested some kind of ghost town with grass and willowherb sprouting up through the paving stones and rabbits breeding among the ruins. Obviously this was nonsense: for most of the week the place was crowded. Later, when the whole area once administered by the London County Council was shown to be declining in population, the same explanation was available – that people had simply lengthened their lines of communication and were sleeping in the dormitory suburbs just outside the border where the rates were lower. Later still, it was learned that the more extensive area administered by the Greater London Council was showing a net population loss too. This was perhaps a sign that London like some American cities was growing hollow at the centre, with its people and its industries tending to cluster in a rough circle around what had once been the outer rim.

By the 1970s however the writing on the wall had become clearer. Over the previous ten years more than 300,000 people had been leaving London every year. People were of course still coming in, from the provinces and overseas, but not nearly as fast as they were getting out – the net loss was an annual 100,000 people. And by the mid-seventies it was no longer possible for anyone to write this off as due to long-distance commuting into ever leafier and more remote suburbs and dormitory villages. A team of planners composed of Department of Environment officials and Local Authority representatives reported early in 1976 that the drift towards the South East region *as a whole* had sharply diminished and that population growth there was declining.

All over America the same phenomenon can be observed.

New York, Chicago, Philadelphia, Cleveland are losing population. In 1960 one in three Americans lived in inner-city areas
and their income was high by national standards. Now only
twenty-nine percent live in those places and their income has
fallen to below the national average. Where the metropolis
used to be a place where people who could afford to would live,
it is becoming a place which almost anyone who can afford
to will quit.

According to urban-studies research coming out of the
University of Chicago, the areas of extraordinary population
growth are places way and gone into the rural outback, like
the Ozarks in Northern Arkansas, the Dakotas, and Vermont,
and the people mainly involved in the exodus are not im-
pulsive flower children but middle-class adults mostly aged
twenty-five to thirty-five who have decided as abruptly as any
Australian abo that they have had enough of that, and no
amount of professional ambition or financial incentive will
persuade them otherwise. As one of them said: 'The extra
money I earned was going in psychiatry and double Martinis.'

These social symptoms have manifested themselves rather
suddenly. Only a few years ago anyone predicting that more
Britons were going to cast an appraising glance at the bright
lights of London and decide to remain in (or move out to) the
'stagnating' provinces, and that significant numbers of rising
US executives were going to say 'to hell with rising, let's fall
a little bit' would have been written off as a raving nutter.
Only a few years ago your average sociologist, asked to en-
vision the City of the Future, pointed without hesitation to
Los Angeles.

That was the lifestyle we were all headed for. We had it
on the authority of the Hudson Institute, no less, that given
another fifty years of growth we could all live like that. That
was Tomorrow's City visible today, the city of multilane freeways, the city of the automobile, to which the inhabitants
adhere as tenaciously as a hermit crab to its shell, where there
are districts where a human biped denuded of any convey-
ance and primitively ambulating along a pavement is so dis-
concerting a sight as to call for instant interrogation by the

police. I suppose there are worse utopias to dream about, for there is no denying the place has its own weird kind of beauty, as anything has that is so superbly adapted to its habitat, its era, and its own inherent strengths and weaknesses. But the same could have been said of the brontosaurus. It is at least as likely that Los Angeles will remain forever unique, a place that travelled further up that particular ekistical *cul-de-sac* than anyone else will ever have the opportunity of doing.

So what went wrong with megapolis? Some sand was discernibly beginning to get into the works from the end of the second World War. As outlined earlier, too many of the advantages of urban living were running into a law of diminishing returns or moving into reverse – big cities were no longer the most gracious, the most convenient, the safest places. Even an index such as literacy – where the city had scored high since the first scribe invented the first hieroglyphics – was no longer reliable, for very few small-town schools turned out as high a proportion of illiterates as some of the blackboard jungles.

The growth in size and complexity increases the city's need for flexibility but decreases its room for manoeuvre. It becomes more urgent to identify future needs with accuracy, but the margin of error grows wider as the number of variables multiplies towards infinity. And the consequences of such errors grow more disastrous as the scale of the project becomes more gigantic.

For example, we have previously considered the consequences of conflicts of interest in an urban context, between the rich and influential sectors and those who are poor and powerless, the outcome being usually a widening of the gap between the two. But the time comes when it is no longer possible for powerful lobbies to advance their interests only at the expense of the weak, or for the authorities to carry out projects which they believe to be in the public interest without coming into conflict with the kind of people who are not accustomed to being inconvenienced.

When protagonists of this calibre lock horns the result is apt to be prolonged stasis or total deadlock, because Community Action takes on a new and more formidable appearance when it is conducted by Top People. They are not in the habit of putting up pathetic barricades or standing on street corners with bundles of petitions; but they will pull wires and spend money and consult lawyers and invite public figures to dinner to chat about old times and explain the fundamental 'unsoundness' of the new project, and hire accountants even wilier and pricier than the official ones to prove that the authorities really haven't done their homework on this. Their letters will appear in top newspapers over well-known signatures, and they will be interviewed on television – not shrill and windblown on a pavement, but silver-haired and calmly authoritative in a studio.

In the case of a projected new airport outside Edinburgh the weightiness of the research and evidence adduced against the plan was so great that the scenario for the Government Enquiry was unexpectedly capsized. The independent Inspector appointed as arbitrator suddenly pronounced himself convinced that the plan should be abandoned. This was highly embarrassing because it drove a coach and horses through the polite fiction that public enquiries are set up actually to inquire into things rather than to allow the indignant populace to blow off steam. The Government simply had to tough it out, explain that the protesters had had a good run for their money, that the result of the inquiry was interesting but that they intended to build the airport anyway. After all the final decision rested with London, from which standpoint Edinburgh is a faraway place of which we know little or nothing. The protesters up there may get pretty riled, but they'll get over it. And fortunately one doesn't have to *live* there, does one? When a similarly high powered lobby got up a campaign to spike the plan for a new London airport at Maplin, the campaign was successful and the plan was quite rightly dropped. In the Home Counties, of course, one *does* have to live. Thus the nearer the centre, the steeper the sums that are involved, the fiercer the in-fighting and the greater the chances of deadlock. World City, if it ever got built had better get everything right first time, because the speed at which it could introduce any urgent major changes would be the speed of an arthritic tortoise.

Another factor that makes urban problems intractable is that once a city has reached those oedematous proportions it is incapable of taking the appropriate actions to cure itself, because it is constitutionally and politically incapable of accepting the radical diagnosis of its disease. If salvation is to come at all, it will have to come from outside.

There was once an expert who was paid to study the problem of traffic in a big city. He studied hard and long. He saw how the commuters were stuck morning and evening in nerve-racking, temper-fraying traffic jams. He saw that the city had reached that inspissated stage of wealth and density when any attempt to cut a swathe through it for a new artery involved costs mounting to the stratosphere and apoplectic resistance from embattled vested interests of the highest puissance. He saw how past experience showed that the construction of any such artery had two direct results – it speeded the flow of traffic in that area and it considerably increased the number of cars travelling on that route.

This invariably led to three indirect effects. By increasing the number of cars it brought public transport another step nearer to bankruptcy, it exacerbated parking problems in the centre and invariably it created another nerve-racking, temper-fraying log jam of traffic somewhere else which would have to be tackled by the same methods and with the same results. After long thought he concluded that the total overall amount of frustration, misery and time-wasting would not be reduced in any case, whereas if the position got any worse than it was some of the people would stop commuting by car – a consummation which the city authorities professed to desire but were, of course, taking all conceivable steps to stave off. He gave as his considered advice that the best thing to do about the appalling traffic congestion was nothing. The advice was not published.

I think he was right, but I ask you to contemplate the fate on the hustings of any urban candidate who included as one plank in his electoral programme: 'What I propose to do about the appalling traffic congestion in my constituency is to let it rip.' He lives there; quite possibly he loves the place; he hopes to represent the place. He cannot humanly do other than accept the proposition that all the frustration and diseconomies of urban scale and growth can and must at all costs be alleviated and compensated for, however inexorably they reappear in modified form or at new locations.

The city's treasurers are bound to be committed to growth; it is their best hope of raising rates and taxes to meet the escalating demands on them. The city's humanitarians are bound to demand extra social security provisions for the city's unfortunates to allow for the higher rent they have to pay, even though that helps to ensure that the rents will never come down, and that the city is never less than the prime magnet for the new immigrants whose arrival they deplore. The city's educators are bound to support higher pay for metropolitan teachers or they would never get enough of them. Its transport authorities, even while agreeing that uneconomic rural railway lines ought to be axed, are bound to urge that uneconomic urban lines must be kept open. Its civil servants and executives, while indignant at the cost of office space and good secretaries, and supporting in principle the dispersal campaigns of the Location of Offices Bureau, are bound to resist any effort to transport their own particular department to low-prestige provincial locations remote from the corridors of power. When the latest figures revealed the extent of London's depopulation the instant reaction from County Hall was that this was getting out of hand, and means must be sought to lure people back again.

For these and a hundred parallel reasons all 'devolutionary' moves originating in, or connived at, by the cities are inadequate and ineffective. They admit they are ineffective; they profess themselves baffled that they are ineffective; but the fact remains that if they were such as to result in directing any significant percentage of real wealth or real influence away from the city, then they would not be supported by the city.

Above all, the Governments in all highly developed countries are unable to combat the inertia of this urban commitment to urban growth because they are in office to further the interests of the nation, and the cities have a built-in majority of the nation's votes. It was safe enough for the US Government to conclude that the decline of villages and rural towns was one of the facts of life, and that the rational response was to accept it gracefully and let those places die, since any other policy would be simply spitting into the wind. But it would take a very brave President to advise Detroit, on the strength of a similar demographic decline, that its day was done and it might as well give up the struggle and sink into the grave without kicking up an undignified fuss about it. The standard prescribed cure for every sick city remains 'more growth', and the problem it submits to every economic consultant it calls in is how to achieve that growth. Any voices from outside querying the wisdom of this have been written off as backward-looking, romantic, defeatist, ignorant or envious.

In the beginning, to be sure, the outside voices were motivated partly by personal predilections. They were the statements of men committed by upbringing and temperament to the green locust's view of life. Noise and crowds and concrete were aesthetically upsetting to them, and ever since William Cobbett in 1821, took one look at London and called it a 'great wen (carbuncle)', there has been a handful of writers in every generation echoing his sentiments. Often they were kind and gentle creatures, anguished that human beings were condemned to live in conditions they personally would find odious, unable to conceive that for millions of those captives the crowded streets were the breath of life.

Later they included more influential figures who concentrated on working out how to mitigate the city's ills, and collected a considerable following, but their approach remained in essence Utopian: 'This is how it could be. This is what you must work towards.' Jane Jacobs, fervent protagonist of urban growth, lined up a whole queue of them in her book and shot them all down, from Ebenezer Howard who 'set spinning powerful and city-destroying ideas', through Patrick Geddes to the later group of 'extraordinarily effective and dedicated people', which included Lewis Mumford, Clarence Stein, Henry Wright and Catherine Bauer. She named them the Decentrists, and denounced their attitude to urban life as morbid and biassed and their influence as malign.

Well, fair enough, and *chacun à son goût*. No one from outside can have any comeback to megapolitans who say: 'That may be how you like it – this is how *we* like it. Don't tell us how to run our show. You simply don't understand.' All I (as an outsider) would claim the right to say is: 'If the way you run your show is draining the lifeblood out of the show *we* are trying to run, you must expect sooner or later to run into some resistance.'

Since the last war the outside voices have been striking an entirely new note, not Utopian but pragmatic. They do not say: 'That is not a good way to live. I have had this vision; aspire to it.' They say: 'I have to warn you that the course you are pursuing will not for much longer remain tenable.'

The archetypal figure here is a professor who began sounding these warnings when he was working, like Dr Jacob Bronowski, for Britain's National Coal Board. (I am unable to determine whether the NCB is particularly good at recognising top-class intelligence, or whether being forced to think hard about coal for a few years stimulates an insight into where humanity is at, and how it got there.)

The professor's name is E. F. Schumacher, and he first hit some rather minuscule headlines in 1958, when he pointed out that the West in general and Europe in particular were recklessly increasing the dependence of their whole economy on supplies of cheap oil, that the supplies were finite, and unless they modified their policy the time would soon come when the oil producers of the Middle East would have them over a barrel. He predicted the date at which the situation might be expected to come to a head, and explained how he had arrived at it. Nobody took any notice. Because of course he would have to say that, wouldn't he? If you work for the NCB you don't go around admitting that coal is obsolete.

A similar warning about oil was included, in more general terms but more graphically, in a book published in 1962 by

Carlo M. Cipolla called *The Economic History of World Population*, which included a reproduction of this little graph drawn by H. Thirring in 1958:

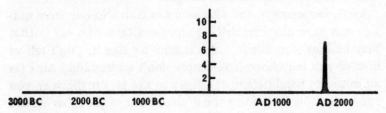

*Source: **The Economics of World Population** by Carlo M. Cipolla, p.59

The black hump is a rough illustration of the rate at which we are using up our reserves of fossil fuel. It is a very moderate presentation of the problem, because the line across the bottom only begins somewhere around the beginning of human civilisation. If you wanted to be sensational and compare the rate of consumption of this energy with the time it took the earth to store it up, you would have to produce the line in a leftward direction for another couple of hundred yards.

The difference between Cipolla and Schumacher is that Cipolla, having pointed out how dramatically the advent of oil-based technology had affected the growth and distribution of world population, and having underlined that the deposits of the stuff were strictly limited, went on to predict that urbanisation would carry on just as before, and that the percentage of people engaged in agriculture would continue to shrink until the numbers involved were comparable to the numbers now involved in hunting and gathering, and World City would prevail.

Schumacher thought not.

When the OPEC crisis arrived, bang on Schumacher's target, immediately all the black-locust futurologists said: 'Well, yes, but. . . .' and began burying their heads in the shale deposits of the Rockies and advising more intensive capital investment in prospecting for off-shore oil wells. Enough additional deposits have been located to convince them that growth can continue as before – or rather, can continue as *never* before, because the theory is that whereas formerly less than half the world was engaged on this binge, in future the whole world can be engaged on it. The predictions of such seers as Herman Kahn are based on extrapolating the trends of the recent past, so that in terms of Cipolla's graph the steep rise is assumed to continue upwards towards infinity.

In so far as the graph needs to be modified by the discoveries of hitherto undiscovered reserves of oil these modifications would make it merely a little taller, but no less narrow, because millions of pounds of capital, public and private, are being invested in prospecting for oil and in new ways of consuming it for every penny that is being invested in discovering ways of doing without it. The net result will not be to delay the moment of truth even for a decade, merely to render the crisis more catastrophic when it arrives.

The thinking behind this policy must be either 'Après moi le déluge' and why should we do anything for posterity when it's never done anything for us? or else a blind faith that an equivalent substitute for oil *must* be discovered, merely because we need it so very badly.

This is the attitude of a spoilt child. If a hundred years ago all the horses and donkeys had suddenly been struck sterile, it would have taken a stupid man to devote his life to improving the design of a four-in-hand and stubbornly insisting that something was *bound* to turn up to fill the equid gap; that somebody would doubtless train a team of sheep or cows or kangaroos to pull the Wells Fargo Express simply because the demand for such a breakthrough was so urgent. It is that brand of stupidity we are manifesting when we continue perfecting supersonic airliners and constructing airports and fourteen-lane highways at this stage of the game. We sometimes fail to appreciate that the fact that the equidae are both fast and ridable was a stupendous one-off piece of cosmic luck for us. The fact that there were pockets of stored up energy hidden in the earth was a second but more ephemeral piece of luck. (The horses can replace themselves, but the oil cannot.)

When our grandchildren look back on the heyday of the

H

coal and oil era and ask how we managed to get through the irreplaceable stuff so fast and precisely what we did with it, there are stories they will find hard to believe. To take just one instance, it will surely seem to them incredible that in our day it was profitable and seemed justifiable that people would take material out of the earth in South America, put it on trucks, drive it to the sea, load it on ships, transport it to the British Isles, unload it, package it with some style and imagination, advertise it, distribute it in vans to shops, retail it, and deliver it to blocks of flats and have it carried up in a lift and laid in a convenient corner in order that a British cat might excrete on it, and then it could be taken down again together with its discarded packaging and surrendered to the further energy-consuming processes of long-distance urban refuse disposal.

But whereas in 1960 the concept of Limits to Growth was a startling one, in 1976 there is no need to labour it. The Club of Rome and scores of other groups have made us familiar with the argument that not only oil but other vital resources are finite. The response has followed a classical pattern. First: 'It is not true.' Later: 'There may be some truth in it, but you are exaggerating.' Later still: 'But of course that is old hat, we have all known that for years, and we have found the answer. Sooner or later we will have to start economising and re-cycling.' (To which is appended, as to St Augustine's prayer to be made chaste and continent, '. . . but not yet.')

If you want a Marxist quote on this part of economics, you will have to look a long way, but Marx was a pretty compre-hensive thinker and he didn't leave it out entirely. Here it is: 'We see then that labour is not the only source of national wealth, of use value produced by labour. As William Petty puts it, labour is its father and the earth is its mother.' At that date the most urgent need was to concentrate on the paternal side of the partnership, because no one had begun to con-template the possibility that Mother Earth's dugs could ever run dry. However, since the last war she has been registering protests that it is increasingly impossible to ignore, and from this point on she will have to be included as a key factor in any long-term economic equation, capitalist or communist.

Inevitably this imparts an entirely new dimension, and if Marx were alive today he would have had to incorporate it.

This is one of the points that Schumacher is making. The only thing that has made it possible and profitable to conduct industrial and agricultural enterprises on such a vast scale, the only thing that has made it possible for half the human race to be sustained in cities, the only thing that has powered the suction of populations into the huge dense urban coagulations of today, is the supply of cheap and ostensibly unlimited resources of fossil fuel.

If the oil dried up tomorow this demographic arrangement would be impossible. Some people who have seen this clearly, alarmed by the reluctance of the people in control of events to see it at all, have left the cities. Many who have not so fled have heard faint alarm bells ringing at some level of their consciousness. Urban librarians in many cities have reported an unprecedented demand for books dealing with basic survival. Seed firms whose catalogues have normally been filled with orders for flowers with a very small sideline in vegetable seeds have found their order books steadily reversing this order of precedence, and have had to rethink their advertising and re-draft the catalogues. Universities who have experimentally offered a course on the techniques of self-sufficiency for any small group of students who might be interested were swamped with ten times as many applicants as they had envisaged.

Well, you know, and I know, and Schumacher knows, that the oil is not going to dry up tomorrow, and it is unlikely that there will be any apocalyptic development which drives us all into the countryside to live off berries and roots and nuts and snails. We didn't live like that before we found the coal and the oil, which was not so very long ago, and we won't live like it when they are gone; the rundown will be gradual and accompanied by an inexorable escalation of fuel prices which will enable us and indeed force us, to modify our habits; we shall have at least as long to adjust to the absence of these resources as we had to adjust to their presence, and probably longer.

The likelier scenario is that from the moment when the

cheapness and availability of coal and oil passes the top of its parabola (which was, roughly speaking, yesterday), the effect will be to reduce the scale on which enterprises – industrial and agricultural – can profitably be conducted, and the effect on the distribution of population will be *anti-coagulant*. The clots will begin to break up and disperse: whether they do it willingly or unwillingly is irrelevant.

If this reasoning is correct, there should already be some straws in the wind to indicate the fact. The initial OPEC crisis was not the crunch nor anything like it – it was merely an advance warning – but some of the reactions to it are interesting.

One we have already noted – the drift out of some of the older centres has become marked, and it no longer consists almost exclusively of drift from city centre to outer suburb. It is, in some instances at least, a move away from the whole conurbation. And it has not been a devolutionary move imposed by Government action or exhortation, but a spontaneous reflex.

An immediate reaction to the oil crisis was a cut-back in investment and 'growth'. Many massive new projects drawn up in the expansive days before OPEC had to be abandoned or postponed for lack of investment capital and a sharp drop in confidence. This was sad for the prosperous and go-ahead areas where most of these projects would have been sited, but it gave a little longer lease of life to the more scattered and smaller-scale concerns which would have been knocked out by their competition.

In Britain in 1973 more than one commentator on the economic situation, having been despatched to travel around the country and report on the national morale, returned to the capital and announced with a mixture of relief and mild bafflement that the provinces appeared to be taking the whole thing far more phlegmatically than London.

A less negative aspect was that firms in the provinces began to take a more realistic look at the ways they were spending their money and what they were getting for it. And this led to a brake being put on the centreward flow of money and business in the more adventitious enterprises such as advertising.

The financial pages featured occasional headlines with an unfamiliar ring about them, such as 'Gravy train pulls out for the
North', covering reports that:

> London is not the place to have an advertising agency
> these days. Many of the large companies are now casting off
> the extravagances of expensive London offices to house their
> market men. . . . The day spent visiting a London agency
> is becoming a luxury the hard-headed businessman of
> England's industrial heartland are becoming more and more
> reluctant to indulge. . . . Manchester is leading the regions
> out of the traps. . . . Combined turnover is up in nearly
> every region. . . . Many a loosely held regional account will
> soon be dropping off and rolling back to its home base.
> Tomorrow unlike all our yesterdays in advertising may be-
> long to the regions.

The significance of this was presumably that the same root-
lessness of many of the white collar jobs which had made it
so easy to magnetise them to London would also make it
easy for them to drift out again in any wind of change.

However it came about, the aggregate effect of thousands
of individual economic reappraisals was an impulse of recoil
from the centre. The motives were manifold ('It also helps,'
The Guardian pointed out, 'if you are paying £1.50 a square
foot compared with up to £18.00 in London's West End'), but
the net result was centrifugal. When combined with the high
rate of bankruptcies among the thousands of egregiously non-
essential service enterprises that sprout like mushrooms in
every metropolis it gave rise to another unprecedented
phenomenon. When the unemployment figures rose they rose
first and fastest in the South East.

That had never happened in any previous economic crisis.
It was one reason why London was for a while more jittery
about the situation than any place in Britain outside it, and
people in responsible positions there were semi-seriously discussing contingency plans for coping with possible breakdown
in the system of law and order. Many people were getting,
for the first time, some understanding of the precarious in-

verted pyramid of employment that constitutes a modern city, and some appreciation of the fact that it is only held upright like a gyroscope by the speed of its spin. If it ever slows down it will wobble, and to sustain the speed there is still as yet no effective substitute for hydrocarbon fuels.

Since that time we have also witnessed the first signs of the development that Schumacher predicted. There has been a tendency to question the wisdom and effectiveness of very large-scale enterprises, and the beginnings of a retreat from them. The questioning is no longer confined to light-hearted thinkers like C. Northcote Parkinson or maverick economists like Galbraith, but is being echoed by voices from the heartland of the orthodox business establishment.

Let us take as an example the second thoughts of a man like Sir Frederick Catherwood, experienced industrialist, director of several major companies, Chairman of the British Institute of Management and former Director General of the National Economic Development Office. When he was appointed chief industrial adviser in the Department of Economic Affairs he was a staunch supporter of the 'economies of scale' theory. Four years in the aluminium industry comparing the efficiency of British and American production had confirmed him in that conviction. In steel, also, the average US company was eight or ten times the size of its British equivalent and was demonstrably able to operate with lower costs and greater efficiency. He accepted without question that there was a causal relationship between the greater size and the greater output. He remained firmly convinced of the economic advantages of large-scale production, until in his capacity as Director General of the National Economic Development Council he tried to track them down and quantify them. He outlined his conclusions for the Council of Engineering Institution as follows:

> Even the economies of scale in the American Aluminium Industry with which I was so impressed were vulnerable to the small extrusion press giving a more local service, more neatly tailored to the precise needs of the customer. They took a very large section of this business away from the

'majors'. And while it was supposed that no smelter could make money under 100,000 tonnes a year, a foreign company came in with a smelter a fifth of the size. On closer analysis the only real economy of scale in the industry was the big hot rolling mill. This had to have about ten percent of the total national market to keep it going. But then someone started up a rolling mill to 'toll' roll other companies' metal, and though the mill required the same large output the toll roller did nothing else and was in itself a tiny business employing very few people. When I was Director General of NEDI we tried to track down the elusive economies of scale and finally came to the conclusion that *they had only existed in the mind.*

His final conclusion was: 'I think that the day of the giant plant is over,' and he was not alone in this view. A few companies had already decided as a matter of policy never again to build another plant employing more than three thousand people. Others again had opted for a future maximum of five hundred employees. A factor in this decision was the discovery that in large plants employing ten or fifteen thousand people work satisfaction tends to be lower, communications between labour and management more garbled, labour turnover higher and stoppages endemic – in situations where a strike by a handful of men can throw thousands of others out of work; whereas at the opposite extreme, the Bolton Committee reported in 1971 that in the period 1967-1969, of all firms with two hundred employees or less, only one-and-a-half percent had been affected by their employees going on strike.

By the end of 1974 the latest figures showed that the size of the median plant in the United Kingdom manufacturing industry had begun to fall, while the Bolton Committee reports that across the Atlantic also, small establishments and plants are accounting for a bigger share of manufacturing employment in the United States and Canada than previously.

How then are we to account for all those statistical tables so closely correlating size and efficiency? I have seen it suggested, and it seems to me by far the likeliest explanation, that it was yet another beautiful example of the self-fulfilling prophesy. People believed that the trend was for plant to become bigger and bigger. Therefore all the new plants with the most up-to-date equipment were built on a larger scale than the obsolescent ones; therefore every investigation confirms that the large (new) plants were more efficient than the small (old) ones. QED. Which was a powerful argument for building the next and newest ones bigger still.

You may object that these instances are of minor importance and parochially concentrated on Britain. This is partly because I live here, but partly because it is the place where the whole thing started and as good a place as any to look for signs that the tide is turning. At the other end of the spectrum, in the oil-poor countries of the Third World, the impact was greater and infinitely more tragic, but pointed ultimately in the same direction.

The scarcity of oil and fertiliser, the check to the Green Revolution and the sight of the immobilised tractors, the cutback in food and other aid from the developed countries, strengthened the conviction that was already growing – that the kind of aid and foreign investment they had been receiving was the wrong kind anyway. The lion's share of it tended to get stuck in the primate city. A research programme financed by the Overseas Development Ministry in 1973 confirmed that in a sample of fourteen Third World countries, agriculture, which employed nearly half the economically active population, received only eleven percent of all investment. Eighty-nine percent of it was strengthening to gale force the wind that was sucking people into cities which had neither jobs to offer them nor houses to put them in; a good deal of the eleven percent was devoted to large-scale oil-intensive enterprises which had the same effect on the villages of the hinterland. Tanzania, which was making the most strenuous efforts to support and stabilise such villages, was the only country in Africa where food production was growing faster than the population. Economist H. W. Singer was one who was driven to the stark conclusion that much of the aid that had been poured in had in the last resort been 'positively harmful'. Many members of the Aid Committees themselves have come to agree with him.

The idea that the processes that had led half the world to affluence could, with a bit of capitalist investment to prime the pump, lead all the world to the same affluence, was always a mistake. It was based on the age-old centralist conviction in the developed countries that they alone, plus oil, had worked the miracle, and that given the know-how anybody could do it, which was not true. Anyone could do it given the oil, and the know-how, and the raw materials, and an unlimited reserve of people somewhere else willing to work harder under worse conditions on a much lower standard of living than the miracle-worker.

It is this last ingredient quite as much as the oil which makes it hard and finally impossible for the latecomers to this feast to get the miracle off the ground by using the same formula that the developed countries used. As Professor Eric Hobsbawm concluded, development *creates* underdevelopment. If you are at the bottom of the league there is nobody you can work the wampum trick on, nowhere where the underdevelopment can be created, except in your own hinterland. And in the poorest countries the people out there are so near the borderline that if you try to squeeze them any further they will either die or get too weak to work at all, or they will promptly get the hell out to the cities. They will have to find another way, and when they do the effect on the rest of us may be more uncomfortable than we have yet begun to calculate.

One result of the growing disillusion was the growing stream of enquiries from the Third World to E. F. Schumacher, who believes as Gandhi did that 'the poor of the world cannot be helped by mass production'. He has never been purely a theorist but a man who wants to get things done, interested in developing the kind of technology which nobody had hitherto been paid to research into, because nobody will ever make a packet out of it and the people most likely to benefit can't afford to pay for it anyway. His Intermediate Technology Group specialises in developing low-cost (or 'no-cost') techniques using indigenous materials, small in scale, and labour-intensive rather than oil-intensive. When anyone tells the Group that you can't produce product X and break even unless you are turning it out in batches of 100,000 a week, they look for a way to divide that figure by a hundred.

Wherever this technique is employed the effect is the direct opposite of previous forms of aid – it decreases rather than increases the dependence on foreign capital and foreign imports; it adds nothing to the national debt; and it slows down rather than speeds up the tide of urbanisation. Among countries where Intermediate Technology projects are in operation are Kenya, Sudan, Brazil, Botswana, Jamaica, Tanzania . . . and Germany is now setting up an Intermediate Technology Institute of her own.

The man whom even more of the Third World countries turned to was Mao Tse Tung, whose particular version of Marxism owes much to the discovery that the poor of vast areas of China couldn't be helped by mass production either, and who was preaching and deploying his own brand of Intermediate Technology before Schumacher's Group had been heard of. One thing that favourably impressed the Africans where teams of Chinese technologists did arrive was that whereas experts from the US and USSR stood around and said: 'I will now explain to you what you should do,' the Chinese were more likely to roll up their sleeves and say: 'Come on, this is how we're going to do it.'

How long Mao's methods will survive his death, and the discovery of copious Chinese oil deposits, and the desire to rule that vast area as a single unit, remains to be seen. The Chinese have this year (1976) announced a policy of building towns and cities with populations limited to 400,000. But it will take not only Mao's revered memory and his *Little Red Book* but a national will of iron, if they are not to let the oil lead them (while it lasts) down the same rollicking road that the rest of us took, and stampede them into a coastal megapolis that will make America's North Eastern conurbation look like Little Muddlecombe-in-the-Marsh.

Most dramatic of all have been the effects on the distribution of population whenever a developing country has become cut off, whether voluntarily or involuntarily, from some or all of the trade with the West which had powered the magnetism of the cities and financed the supply of oil. They were demonstrated for a while in Cuba, where parts of Havana took on the aspect of a ghost city, with houses, hotels, and department stores left empty and hollow, boarded up and invaded by vermin; again in Saigon; and even more dramatically in Cambodia where the exodus has been enforced with speed and ruthlessness. There can be no doubt that if anyone could supply a sudden and effective tourniquet to the supply of oil, the viability of Paris or Bonn or London or Brussels would suffer as complete a collapse, and necessitate similarly drastic measures. To my mind there can be no doubt either of the likelier less alarmist corollary, that the gradual and inevitable rundown of those supplies, even if it takes a century, will be accompanied by the gradual and (hopefully) painless decoagulation of these inspissated demographic clots.

This is one reason why Schumacher calls it 'almost a providential blessing' that we have been forced to think about this kind of technology for the sake of the people in the poorest countries, because 'they need the very thing which we also need'.

He means this partly in an aesthetic sense – 'technology with a human face' – because he is psychologically cast in the mould of many of his decentrist predecessors – patently good guys, wanting people to be happier rather than richer, worrying about the quality of life. There are only two new things in his brand of decentrism. Where the Garden City boys tried to tackle the problem from the centre, he wants to tackle it from the outer edges, a far more practical policy. And where previous idealists had tried to appeal to men's finer natures and hoped they could be evangelised into standing firm against materialism and the profit motive, he has the same conviction that Marx had (and with as much reason) that history is on his side. We don't have to fight against market forces – they're coming our way.

An example he's fond of is bricks. The profitable way to make them now is in factories that can turn them out by the million and despatch them to where they are needed. But clay is heavy stuff to haul in and bricks are heavy things to haul out – the economies of scale would never have accrued if the haulage had always been done by horse and cart. You could put the figures into a computer and predict at what point the rising costs of transport will make it possible for a man with moderate outlay and a couple of employees to set up a kiln to supply enough bricks for local building needs and undercut the distant mass-producer by a handsome margin. When that time comes if he wants any advice about methods and equipment, the Intermediate Technology Group will be able to send him a leaflet: they've been designing those things for the Third World for a good many years. (Actually for Third World housing they've now turned to ways of modernising mud, but the principle is unaffected.)

This week, as I write, commuter fares in London have gone up again – for some of the victims interviewed on television, up past the point of no return. One or two of them said – it's the end. It's impossible. I can't afford the rents in the centre, and there aren't any jobs near where I live – I'll have to move away altogether. Next time the prices go up and the time after, there will be more incentive for more people to find a place less sprawling, where home and work can be closer together. A smaller place. It's a straw in the wind and would mean very little, except that so many straws are blowing one way. If they continue to do so, a good many of the political attitudes we have got stuck in since the eighteenth century are going to have to be modified or abandoned, and it's not too soon to start thinking about some new ones.

11 The politics of exodus

There is very little in the foregoing that has not already been stated by different people in different countries who have perceived this underlying pattern of events and expressed it repeatedly in their own fashion and from their own particular standpoint.

It is in essence what Professor Raul Prebisch was saying when he formulated his 'Law of increasing Peripheral Neglect'. I heard Professor Harold Laski outline it in Oxford over thirty years ago and encapsulate it in the quotation about 'apoplexy at the centre and anaemia at the extremities' from some European thinker whose name I failed to catch and have never been able to track down. It was implicit in what J.-F. Gravier was saying to France in his best-selling *Paris et le desert francais*. But however often it has been said it has not made a great deal of impact and it is not difficult to see why.

Professor Peter Medawar has said that scientists tend not to ask themselves a question until they can see the glimmerings of an answer. Statesmen and politicians of every colour have a similar blockage: they are not particularly interested in either questions or answers that will not help them to weld together a section of the people which they can use as a power base. They want the kind of answers which will enable them to say:

> I am your champion. Your interests are identical and I have a simple and clear-cut policy which will further them. Those people over there are your enemies and are acting wickedly and working against you. Therefore stick together and support me.

A theory of that kind, whether it is right or wrong, can move mountains. Marx had one – so did Hitler.

The first essential for commanding such political leverage is to propose an analysis that clearly defines and delimits a group susceptible of being welded into solidarity. You may define the group geographically (Australia, Great Britain) or racially (Aryanism, Black Power) sexually (Women's Lib) or economically (Marxism). It is fairly easy for people to be clear about where they live, what sex and colour they are, and whether they are workers or employers. A second essential has always been, historically, that the section to whom you are appealing should be geographically concentrated as far as possible, so that you can assemble them, make speeches to them, and by standing shoulder to shoulder and hearing the volume of their own cheers they can gain confidence in their collective strength – which is why Marx and Engels were so firmly convinced that their particular form of revolution must begin in an industrialised state.

Now, by every criterion of practical politics the concept of peripheralism is a non-starter. Academics who are merely intellectually curious about what makes things tick may keep returning to the idea and running it up the flagpole, but nobody ever salutes; it sinks without trace because the kind of men who actually run the world can see at a glance that it is pragmatically sterile.

Let us consider some of the reasons why they write it off. The people to whom it should have most appeal are the people with the least power and the least money. They have the least confidence in themselves because they very rarely have a memory of any conflict with the centre that did not end in their own defeat. They are more widely scattered, less uniform in habits of speech, thought and lifestyle, less adept in forming alliances. They have least access to information. Wherever there is illiteracy and malnutrition theirs is the deepest ignorance and the sharpest hunger. Most of their education and employment – and their capital equipment where it exists – is supplied by, and geared to the needs of, the centre. If it was withdrawn from them they could be plunged into penury.

That looks already like a prohibitive imbalance of advantages and a foregone conclusion of no change. Of course it is nothing of the kind. If you look carefully at that list you will see that it is a list of reasons why the wageslaves of nineteenth century Europe could never hope to emerge from poverty, insecurity and squalor. It is a list of reasons why the British, French, Dutch and all the other Empires could never be ousted by their colonial dependencies, and why the coloured peoples in the United States could never hope to secure civil rights. Yet all these things happened.

Also the rumbles from the periphery are written off because so far they are muted and inarticulate. They do not speak with one voice : their grievances are amorphous and sometimes contradictory. Where you live you may not have heard or understood them. You may not believe discontent really exists except in the minds of a few shrill fanatics, or that even if it did it could attain to any effectiveness, operating from such an inchoate and economically enfeebled base, still less that it could leap across frontiers and that small victories in one country could feed hopes in another. But remind yourself how long ago it is – the day before yesterday? – that people were saying every one of those things about the women's movement, and how swiftly nevertheless it has changed the aspect of life and work and statute books in countries all around the world.

However, there is one handicap that is unique, and did not apply to any of the other disadvantaged groups that have made such striking progress. If you were a sweated factory hand, if you were black, if you were female, in the times and places when the status of those groups was at its lowest, you were virtually locked into that status. However much you chafed under it you could not say : 'I've had enough of this. Tomorrow I will be a mill-owner instead – or tomorrow I will be white – or tomorrow I will be a man.' Therefore many of the best, proudest, most vigorous, most intelligent representatives of those groups found no other way of reacting to their feelings of frustration than by devoting their lives to trying to raise the status of *the whole group*. But if you are born in a tribal village, a hick town, a stagnating industrial scrap heap, and are proud and vigorous and intelligent and resentful of the low status that clings to the place, you are not locked in at all. You can say:

> I've had enough of this. Tomorrow I will be metropolitan. I will learn their ways and pick up their accent and this time next year I will be indistinguishable from them. These people can stay here and rot if they like, but not me.

The next day you can leave.

It is a better trick than Herod's, even though no one has villainously sat down and planned it. It would be pretty debilitating for any community to lose all its first-born indiscriminately at birth, but more debilitating in the long run to rear them all and in every generation to hear the best, the white hopes, saying 'Include me out.' So what hope has any place of fighting for regeneration once that starts happening? The answer, for centuries, was 'little or none.' For idealists and devotees of lost causes the answer was 'First you will have to change human nature', and there has never yet been a politician who lost a night's sleep worrying about any opposition group that staked its all on the hope of changing human nature. *Plus ça change, plus c'est la même chose.*

All the same if change is due it will come, and if any existing political institutions are incapable of adapting to it, then they will be superseded, or else new ones will come into being (as the trade unions came into being) which more faithfully reflect the new economic realities. The first signs are invariably psychological – a slight diminution in the self-confidence of the previously dominant group and a corresponding rise in the morale of the underlings. It is a political truism that the French and Russian Revolutions did not take place when the plight of the *sans culottes* and the Russian peasants hit an all-time low, but when it began to improve. So let's look for signs and portents of what is happening to the balance of morale.

One omen which has created a good deal of personal trauma in the last decade is the novel phenomenon of the white-hope offspring of civilised urbanised successful professional parents in Western countries doing the Herod trick in reverse: just when they are ripe to contribute their expensive talents to the kind of community which bred them, they say 'These people can stick here and rot if they like, but not me,' and they light out for some place as far away from the city as they can get, and organise a copy of the *Whole Earth Catalogue* and practise Intermediate Technology.

For the most part they appear and operate in the places nobody wants, depopulated areas where the peripheral gangrene is far advanced. (It was in just such empty niches, as pickers-up of unconsidered trifles, that the first mammals the size of tree-shrews began to try out a new life-style when the dinosaurs were running themselves into a *cul-de-sac* of gigantism.) The numbers involved are not great and no one rates them as a political force, but they are an irritant to the status quo and they serve to undermine the forces of centralism in two small ways and one big one.

For one thing most of them manage to escape the tentacles of that indispensable servant of centralisation, the Inland Revenue, because one foolproof and perfectly legal way of avoiding income tax is to live off the land or by barter and arrange to have no net monetary income to tax. Governments in previous ages have always found a way around this – hut taxes, poll taxes, etc, with payment exacted, if necessary, in kind. But most Government Departments have troubles enough these days without undertaking to send a truck up a mountain to collect for auction a wheelbarrow full of carrots, six duck eggs and a half-grown billy goat.

The second effect is more or less fortuitous. When they arrive and settle in or near a small village they are often initially unwelcome because of beads and beards and cannabis and carryings-on. But if they stay, and the strangeness wears off, the village benefits. They don't come like second-home buyers with a wallet full of cash to push up house prices to the point where locals are priced out of the market – they move into places that were empty or falling down, and stave off the decline. The bus service into town that was on the verge of packing up has a few more regular customers and may find it can just break even, for a few more years at least. The local store finds its takings have gone up a bit. The local school, due for closure if the numbers drop any lower, gets an influx of five or six toddlers and can apply for a reprieve. The local farmer for the first time in years has a local reserve of unskilled labour he can tap for harvesting or fruit picking, can barter some of his produce for odd-jobs of fence mending and ditch clearing and maintenance; oftener than not, the buzz of outrage that greeted their arrival diminishes and becomes perfunctory. The economic effect of a scatter of these communes over a rural area is like sowing clumps of marram grass on a sand dune – they look sparse and tatty, but they serve to halt the erosion.

But by far the greatest influence of the Alternative Society has been its moral impact. It has helped to trigger off a world-wide consciousness of, and guilt about, the filth and poisons that industry and agribusiness have been allowed to spew over the globe. They have been among the founders of the first really effective political lobby for a century which can answer the question of 'What's in it for you, then?' in non-material terms. 'A blue sky. Bird song. Quietness.'

At a time when half the world is so deprived that their necessary answer to 'What do you want?' is 'More', one of the signs of hope is that there are some among the young of the overstuffed West who are answering 'Less'. In the beginning the people who protested about the Quality of Life were the kind that practical men felt they could dismiss with impatient contempt as dreamers and weirdos. But the practical men tread a little more softly since they found that the streak of idealism can sometimes be welded to political acumen of the highest order, and then they are faced with somebody like Ralph Nader who doesn't dismiss so easily.

They tread more softly still since (especially in America) the Ecological Lobby got rolling and the old slogan that 'there are no votes in sewage' turned out to be a monumental miscalculation. It will be a serious blow to thousands of massive-scale enterprises if (or when) they are made financially responsible for clearing up all the messes they make and paying compensation for all the nuisances they commit. Most of them have too long been content to shift all the clean-up expenditure on to

the public sector, and as for the nuisance factor they have assumed that the old adage 'Let the buyer beware' could be extended to cover 'and let anyone living within range of our
smoke, stink, noise, effluents and general contamination beware'. That 'beware' could boomerang on them yet.

Another early-warning signal that was written off a few
years ago as a vagary of the lunatic fringe was the appearance
(especially, this time, in Europe) of romantic figures flying the
tattered banners of some semi-defunct and half-digested cultural
minority or one-time nation, writing passionate tracts about
'old forgotten far-off things and battles long ago' – the Scots
and the Welsh, the Basques and the Bretons, and various other
peripheral enclaves and off-shore islands. It was so clearly
another of those lost causes – earnest young schoolmasters
swotting up the Gaelic, or sitting at the feet of the last surviving native speaker of the Cornish tongue and hoping to blow
on its embers and bring it back to life. It was quite charming
in its way, and innocent, like the craze for steam locomotives
or vintage cars. But anyone who seriously imagined that actual
political separatism for any of those groups was anything more
than a pipe dream was out of his tiny mind. Gaelic was like
sewage – there were no votes in it.

Or, as Professor Esmond Knight wrote in 1970 in a grotes-
quely unlucky turn of phrase:

> Some of the Scottish National Party's leaders take pride in
> claiming that they want an independent Scotland to sit at
> the UN between Saudi Arabia and Senegal – apparently as-
> suming that either of these has any influence there whatso-
> ever.

Six years later it is painfully apparent that Saudi Arabia
wasn't the only nation he was treating too lightly. The British
Government is currently getting ever deeper into the coils of a
devolution crisis that seems to have crept up on it stealthily
and almost by accident, and no one seems at all sure any longer
where it will end. A national newspaper compared the mood
in the Westminster Parliament with that of the lost sinners
in hell crying up to heaven: 'Lord, Lord, we didna ken!' to

which the Scots reply with the Lord's stern Calvinist retort:
'Weel, ye ken the noo!'

The problem is made no simpler by the fact that sizeable
sections of the Scots and the Welsh according to opinion polls
are themselves slightly taken aback by what is happening, not
sure if it's quite what they wanted or how far they want it
to go. Certainly a majority in both countries has only a minimal interest in the ancient language or the ancient culture,
though they may feel vaguely benevolent towards it as long as
it doesn't do them any harm. A lot of protest votes were cast,
out of a fairly new and heady feeling that they were as good
as anybody, that they were being neglected and pushed around
and ignored, and it was time that Westminster was made to
sit up and take notice – a feeling that was quite as strong in
other peripheral areas that had no national hook to hang it
on.

It might have been thought that the threat of the Welsh and
the oil-rich Scots getting in future possibly more than their
share of any redistribution of power and resources would have
at least one reassuring spin-off for the central government –
that the English themselves, sick of the Celtic sniping, would
draw closer together in Anglo-Saxon solidarity and flock to
support a policy of English nationalism and loyalty to London.
On the contrary, many indignant spokesmen from areas like
Tyneside pointed out that they too were as good as anybody,
and they had just as much to beef about as their Celtic neighbours (which was entirely true), and that if that was the pay-
off for kicking up a separatist fuss then it was time *they* kicked
up a fuss. How about UDI for the North of England?

In Spain as Franco's dictatorship dragged on, the fiercest resistance came not from any political party or trade union
but from separatist elements among the Basques and Catalans.
In France the regional rumbling grows louder and Paris vacil-
lates between trying to placate it and trying to slap it down.
The prospect of outlying pieces of Europe following the example of the distant colonies and flaking away seems less
impossible than once it did. Eire went long ago; Sicily has
gone; Scotland, unless very adroitly handled, could easily go.

Some of the Corsicans have taken to direct action and have been sharply reminded that Corsica is immutably *française*, but it is not very long since Algérie was being as sternly told that very same thing. In the whole of Europe the two nations least troubled by these murmurings are Germany and Switzerland, whose federal constitutions already afford the greatest degree of local autonomy.

The Soviet Republic of Georgia, though nobody imagines it will be allowed to flake away, is hearing complaints from Moscow that would be wearyingly familiar to dozens of similarly placed areas in capitalist countries – that its industrial productivity is becoming stagnant, it is not keeping up, it is being carried by the rest of the country, that all this must be blamed on the unique corruptibility of its local dignitaries, that its attempts to revive interest in its indigenous culture are phoney and reactionary, that it must pull itself together and get Russified.

In America the phenomenon is harder to identify because the growth centres are around the edges and the 'periphery' in the middle; and less novel because its constituent states have always been so uppity that it has acquired great expertise in coping with them. But campaigning candidates have been getting deeper-throated cheers than formerly for any attack on the top-heavy bureaucracy in Washington, and a more exuberant reception of any reference to how very easily and comfortably California, for example, could survive, if necessary, all on its own if things got in *too* much of a mess back East. . . .

All these and other disparate events are not often seen as constituting a pattern.

But it is significant that almost everyone has silently abandoned a pattern that was widely believed in up to the first World War and quite a long time after it. Up to that point the trend had been in the opposite direction. We had seen a lot of separate independent cities and dukedoms and principalities in the north of Europe struggling to form themselves into a united Germany; in a similar litter of little states in the south, reformers and idealists were hell-bent on realising the dream of a united Italy and achieved it; in Canada the French and

English-speaking provinces were learning to think of themselves as all Canadians just as the Scots and Welsh and English thought of themselves as all British; in the Indian subcontinent a host of races and religions and languages and tribes and sects were being welded into one mighty nation; the fight for separatism in the Southern States of the US was felt in hindsight to have been foredoomed to failure as being contrary to the tide of history; and a good many people of the highest intelligence and idealism and political experience looked forward with confidence to the day when this powerful urge would reach its logical conclusion with the setting up of a World Government. It is a very long time since I have heard those words uttered. Today I imagine anyone who dreamed the day had arrived, and saw a vision of World Government's skeleton force of 100,000 multilingual bureaucrats with their computers and their secretaries annually increasing and multiplying, briskly deciding the fate of obscure communities they had never previously heard of and burying the continents under a torrent of paper, would wake up in a cold sweat, screaming.

At the time when the blocs were being built up and Britain and the others were constructing their Empires, morale at the centre was impregnable. There was an unshakeable conviction not only of superior power but of superior wisdom and superior virtue. Those people were never troubled by any tremor of doubt that when they barged on to some foreign strand, destroyed heathen idols, preached monogamy, inculcated the work ethic and put trousers on the natives, they were combating evil and spreading light.

Today when they look back they are not so sure. The strengthening conviction among once-subject nations in the Third World and once-submerged regions in the homelands that they are as good as anybody, is only one aspect of the shift in morale. The other side of it is a lessening of the certainty among those at the centre that they are better than everybody.

One striking change has been in the attitude of the civilised peoples of the world to the uncivilised ones. Where any tribes still exist that have not encountered the blessings of civilisation they are not nowadays pounced upon by proselytisers pointing out the error of their ways; they are far more likely to be visited by anthropologists who approach them with something nearer to humility, hoping not to teach them but to learn something from them, about our common humanity and the different social patterns it may spontaneously crystallise into.

Former 'civilisers' have contracted guilt feelings – Edmund Wilson's 'Apology to the Iroquois' echoed the compunction of many people in the United States about how the Red Indians were treated. The influence of people such as Margaret Mead has been considerable. Nowadays liberal white America shows great respect for the beliefs and folkways of far-flung tribes in jungle, desert or icefield. It admires and covets their carvings and sculptures, would not willingly infringe their taboos, and asserts that their social mores are right 'for them', and ought not to be tampered with. It believes it has purged its soul of any taint of patronage.

That is not wholly true. The touchstone is applied when the folkways belong to communities in, say, West Virginia, who desire to persist in behaviour patterns that have for centuries been 'right for them' – namely, to bring up their children as far as possible ignorant until puberty about the facts of life and believing in Genesis as literally as the Indians once believed in Miche Manito. It immediately becomes obvious to all right-thinking people that they can't be allowed to *do* that, because those are not savages but *American* kids, for God's sake, whose heads they are filling with all that guff. So this time it matters, and it's high time they were forced into educational conformity with New York and Los Angeles. (A belief in Papal infallibility, or in circumcision, is still OK to pass on to your children, but if you want to stay out of line in such matters you had better be 'ethnic', that's all.)

Nevertheless they are trying hard. I suppose even Alvin Toffler was trying hard in his book *Future Shock* when he sprang to what he imagined was the defence of places like West Virginia, with a conservationist's zeal. 'Such slow paced committees,' he proposed, must be consciously encapsulated. . . . Radio and TV should be broadcast only for a few hours a day. . . . Such communities not only should not be derided; they should be subsidised by the larger society as a form of mental and social insurance. We may even want to pay people not to use the latest goods.

I am not sure where he is going to find such communities, willing to submit to metropolitan censorship of their viewing habits, suitably grateful for not being laughed at, and accepting allowances of real money to spend on condition they don't go wild and splash out on things like washing machines, as if they were the same as city folk. I should very much like to be present if he tried it out anywhere in the United States.

In Britain the time is long past when any Londoner would have been tempted to propose turning any part of its provinces into a kind of Serengeti for human specimens. If you want to discern what is happening there to the balance of morale you can do it with your eyes shut. You only have to listen to the voices – on the media, at the dinner parties, in the boardroom, on the stage. Right up to the last war if you aspired to hold a public position in almost any sphere, to be listened to as an authority on any subject, to get a job with the BBC, to become an officer in the Army, or to act, or to sing, the first thing you had to do was to acquire the accent of the Home Counties. If you came down from the North with any such ambitions and couldn't acquire it fast enough, you could pay to have your voice fixed, the way American coloured girls paid to have their kinky hair straightened, and then you could be an announcer or a headmistress or a saleslady or tread the boards as a Charles or a Pamela in the only kind of plays that were then being written.

The devaluation of this asset set in soon after the war, and the people who administered the final *coup de grâce* were the Beatles. For a dizzy few months even young Etonians were reported to be vying with each other trying to speak Scouse, and from that point on the regional accents rushed into bloom everywhere almost overnight, like Afro haircuts. A debutante hoping to get work in the London theatre today complains that the heaviest millstone round her neck is being cursed with the accent that Eliza Doolittle laboured so hard to acquire. If Shaw were alive and writing a sequel, he would have her hammering on Higgins's door crying 'Please – take it away, take it away, take it away!' She would settle no doubt for the voice she started with. I'll grant you that Cockney is just as 'demotic' and acceptable as Leeds or Liverpool or Devonshire – but not a whit better.

You will protest that none of this is politics: it is merely a general assertion that in some countries there is beginning a quantifiable drift of people away from the large cities and – less quantifiable but unmistakable – a heightening of self-esteem in areas far removed from them. But that is precisely the kind of indispensable compost necessary to any kind of political change before it can get under way. It has long been a standard jibe that any Scotsman on the make heads straight for London, but it is no longer true; the cream-off is slowing down, and some of the best would not cross the border now for any money. And it's not only the oil, because the same is true of Welsh-speaking areas of Wales which have had no such economic shot in the arm, and the only change is in the hearts and minds.

The next step is to put out feelers and try to find out who your allies are, and to lay down the first synapses of new kinds of combination; and to decide who your enemies are and select the best weapons – or design new ones – for resisting them.

That is one of the dangers of using nationalism as a lever. It is a powerful force and potentially an effective bloc-breaker, and in the areas where it is lying to hand it is inevitably going to be picked up. It may help to identify *some* of your natural allies: a Welsh Nationalist will be heartened by a Scottish Nationalist victory, and will know where he stands about the Bretons and the Basques. But it can be two-edged and it is an oversimplifier.

For one thing, a multiplication of frontiers will not in itself solve the basic problem. Independent Eire is no nearer than independent Nigeria to solving the problem of depopulation. Eire is independent but its economy remains essentially peripheral to Europe's. Internally nearly all of the eagerly enticed foreign investment is poured into the districts of Dublin and Shannon, while in the west the shrunken population shrinks further still.

Independence has not stemmed the exodus of Irishmen either, though it has probably done something to change the composition of it: more of the professionals stay put to run the country and the emigrants have a greater preponderance of the unskilled, which is presumably better than the other way round. But the depopulating Highlands and the depopulating counties of Wales would not be appreciably better off if they lost less of their people to London and Liverpool and more of them to Edinburgh and Cardiff.

The greater danger lies in failing to identify the enemy, and imagining that the enemy is 'England'. The forces that have brought stagnation to Durham and Newcastle are precisely the same as the forces that have debilitated Ebbw Vale and Clydeside. Their natural claim to figure in any devolutionary alliance is at least as strong as Brittany's, and to lump them in with the enemy because some of them had no Celtic grandparents is a nonsense. Fortunately though, the things people do has more influence than the things they say, and there is every indication that greater independence for the Celtic fringe will strengthen rather than weaken both the claims and the determination of similar areas to stand up and demand more control over their own destinies, and that when they do the voices from over the border will not be saying 'dirty Sassenach' but 'Right on, brother!'

A tentative move towards a new and potentially more significant kind of political grouping was marked by the formation of an organisation called Peripheral Maritime Regions of the European Community. This includes representatives of areas within the EEC itself, such as Scotland, Schleswig-Holstein, North Jutland, Wales, Aquitaine, the West of Ireland, Pays de Loire, etc, and its very first meeting in Brittany also attracted observers from outside the EEC altogether – from regions of Portugal and Spain and Norway who face the same problems and felt that here were people talking their own language, in a gut-reaction sense if not a philological one.

The EEC itself looks like an organisation that could only foster and strengthen centralising tendencies. But one thing that has become much clearer since its inception is that peripheral anaemia operates on a continental scale. It is one of the most intractable problems the Community has to deal with, and a drain down which increasing amounts of its resources are being pretty fruitlessly poured. There are, it emerges, two Europes, just as Disraeli pointed out in the nineteenth century that there were two Britains – and the problems of the submerged Britain never got solved until it took them into its own hands and began forging its own political weapons.

So far the first Europe has done most of the talking. Delegates from its constituent nations have brought along begging bowls on behalf of their Special Areas and tried to outbid one another for the size of the handouts they can reasonably claim and send home to be distributed, while the Other Europe has for the most part sat at home and waited. There is no reason to think it will sit there forever. The Peripheral Maritime Areas group could be extended to or supplemented by other such ancillary groups. All this would take some time. The kind of delegates liable to be appointed would possibly have been trained in local grassroots administration and be orientated in their thinking towards specific local problems. But the longer they go on talking and the wider the spectrum of areas from which they are drawn, the more clearly they will be able to recognise the nature of their common problem, and perhaps make the imaginative leap required to recognise that the begging-bowl approach will never solve it, that in the long run the kind of aid dished out to them, like the aid dished out to the Third World, could, as Singer phrased it, be 'positively harmful'. Their real natural allies are world-wide and come in many colours.

If it doesn't happen in that way it will happen in another. The two EEC members most deeply penetrated by the problem are Italy and Great Britain. Italy is split across the middle, with the bottom half pretty solidly Other-Europe. It is trying to survive half-winner and half-loser, as the United States tried to survive half-slave and half-free. But the free trade philosophy of the EEC is designed to benefit the winners, and Italy is already beginning to find that as long as it is trailing the dead weight of the south it is not possible to maintain economic viability and national unity and observe the pure milk of the EEC gospel all at the same time. It has asked for an exception to be made in its favour, and voices are being raised in Britain (mainly from the provinces) demanding the same thing. In the end something's got to give. Either the EEC will have to modify its policy, or else Britain and Italy will be the first two members to be forced to resign, or else the presently unthinkable will happen – the flake-off will be on in earnest, and the nations will split.

A lot more people will then be listening to Schumacher's idea that the real enemy of all of us is the scale we are trying to operate on. If you're Third-World or Other-Europe and hold out the begging bowl what do you get? You may get a loan – it's called Aid because the interest is lower than you might have been charged elsewhere, but it's a loan all the same and will have to be paid back and the interest too: you're another day older and deeper in debt. Or it may even be a Grant – to build the infrastructure of a site so that you can sit there like a spider in its web hoping to lure someone from outside into building a factory on it, and you make speeches telling him how grateful you are. A hundred-to-one it will be a branch factory belonging to some large concern – which is naturally not in the business for the sake of its health so the profits will go back to base, and naturally too if there's any dip in demand the branch factory is the first to close down. Quite possibly, because the big concerns are founded on Specialisation and the Economies of Scale, it will be making *parts* of something, so every time somebody four hundred miles away gets sworn at by the foreman and it leads to a strike, the doors will be closed on you too until it's settled.

Or you might get a real break and the company will build a big new plant employing 17,000 men which will be so competitive it'll keep you going until someone, in your country or another, builds another one more competitive and it closes down and the men are unemployed. Why are they unemployed? Surely it takes an awful lot of work to supply all the needs of 17,000 men and their wives and children? It does take an awful lot of work, but they are not able to do any of it. They have all been trained to do one thing, and besides the economies of scale will dictate that all the things they need have to be grown and made and processed and packaged and marketed by mass-production methods, and it's more economic to pay them social security to sit on their backsides and simply consume the stuff and be told how stagnant they are, rather than reduce the scale and diversify their skills and let them do some of it themselves, even if they would find it more rewarding than sitting on their backsides, and probably more interesting than turning knobs on an assembly line. Besides, if they stopped buying the mass-produced objects they would only damage some other town where the people have also been trained to do one thing only.

Centralists are dead set against the idea of outlying communities trying to regenerate themselves by small-scale enterprises. Jane Jacobs, worrying about stagnation in the big city, recommends that one of the major moves cities need to make to save themselves is by 'import-replacing': they must start manufacturing the things their own citizens need to consume, and that will be their salvation. Fine. But when she sees a small community applying the same policy she regards that as reactionary, and demands 'where is the need' for these people to try to make things which the city can make so much better? This is the old Venetian cry of 'ande arar' – you get back to the plough, brother, and leave the clever stuff to us.

Exporters are dead against it too. You need a vast docile domestic market if you are to manufacture things on a large enough scale to undercut foreign competition, but exporting is not as simple as it used to be. The original idea of free trade was that a country exported the things it was best fitted to produce and imported the things it was less fitted or unable to produce – we'll swop our cod for your oranges. It was simple too when only a few countries had embarked on large-scale production, and Britain could say: 'We'll swop our shirts and bicycles for your tea and coffee.' It has now got to the stage when our manufacturers are trying to sell cars to Japan to earn the currency to pay for the cars which the Japanese are trying to export to us, and those are the economies of lunacy.

In the West they can only be pursued by an endless striving for greater scale, eternally spiralling consumption, planned obsolescence, the stimulating of the demand for ephemeral products to fulfill non-existent needs, and a ruthless competitive cutdown in the number of man-hours required to produce any given object so that the workers can be released to – to do what? Some are wafted upwards to cope with the paperwork, some are absorbed into transporting the products over ever-longer distances to consumers whose local production units have been knocked out of the running, and some have been thrown on to social security paid for by rising taxes, of which the company pays its share with shrill yelps of indignation. And some find jobs with yet another go-ahead concern with even better ideas for giving the spiral another spin.

There are limits, of course, to Small is Beautiful, as Mao found when he tried to popularise the back-yard blast furnace; but no one has ever tried to define what those limits are. A society which can miniaturise a television set to the point where you can strap it on your wrist like a watch has made no scientific attempt to establish the optimum, let alone the minimum, economic size for its units of production. Sometimes, as Galbraith and Catherwood have pointed out, the size is above the economic optimum even from the point of view of the shareholders. What we more badly need to know is the optimum size not for the company but for the society as a whole, which bears most of the burden of the diseconomies of scale – the pollution, the tax burden, the unemployment, and the plight of the strangling cities and decaying rural areas.

One thing is sure – it's the poorest and smallest communities which will be the first to listen to Schumacher's slogan and accept that small is stable; small is anticoagulant; small gets you free from the begging bowl and the butter mountain and the bottleneck; it gets you further from 'live now – pay later' and closer to 'pay now – live freer'.

It may be a long time yet before more than a small minority in the West will listen. For the Third-World village, Inter-mediate Technology is the brightest hope not only of greater independence and self-respect but of immediate material advantage. In the developed countries, as long as the oil holds out, it will only be an option for the kind of people who don't put material affluence at the top of their priorities. But that's not as small a subsection as we sometimes imagine. If it were, who would ever have opened up the American West?

For the Communist countries, the situation differs only insofar as the shift cannot take place by means of a multitude of individual options. The major decisions are consciously and politically determined at the top level, and there is nothing in the pure milk of socialism to determine which way they should go.

Some years ago in the Soviet Union this was recognised by throwing the issue open to public debate of a more unin-hibited and free-ranging nature than is common there, with both sides quoting the Marxist-Leninist scripture to support their own contentions. One of the contenders was geographer B. S. Khorev, who put up an eloquent case against centralism and unrestrained urbanisation. Subsequent indications would indicate that he failed to carry the day. So how will it work out there? Who is going to convince the winners that history was on his side?

Presumably it will have to be left to the third force, Marx's Mother Earth. Even the most intransigent Soviet centralists must have noted, without pleasure, Earl Butz's discovery that 'food is a weapon', and the buzz of speculation that arose in some circles in America as to how it might be used as a diplomatic lever: 'How many cargoes of grain would they take to soft-pedal their intervention in which particular hot spot in Africa or the Middle East?' It is not a comfortable situation, and meatless days in Moscow restaurants are not a comfortable thing to have to introduce either. So what do you do about food production? Dismiss a few scapegoats, but that won't solve much. Coercion has been tried and was counterproductive. . . .

It is impossible, from outside, to detect what is happening in that country to morale either at centre or periphery, except by looking for straws in the wind in the snippets of news that emerge in the Western press, of which I offer you two that appeared in the last month.

There was a prolonged and animated correspondence in the columns of *Pravda* concerning one Comrade Bogomolov, who had fantastically exceeded the individual norms of industrial output in his factory – the very feat for which the miner Stakhanov had once been fêted all over the USSR and rocketed to world-wide fame. Some letters attacked the new Stakhanovite for greed (he was earning more than the factory manager) and others defended him, but the net impression was a rather grudging: 'OK, but cool it, brother.'

At almost the same time it was announced that any agricultural commune which put on a similar spurt and exceeded its target would be rewarded with prizes of colour television sets. It's not much – a kind of Soviet equivalent of green stamps – but it's a beginning.

Throughout the Third-World countries too this is the great divide, of greater significance in the long run than whether their foreign policies are pro- or anti-Communist, and showing no perceptible correlation with that factor. At one extreme are countries like Thailand, run by a highly centralised bureaucracy which channels the lion's share of all education, health care and investment into the city. 'The economic history of at least the last twenty-five years in Thailand,' wrote one Thai economist in the *Bangkok Bank Monthly Review*,

'has been one of systematic transfer of resources from the farmers to the upper classes, by a variety of devices – the taxes on rice, the high interest rates on agricultural credit, and the land rents paid to rich farmers and absentee landlords.'

The resulting decline and stagnation of agricultural production is hardly more devastating than the effect on Bangkok itself – an area of urban disaster, with potholed streets, chaotic traffic jams, drainage at breakdown point, 300,000 drug addicts, a soaring crime rate, 110,000 new immigrants from the hinterland every year, and city health officials who believe that the best and cheapest solution of its problems would be to abandon it and build again somewhere else.

At the other extreme are countries whose leaders tilt their policies in the opposite direction, like Julius Nyerere, who faced the indignation of his urban sector when he cut back the indent of the up-to-date hospital in his capital city for new and very expensive up-to-date diagnostic equipment, because the same amount of money spent in the villages would save a hundred lives for every one the machine would save, and restore to health and vigour hundreds of men and women who are dragging themselves around riddled with crippling and unnecessary disorders like hookworm.

It was felt as a blow to the prestige of the hospital and the city and therefore, some felt, to the nation. The money saved by the decision was used to scoop up one or two raw volunteers from each of a large number of villages, take them to a centre where they were given a crash course in diagnosing and administering the standard treatment for a range of the commonest ailments, and send them back home with a glorified First Aid box of drugs, hypodermics, etc, backed up by a system of referral for cases they could not cope with. 'Dilution' of the profession on that scale would send shudders through any Western Medical Council, but the life and the health of the villages were transformed.

That is another example of intermediate technology and it may superficially seem as far out of our ken as introducing a hand-guided metal plough. But the world is one, and there can be few doctors from Leningrad to San Francisco who cannot now foresee the time as the potentialities of intensive care units and replacement surgery continue to advance, and the cost per patient in man-hours of skilled professional attention advances even faster, when they too will have to take equally difficult decisions about either pulling the progress plug out

I

or having to define the particular elite which is to benefit from it. Obviously everybody can't.

The dichotomy that is beginning to manifest itself and will ultimately find political expression is not between so-called Left and so-called Right, nor between Socialism and free enterprise, but between those who think that decisions like Nyerere's are 'progressive' because they mean greater equality, and those who think they are 'reactionary' because they mean calling a halt to some kinds of technical advance until those at the bottom have caught up. Which would mean deciding, for instance, that the civilised answer to the ringing question of 'After Concorde – what?' is something smaller, and slower, and cheaper.

It is not an easy choice; it is one that everybody could conscientiously avoid making as long as we persuaded ourselves that the 'growth' curve could go on rising eternally, and those at the advancing tip of it were not arrogating more than their share of finite resources but blazing a trail into a land of plenty where everybody in the end, at however long a remove, could follow them. We could live with the idea that six percent of the world was consuming fifty percent of the world's energy as long as we believed there would always be plenty more where that came from and the arrogators were only showing the rest of the world what they too would be able to do with it, once they joined in the bonanza.

The last hope of retaining belief in that kind of infinite growth curve lies in nuclear energy. After the last war there was a great surge of optimism that coal and oil had been nothing but a springboard to catapult us into infinitely greater realms of undreamed of affluence.

This is where the crunch comes. Suppose that nuclear power were to take over where oil left off, then the GNP really could go on rising, and Herman Kahn's airy talk of redesigning the continents and redistributing the Arctic and issuing arbitrary edicts to the sea and the clouds like some latter-day Prospero would begin to look feasible. He would reckon he's in with a chance of being a true prophet and ushering in Utopia and Ecumenopolis, those heavenly twins. Mother Earth, having thrown open the last of her coffers, would find herself as powerless as Lear to curb the wildest whims of any of her unruly brood.

Utopia, I doubt. A few steps nearer to World City, beyond question. The centripetal spiral would pick up speed again. The sectors that had grown rich on oil would hope to grow a hundred times richer on atomic fuel, and anyone who had begun to hope that the lower end of the see-saw was beginning to lift would be unlucky. Every technology dictates its own scale – you can't travel three miles on a Jumbo jet – and nuclear technology would dictate a massive scale and a pace of change much faster than anything we have dreamed of.

The energy problem would be solved: all the others would be intensified. The complexity of urban problems would increase in geometric progression. There is no earthly reason to believe that stress and psychological disorders and anomie and fear and crime would not keep pace with that progression; there is every reason to believe that neither the increase in human wisdom nor in human happiness would keep pace with it at all. The throw-away society would achieve new heights of profligacy. People would not only abandon Bangkok: they would throw away New York when the problem of what to do about it grew too tedious, and move down to the sunbelt until they'd turned that into the same kind of mess.

But after all, when you're really hooked on energy almost anything is better than the prospect of quitting cold. The only other option is to turn to the renewable energy sources – the sun, and the wind, and the force of gravity on falling water, and the heat of the earth, supplemented where necessary by the renewable source that in 1850 supplied *ninety percent* of all the energy expended in the whole of the United States of America. (In case anybody has forgotten what it was, it was muscle power. It's still around.)

The common factors among all these renewable resources is that they are devolutionary; they are anticoagulant (it would be very difficult for one-sixth of the world to commandeer fifty percent of the wind or the sunshine); they would decrease differentials instead of increasing them. You can't build World

City with them because the scale of technology they would most efficiently serve is a small one. To benefit from them you would not necessarily have to live somewhere within reach of an umbilical cord stretching out from the nearest city or power station, and you wouldn't have to wait until some great institution with access to virtually unlimited financial resources – a powerful nation-state or a top-scale commercial enterprise – had erected the installation and geared it to serve its own ends and hired some of the energy out to you.

Alternative technology is presently in a very primitive state – at the stage that aviation had reached with the Wright brothers, or television when Baird transmitted the blurred image of a face from one room to another – and much of the effort put into it to date has been by amateurs not too unlike the Wright brothers, operating on a shoestring and barracked by derisive predictions that it would never get off the ground. As to why the job was largely left to them in an energy-hungry world where any additional sources would be welcome, Tom Stonier, an American professor now at Bradford University's School of Science and Society, claims:

> The greatest impediment to the rapid development of solar energy has been the obstruction by the nuclear energy establishment. If we had spent as much money subsidising solar energy, we would have had energy coming out of our ears by now.

That, as they say, figures.

Fifteen years ago no one would have given a cat in hell's chance to any hopes of overcoming that obstruction. The kind of people who opposed it were at the furthest possible remove from the corridors of power.

It was opposed by the members of the nascent ecological lobby. They were worried about the leakage into the earth and the sea and the rain and the foodchain of radio-active substances which had never existed before and need never have existed at all, which are readily incorporated into the tissues of living things (including ourselves) with hideous and irreversible effects, and which mankind is powerless ever to destroy. They were not too happy with the assurance that radio-active waste could be disposed of quite safely as long as the structures in which they were stored were continually guarded and renewed every fifty years for the duration of man's time on the planet.

They kept asking awkward questions but got very few answers. The nuclear establishment is about as prone to press conferences as the CIA or the KGB, and for the same sincere reasons – they believe that what they are doing is ultimately in the interests of the people as a whole, but they do not trust the people as a whole to perceive this as clearly as they do, so they prefer them not to bother their heads about it at all.

In some parts of the world they also ran into stiffening opposition from the inhabitants of the places where they planned to erect nuclear plants. Such things can't be built, of course, close to 'centres of population' (ie cities) because it's too risky, but if the place was only a village on a depopulated coast the people were assured that there was absolutely no danger and the installation would help to relieve their unemployment. They took to protesting with increasing passion that no, thank you, they'd rather settle for the stagnation.

Fifteen years ago all this would have been dismissed as peanuts. A world-wide switch-over to nuclear power looked inevitable. But now everything has changed. California has been to the polls in a referendum urging that all further nuclear power development in the State should be stopped. This move failed, but others will follow. General Electric, one of America's biggest backers of nuclear energy, is beginning to pull out. And America is putting up a £60 million-budget for solar energy research.

It is doubtful that this *volte face* was achieved purely by sweet reason, or that the nuclear programme couldn't have been driven through far less flimsy barriers of public opposition if there had been enough money in it for anybody. But there wasn't enough money coming out of it, and there was alarmingly too much money going into it. When we were soaring to the top of the oil parabola this wouldn't have mattered so much ('Money? Who's counting?') but now we are on the way down. The richest countries as well as the poorest are trying to steer a tricky course between the Scylla of inflation and the Charybdis of recession, and there are too many other things needing to be done with a million dollars' worth of power than using it to prime a nuclear pump that never gets satisfactorily primed.

Today there seems to be at least an even chance that the world may not after all be travelling down that poisonous road, but may choose a cleaner and a greener one.

That doesn't mean necessarily an easier one. There will be dauntingly difficult problems of adjustment. It will still be very hard for the poorest countries – but hopefully the wind from overseas sucking them into the cities will somewhat abate, and the kind of hardware being perfected by the top brains of the developed world will be much better fitted to their problems and to their pockets.

It will be very hard for the richest countries. They will have to produce governments and political parties with the courage to say to them, like Barbara Ward: 'We have been on an energy jag,' and like Schumacher: 'The party's over.' It is not at all easy to win elections with a platform like that. But people have learned to take that kind of advice from their doctors under the threat of a coronary or a fifty-inch hip measurement, and they would take it from a government once they were convinced it was telling them the truth and knew where it was going – two provisos that very few governments recently have seemed able to fulfill.

It will be – it is already being – very hard for the big cities whose existence was based on assumptions that are ceasing to correspond with reality. Their financial power-base will shrink; their resources will shrink; their morale will decline; they are liable to hear from outside the same cold comfort that they were in the habit of dishing out: 'well, you don't have to stay there.' As always it will be the well-heeled who are best able to follow this advice; they are already staging their retreat, and leaving behind a population which has become specialised in the obsolescent arts of serving their needs and living off the wealth that trickled down from them.

Many of the young will clear out, to the smaller places of the new frontier where their arrival will have a considerable impact on styles of life and thinking: it is much easier to absorb the ideas of evolution and racial equality in daily doses from people who are working beside you than through the diktat of a faraway bureaucrat.

For the ones left behind, it would take a Pollyanna to deny that any future light is at the end of a pretty long tunnel. It may not come until the differentials are much further eroded, and the exit of the affluent is no longer accompanied by the influx of poorer immigrants to whom the city still looks like Eldorado compared with what they have just left; till the places are being run by people with soberer expectations and fewer delusions of grandeur, and the overheated values attached to once-'prestige' locations have come tumbling down, and the racketeers have decided the place is no longer worth the trouble of looting; till bureaucracy as well as wealth and production has been reduced in scale and more evenly dispersed throughout the country; till the frantic pace of oil-fuelled urban change slows down and the overwhelming problems can be tackled maybe ten at a time instead of three hundred at a time; till the bulldozers grow thinner on the ground and people can stay long enough in one community to get to know their neighbours and stop being afraid of them; till the pace on the pavements slackens to allow of once in a while stopping to say 'Hullo'.

That is a far cry from Doxiadis and Ecumenopolis and the irresistible tide of mysterious forces sweeping us into ever greater conurbations which we are powerless to, and dare not, resist. But I don't believe in mysterious forces. I believe in economic ones – that the tide was a tide of oil and is now showing signs of having spent its force, and in the West at least the demographic tide is doing the same thing.

If you stand still in one place for long enough and watch, you can see it turn.

Bibliography

ABRAMS, C., *Man's struggle for shelter in an urbanising world*, MIT, 1970

ARVILL, R., *Man and Environment*, Penguin, 1967.

BELL & TYRWHITT (eds), *Human Identity in the Urban Environment*, Penguin, 1972.

BERRY, B. J. *The Human Consequences of Urbanisation*, Macmillan, 1969.

BRAUDEL, FERNAND, *Capitalism and Material Life 1400–1800*, Weidenfeld and Nicolson, 1967.

BREESE, G. (ed.), *The City in Newly Developing Countries*, Prentice Hall, 1969.

BROWN, M. BARRETT, *The Economics of Imperialism*, Penguin, 1974.

CIPOLLA, C. M., *The Economics of World Population*, Penguin, 1960.

CLUB OF ROME, *The Limits to Growth*, Earth Island, 1972.

COMMONER, B., *The Closing Circle*, Cape, 1972.

COPPA & DOLCE (eds), *Cities in Transition*, Nelson Hall, 1974.

DENNIS, N., *Public Participation and Planners' Blight*, Faber & Faber, 1972.

DICKSON, D., *Alternative Technology*, Fontana, 1974.

DOXIADIS, C. A., *Ekistics*, Hutchinson, 1968.

DYOS & WOLFF (eds), *The Victorian City: Images and Realities*, Routledge & Kegan Paul, 1973.

FRIEDLY, P. H., *National Policy responses to Urban Growth*, Saxon House, 1974.

GANS, H. J., *The Urban Villagers*, Free Press, 1962.

GOTTMANN, J., *Megalopolis*, M.I.T., 1961.

HALL, P. (ed), *The Containment of Urban England*, Allen & Unwin, 1973.

HARVEY, D., *Social Justice and the City*, Edward Arnold, 1973.

HATT & REISS (eds), *Cities & Society*, Free Press, 1951.

HOBSBAWM, E. J., *The Age of Capital*, Weidenfeld & Nicolson, 1975.

JACOBS, J., *The Death & Life of Great American Cities*. Cape, 1961.

JACOBS, J., *The Economy of Cities*, Cape, 1970.

JANSEN, C. J. (ed.), *Readings in the Sociology of Migration*, Pergamon, 1966.

JONES, E., *Towns & Cities*, O.U.P., 1966.

KOHR, L. *Development without Aid*, Christopher Davies, 1973.

MARX, KARL, *Das Kapital*, 1867.

MUMFORD, L., *The City in History*, Secker & Warburg, 1961.

PAHL, R. (ed.), *Readings in Urban Sociology*, Pergamon, 1968.

PLOWDEN, S., *Towns against Traffic*, Deutsch, 1972.

SCHUMACHER, E. F., *Small is Beautiful*, Blond & Briggs, 1973.

SINGER, H. W., *The Strategy of International Development*, Macmillan, 1975.

SMITH, ADAM, *The Wealth of Nations*, 1776.

SOUTHALL, A. W., *Urban Anthropology*, O.U.P., 1973.

STEIN, M. R., *The Eclipse of Community*, Princetown U.P., 1960.

TIMMS, D. W. G., *The Urban Mosaic*, C.U.P., 1971.

TOYNBEE, A. J., *Cities on the Move*, O.U.P., 1970.

WILLIAMS, R., *The Country & the City*, Chatto & Windus, 1973.

WILSHER, P. & RIGHTER, R., *The Exploding Cities*, Deutsch, 1975.

Index